S0-BCC-504

MPLS AND NEXT-GENERATION NETWORKS

FOUNDATIONS FOR NGN AND ENTERPRISE VIRTUALIZATION

Monique Morrow and Azhar Sayeed

Cisco Press

800 East 96th Street
Indianapolis, Indiana 46240 USA

MPLS and Next-Generation Networks

Monique Morrow and Azhar Sayeed

Copyright© 2007 Cisco Systems, Inc.

Published by:

Cisco Press

800 East 96th Street

Indianapolis, IN 46240 USA

All rights reserved. No part of this book may be reproduced or transmitted in any form or by any means, electronic or mechanical, including photocopying, recording, or by any information storage and retrieval system, without written permission from the publisher, except for the inclusion of brief quotations in a review.

Printed in the United States of America   1 2 3 4 5 6 7 8 9 0

First Printing   November 2006

Library of Congress Cataloging-in-Publication Number: 2003115150

ISBN: 1-58720-120-8

Trademark Acknowledgments

All terms mentioned in this book that are known to be trademarks or service marks have been appropriately capitalized. Cisco Press or Cisco Systems, Inc. cannot attest to the accuracy of this information. Use of a term in this book should not be regarded as affecting the validity of any trademark or service mark.

Warning and Disclaimer

This book is designed to provide information about Cisco Unity. Every effort has been made to make this book as complete and as accurate as possible, but no warranty or fitness is implied.

The information is provided on an "as is" basis. The authors, Cisco Press, and Cisco Systems, Inc. shall have neither liability nor responsibility to any person or entity with respect to any loss or damages arising from the information contained in this book or from the use of the discs or programs that may accompany it.

The opinions expressed in this book belong to the author and are not necessarily those of Cisco Systems, Inc.

Feedback Information

At Cisco Press, our goal is to create in-depth technical books of the highest quality and value. Each book is crafted with care and precision, undergoing rigorous development that involves the unique expertise of members from the professional technical community.

Readers' feedback is a natural continuation of this process. If you have any comments regarding how we could improve the quality of this book, or otherwise alter it to better suit your needs, you can contact us through e-mail at feedback@ciscopress.com. Please make sure to include the book title and ISBN in your message.

We greatly appreciate your assistance.

Corporate and Government Sales

Cisco Press offers excellent discounts on this book when ordered in quantity for bulk purchases or special sales. For more information, please contact:

U.S. Corporate and Government Sales 1-800-382-3419 corpsales@pearsontechgroup.com

For sales outside of the U.S. please contact:

International Sales international@pearsoned.com

Publisher   Paul Boger

Executive Editor   Brett Bartow

Cisco Representative   Anthony Wolfenden

Cisco Press Program Manager   Jeff Brady

Managing Editor   Patrick Kanouse

Development Editor   Betsey Henkels

Project Editor and Copy Editor   Deadline Driven Publishing

Technical Editors   Tom Nadeau, Christophe Masiero, and Joseph Fusco

Team Coordinator   Vanessa Evans

Cover and Book Designer   Louisa Adair

Composition   Tolman Creek Design

Indexer   Julie Bess

Americas Headquarters
Cisco Systems, Inc.
170 West Tasman Drive
San Jose, CA 95134-1706
USA
www.cisco.com
Tel: 408 526-4000
800 553-NETS (6387)
Fax: 408 527-0883

Asia Pacific Headquarters
Cisco Systems, Inc.
168 Robinson Road
#28-01 Capital Tower
Singapore 068912
www.cisco.com
Tel: +65 6317 7777
Fax: +65 6317 7799

Europe Headquarters
Cisco Systems International BV
Haarlerbergpark
Haarlerbergweg 13-19
1101 CH Amsterdam
The Netherlands
www-europe.cisco.com
Tel: +31 0 800 020 0791
Fax: +31 0 20 357 1100

Cisco has more than 200 offices worldwide. Addresses, phone numbers, and fax numbers are listed on the Cisco Website at **www.cisco.com/go/offices.**

©2006 Cisco Systems, Inc. All rights reserved. CCVP, the Cisco logo, and the Cisco Square Bridge logo are trademarks of Cisco Systems, Inc.; Changing the Way We Work, Live, Play, and Learn is a service mark of Cisco Systems, Inc.; and Access Registrar, Aironet, BPX, Catalyst, CCDA, CCDP, CCIE, CCIP, CCNA, CCNP, CCSP, Cisco, the Cisco Certified Internetwork Expert logo, Cisco IOS, Cisco Press, Cisco Systems, Cisco Systems Capital, the Cisco Systems logo, Cisco Unity, Enterprise/Solver, EtherChannel, EtherFast, EtherSwitch, Fast Step, Follow Me Browsing, FormShare, GigaDrive, GigaStack, HomeLink, Internet Quotient, IOS, IP/TV, iQ Expertise, the iQ logo, iQ Net Readiness Scorecard, iQuick Study, LightStream, Linksys, MeetingPlace, MGX, Networking Academy, Network Registrar, Packet, PIX, ProConnect, RateMUX, ScriptShare, SlideCast, SMARTnet, StackWise, The Fastest Way to Increase Your Internet Quotient, and TransPath are registered trademarks of Cisco Systems, Inc. and/or its affiliates in the United States and certain other countries.

All other trademarks mentioned in this document or Website are the property of their respective owners. The use of the word partner does not imply a partnership relationship between Cisco and any other company. (0609R)

About the Authors

Monique Jeanne Morrow is currently a Distinguished Consulting Engineer at Cisco Systems, Inc. She has more than 20 years experience in IP internetworking that includes design, implementation of complex customer projects, and service development for service providers. Monique has been involved in developing managed network services, such as remote access and LAN switching in a service provider environment. Monique has worked for both enterprise and service provider companies in the U.S. and in Europe. In 1999, Monique led the engineering project team for one of the first MPLS-VPN deployments for a European service provider.

Monique has presented in various conferences on the topic of MPLS. Additionally, Monique is coauthor of the book *Designing IP-Based Services: Solutions for Vendors and Service Providers*. Monique is also the coauthor of *MPLS VPN Security* and *MPLS for Decision Makers*. She is working on a book that presents enterprise drivers and concerns for IP-based service delivery.

Monique is active in both the IETF and ITU-T SG 13 with a focus on OAM. She has a master's of science degree in telecommunications management and an MBA. Additionally, Monique is vice chair of IPsphere Forum.

Monique is currently engaged in MPLS OAM standards development and has been engaged in international carrier discussions on the topic. Monique was a co-guest editor of a special issue of the *IEEE Communications Magazine* on the subject of "OAM in MPLS-Based Networks," which was published in October 2004. She was also a guest editor of a special issue of the *IEEE Communications Magazine* on the subject of "Challenges in Enabling Inter-Provider Service Quality on the Internet," published in June 2005 and on the subject of, "GMPLS: The Promise of the Next Generation Optical Control Plane," published in July 2005. Finally, Monique is working on NGN for service providers and GRID technology.

Azhar Sayeed is currently the director of product management for the Cisco Network Software and Systems Group. He has more than 16 years of networking and communications industry experience. Azhar is currently responsible for product management and roll out of MPLS, Layer 2 and Layer 3 VPNs, broadband technologies IP routing, and Qo) features in Cisco IOS software. Cisco IOS software is the network system software that powers the majority of Cisco hardware platforms.

Prior to joining Cisco in 1998, Azhar worked for Cabletron Systems as a product line manager for the ATM group. He designed and implemented product development strategies and brought products to market. He has held additional industry positions including that of an ATM aviator with Digital Equipment Corporation where he supported presale operations of the High Performance Networks group for Digital.

Azhar started his career as a field engineer, installing X.25 and Frame Relay gear for large service provider and enterprise networks. Since then, he has been involved with ATM and MPLS in DEC, Cabletron, and Cisco.

Azhar has published several research papers from his master's thesis and dozens of magazine articles on MPLS and QoS. He has been invited to speak at several conferences, such as MPLS 2002 through MPLS 2005. He has also spoken at MPLS Con 2002, Broadband Year, Comdex, N+I, Supercomm, APRICOT, MPLS World Congress, and so on.

Azhar's interests include network protocols and wireless and broadband technologies. Azhar holds a bachelor's degree in electronics and communications and a master's degree in electrical engineering. He is also a member of IEEE and IEEE communications society.

About the Technical Reviewers

Joseph Fusco is the product director for BT Infonet's global MPLS Cisco-powered network, a network that serves over 1000 clients around the world. He has provided consulting services in the area of global service provider network features and deployment. He has published articles and spoken at industry forums on MPLS. He is a graduate of the University of San Francisco and obtained his master's degree from National University of San Diego. He worked for Xerox Corporation as an instructor in the early release days of Ethernet and prior to joining BT Infonet, he held senior management positions at Symantec Corporation.

Thomas D. Nadeau works at Cisco Systems where he is a technical leader who is responsible for the leadership of operations, management, network management standards, and development and architecture for MPLS-related components at Cisco.

Tom is an active participant in the IETF, ITU, and IEEE. He is coauthor of many IETF MIBs, protocol, and architecture documents in the L2/L3VPN, TE, PWE3, GMPLS, and MPLS areas. Tom is coauthor of RFC 3564, RFC 3811, RFC 3812, RFC 3813, RFC 3814, RFC 3815, RFC 3916, RFC 3945, and RFC 3985. Tom was recently coeditor of the October 2004 *IEEE Communications Magazine's* special section on "MPLS Operations and Management." Tom has filed a number of patents in the area of networking operations and management.

Tom received his bachelor of science in computer science from the University of New Hampshire, and a master s of science degree from the University of Massachusetts in Lowell, where he has been an adjunct professor of computer science since 2000. Tom currently teaches courses on the topic of data communications. He is also on the technical committees of several prominent networking conferences where he provides technical guidance on their content. He also serves on the technical advisory board of Westridge Networks. He is the technical editor of *Enabling VPN Aware Networks with MPLS* (Prentice Hall Publishers, 2001) and author of *MPLS Network Management: MIBs, Tools, and Techniques* (Morgan-Kaufman, 2002).

Christophe Masiero is head of VPN Services at Equant Network Services. In this capacity, he leads the team that manages the Equant flagship product MPLS-based IP VPN as well as traditional data services such as X.25, Frame Relay, and LAN access. His responsibilities include P&L ownership, definition of the marketing, pricing, development strategies, and cost optimization as part of the life-cycle management of each product.

Prior to assuming this product management position, Masiero was a senior research consultant in Equant's Technical Strategy group. In this role, Masiero provided strategic recommendations to Equant senior management for the introduction of leading IP technologies, such as MPLS, class of services, and IPsec.

Prior to joining Equant in 1999, Masiero held a series of sales support positions for Alcatel in both the U.S. and France. In these roles, he participated in sales efforts, delivering FR, ATM, IP solutions, and turnkey voice network solutions to international carriers.

Masiero was a French Air Force reserve officer, holds a French master's degree in computer sciences and electrical engineering from ESIGETEL, France, and an MBA from Kennesaw State University, GA.

Dedications

Monique Morrow: I dedicate this book to my parents Sam and Odette Morrow who have always encouraged me to strive for the very best where nothing is impossible. Additionally, to my dearest friends Veronique Thevenaz and Irene Hoehn who have provided me with the greatest gift of friendship. Thank you!

Azhar Sayeed: I dedicate this to several people who have shaped and affected our lives. Some notable mentions are my family members: my wife Sameena; my two wonderful daughters Abeer and Areej; my parents for all their love, affection, wonderful support, encouragement to be the best, and their hard work throughout my life; and my only brother Mazhar for his encouragement to take on challenging tasks. Several friends have shaped my career and I am indebted to all of them for their help, guidance, and friendship. But the one who left his mark and passed away very young, always smiling, is my friend and buddy Vijay Krishnamoorthy.

Acknowledgments

We wish to acknowledge a number of people who have made this book possible, namely our employer Cisco Systems, our managers Daniel Scheinman and Christine Hemrick, Steven Steinhilber, Chip Sharp, Ben Goldman, and Sangeeta Anand. Without their support, this book would not have been written. We are grateful to our technical reviewers, Tom Nadeau at Cisco Systems, Joe Fusco at Infonet, and Christophe Masiero at Equant. They ensured quality content and relevance to the industry. We would also like to thank these reviewers for their time and effort in helping to shape this book for publication. Additionally, we would like to acknowledge the following Cisco Systems individuals who have contributed to this effort (unknowingly): Sangita Pandiya; Jim Guichard; Gery Czirjak; Craig Mulholland; Ripin Checker; George Swallow; Jeff Apcar; Hari Rakotoranto; and Jaak Defour. It has truly been a team effort! We also would like to thank Susan Scheer, vice president of engineering at Cisco Systems for taking the time out of her very busy schedule to write the foreword to our book. Finally, we are most grateful to our editors and the Cisco Press team: Reina Han, Betsey Henkels, Brett Bartow, Jim Schacterle, and Tammi Barnett for working diligently with us on this book and keeping the book on schedule for publication.Contents at a Glance

This Book Is Safari Enabled

The Safari® Enabled icon on the cover of your favorite technology book means the book is available through Safari Bookshelf. When you buy this book, you get free access to the online edition for 45 days.

Safari Bookshelf is an electronic reference library that lets you easily search thousands of technical books, find code samples, download chapters, and access technical information whenever and wherever you need it.

To gain 45-day Safari Enabled access to this book:

- Go to http://www.quepublishing.com/safarienabled
- Complete the brief registration form
- Enter the coupon code N9AM-REVB-KYRN-K7BD-4T01

If you have difficulty registering on Safari Bookshelf or accessing the online edition, please e-mail customer-service@safaribooksonline.com.

Contents

Icons Used in This Book

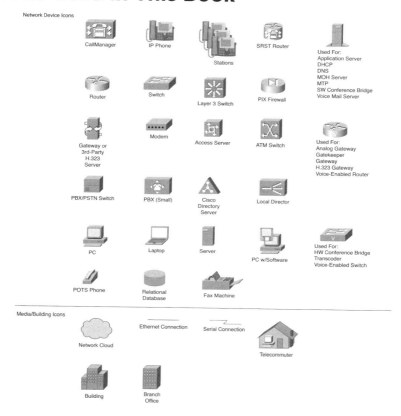

Command Syntax Conventions

The conventions used to present command syntax in this book are the same conventions used in the IOS Command Reference. The Command Reference describes these conventions as follows:

- Boldface indicates commands and keywords that are entered literally as shown.
- *Italics* indicate arguments for which you supply actual values.
- Vertical bars (|) separate alternative, mutually exclusive elements.
- Square brackets [ ] indicate optional elements.
- Braces { } indicate a required choice.
- Braces within brackets [{ }] indicate a required choice within an optional element.

Foreword

In 1996, Cisco took a dramatic step at the IETF in requesting a BOF to discuss standardizing tag switching. Tag switching is a technology that was pioneered by Cisco to establish a common control plane across IP and ATM networks. That same year, Cisco shipped the first implementation of tag switching in software release 12.0(1)A.

In less than a decade, tag switching, or as it later became known through the standardization process, Multiprotocol Label Switching (MPLS), has become a leading technology for IP-enabled services. More than 250 service providers around the globe have delivered services based on the robust Cisco MPLS roadmap, and a growing number of enterprises are also deploying MPLS to meet internal IT demands.

Why is MPLS such a driving force in the industry? The attributes of MPLS enable customers to easily separate customer or user traffic through a label (or tagging mechanism) much like the postal service forwards mail with a postal or zip code rather than the full address. Separating traffic based on labels lends itself to a virtual private network (VPN) service. Furthermore, MPLS allows providers to direct or reroute traffic through the Cisco traffic-engineering mechanisms. Providers can differentiate services through quality of service (QoS), delivering a gold, silver, and bronze offering. MPLS is now advancing to meet increasing requirements for voice- and video-based services and supporting interconnections across service provider domains to reach new markets or meet multinational customer sites. Ultimately, MPLS is evolving to enable a converged packet network that allows providers to migrate existing Layer 2 services and their IP-based services across a robust common infrastructure.

The concept of MPLS is also extended to General MPLS or GMPLS for IP + Optical requirements to deliver dynamic bandwidth allocation.

Here are just a few examples of the impact MPLS has on the industry:

- In 1999, British Telecom Global Services launched BT MPLS to deliver global multipoint, data, voice, and video network services that prioritize and support any mix of IP applications. BT MPLS offers comprehensive Service Level Agreements that cover delivery, availability, and network performance.

- Equant IP-VPN service offers five distinct classes of service for their MPLS VPN service with each class tied to particular applications. Equant allows customers to monitor their network services through a web interface.

- Infonet offers an IP VPN Secure product delivered over their MPLS-based private IP infrastructure. The service offers five or more classes of service targeted to multinational corporations in the pharmaceuticals, financial services, manufacturing, logistics, and chemical segments. Infonet has engineered voice, video, and data class separately.

- Bell Canada and St. Joseph's Healthcare partnered to deliver a telerobotics-assisted surgery over Bell Canada's VPN enterprise service to provide healthcare services in remote regions of Canada.

- The authors of this book, Monique Morrow and Azhar Sayeed, have been at the forefront of the MPLS technology revolution. They collectively have 35 years of experience in the telecommunications industry, and they have worked with service providers and enterprises around the globe to guide their service definitions and assist with their network designs. They both have hands-on, practical experience at the business and engineering levels. They have shaped the Cisco product portfolio, identifying new capabilities to meet increasing customer requirements for new applications, higher availability, and better operational controls.

We hope that this book will help you realize the business opportunity from MPLS-based services.

—Susan E. Scheer, vice president of engineering
Cisco Systems, Inc.

Introduction

MPLS is becoming the technology of choice for Layer 2 and Layer 3 service delivery. More than 250 service providers and enterprise customers have integrated MPLS into their networks to provide Layer 3 VPNs, implement traffic engineering, reduce costs from operating multiple networks, and increase revenues from new service options based on MPLS technology.

Chief technology officers, IT managers, network managers, service provider product managers, and service architects have many different choices in architecting and building their backbones. For example, they can build on existing Layer 2 networks and add IP routing functionality, or they can build a new high-speed packet core using multiservice devices and add Layer 2 or Layer 3 services to it. These decision makers also need a technology that can scale to their network for various services and track the growth curve without radically changing the design midway through deployment. For these individuals to make intelligent choices, they require a comprehensive overview that includes service management, technology management, and network management, so the total cost of ownership can be determined. This book discusses a series of steps that network managers can follow for the introduction of a new Layer 2 or Layer 3 service using MPLS.

Who Should Read This Book?

The primary audience for this book include CTOs, IT managers, network managers, service provider product managers, and service architects who are responsible for assessing technology and architecture as a basis for service and solutions deployment. Industry analysts, focusing on telecommunications, constitute the secondary audience for the book.

Network managers often question the value that MPLS brings to their business environments. This book provides them with a precise guide for evaluating the benefits of MPLS-based applications and solutions. The book guides the network manager through the business case for MPLS by exploring other technology alternatives, including applications, benefits, and deficiencies. Understanding the service creation process as the basis for MPLS-based solutions is pivotal when describing the benefits that MPLS offers. The book explores MPLS technology and its components, providing the reader with an overview of the architecture necessary to reap the true advantages that MPLS brings to a service provider or enterprise network. These advantages include new revenue opportunities and a total cost of ownership reduction that positively impacts a company's bottom line. Return on investment (ROI) models and case study examples further confirm the business impact and help the decision maker create a blueprint for MPLS service creation. Specific aspects, such as security, network management, advanced services, and the future of the technology complete the book, helping decision makers assess MPLS as a candidate for implementation.

How This Book Is Organized

The book is divided into four major sections as follows:

Part 1, "The Business Case for MPLS," includes Chapters 1, "The Dynamics of Service Creation and Deployment," and 2, "The Scope of Service Types."

- Chapter 1 details the industry dynamics, competitive outlook, business motivation, and drivers for service creation and deployment. It provides examples of service types and discusses how service providers build network infrastructures for service deployment. It also outlines why large enterprise customers need such services for either do-it-yourself (DIY) or outsourcing.

- Chapter 2 discusses the breadth of services that are available to the service provider and the enterprise and includes a detailed description of each service type. It describes Layer 2, Layer 3, remote access, and value-added services such as managed VPN, web-hosting, and managed shared services, as well as their applicability in the current environment.

Part 2, "The Technical Case for MPLS," includes Chapters 3, "Technology Overview: Making the Technology Case for MPLS and Technology Details." This chapter highlights all the available technologies for creating the services described in the previous chapters. It provides pros and cons for each option and builds a case for MPLS as a baseline technology for service creation.

Part 3, "MPLS Services and Components," includes Chapters 4, "Layer 2 VPNs," Chapter 5, "Layer 3 VPNs," Chapter 6, "Remote Access and IPSec MPLS-VPN Integration," and Chapter 7, "MPLS Security," Chapter 8, "Traffic Engineering," Chapter 9, "Quality of Service," Chapter 10, "Multicast and NGN," and Chapter 11, "IPv6."

- Chapter 4 provides an overview of Layer 2 VPNs and how MPLS can be used to deliver Layer 2 frames across a packet network. It also compares and contrasts other Layer 2 transport mechanisms that are available to do the same and highlights the benefits of MPLS in building Layer 2 VPNs.

- Chapter 5 provides a technology overview of Layer 3 service components, describing their functions and operations. It also discusses how MPLS Layer 3 VPN technology can be used to build managed central services for developing value-added models over and above VPN connectivity.

- Chapter 6 provides a technology overview and discusses the options available for remote access integration into MPLS.

- Chapter 7 discusses reasons why customers are interested in security overall. It also identifies security components inherent in MPLS and discusses government regulatory issues that may require customers to deploy encryption that is implemented jointly with MPLS.

- Chapter 8 describes the need for MPLS traffic engineering and how MPLS traffic engineering can solve problems in the networks. It also provides a technical overview of how MPLS traffic engineering works and the various benefits and applications of MPLS traffic engineering.

- Chapter 9 provides an overview of QoS and how it applies to MPLS networks. It describes how IP QoS mechanisms can be leveraged to build an MPLS DiffServ architecture that can be further strengthened by combining IP QoS and MPLS traffic engineering.

- Multicast is increasingly becoming useful for content distribution and video in networks. Chapter 10 describes how multicast can integrate into MPLS networks for easy migration from existing environments to MPLS VPN environments.

- Chapter 11 provides a description of how IPv6 can be transported in an MPLS network using 6PE as a model. It also highlights the need for IPv6-based VPNs.

Part 4, "Bringing Your MPLS Plan Together," combines the technologies that have been discussed in the previous chapters to build a comprehensive service with design, provisioning, and management taken into account. It includes

Chapters 12, "Network Management and Provisioning," Chapter 13, "Design Considerations: Putting it All Together," Chapter 14, "MPLS Case Studies," and Chapter 15, "The Future of MPLS."

MPLS architecture provides a challenge in troubleshooting and debugging due to the separation of control and data planes. Features such as MPLS OAM help trace issues and problems that are critical to deploying and managing a service. Chapter 12 describes the management and provisioning aspects for Layer 2 and Layer 3 services.

Chapter 13 provides checklist items to keep in mind when building Layer 2- and Layer 3-based services. It discusses various scalability aspects, feature protocol aspects that the designer and network manager must be aware of before making a decision to start deployment of MPLS-based Layer 2 or Layer 3 VPNs that can affect the design of the Layer 2 and Layer 3 services.

Chapter 14 discusses two case studies and both real and hypothetical customer examples, builds ROI models, and shares their lessons in deploying MPLS technology.

Chapter 15 discusses the future of MPLS and how MPLS VPN mechanisms can be leveraged to build a transport-independent infrastructure.

PART 1

THE BUSINESS CASE FOR MPLS

CHAPTER 1

THE DYNAMICS OF SERVICE CREATION AND DEPLOYMENT

This chapter details the industry dynamics, competitive outlook, business motivation, and drivers for service creation and deployment toward service provider–based next-generation networks (NGN) that use IP/MPLS as a service architecture foundation. Additionally, enterprise organizations can use IP/MPLS to segment their networks into LAN, campus, and WAN functions as a basis for service virtualization. It also outlines the needs for such services by large enterprise customers for either do-it-yourself (DIY) or outsourcing. We use the term *service provider (SP)* to refer to a telecommunications company, such as a carrier that offers services like voice, data, video, and possibly mobile.

This chapter further identifies how MPLS as a technology can be used to facilitate the service creation process for both SPs and enterprise organizations. The chapter discusses motivations for Layer 2 VPN and Layer 3 VPN deployments and compares existing technologies, such as Frame Relay, ATM, and IP. The chapter concludes with service examples, such as transparent LAN service (TLS) and multicast VPN service using MPLS as a service creation foundation.

This chapter serves as the basis for the book's subsequent chapters that discuss service types and explore the feasibility of MPLS technology for deployment in service provider NGN-based networks, in addition to enterprises that develop virtualized architectures. We also examine the service components of MPLS, such as IPv6, quality of service (QoS), traffic engineering, Layer 2 and Layer 3 constructs that are used to build services such as remote access, and Layer 2 and Layer 3 virtual private networks (VPN). We begin with a view of industry dynamics and challenges to NGNs, IP/MPLS convergence, and enterprise virtualization.

Industry Dynamics and Challenges

Since 1999, service providers have been in the process of evaluating and evolving their multiple networks to a single converged infrastructure upon which they will deploy existing and future services.

IP/MPLS is recognized by most service providers as the service-aware technology that facilitates convergence and provides operating efficiencies and service flexibility. Further, IP/MPLS is the foundation for the service provider

NGN evolution or network convergence. To be *service aware*, the architecture should offer a differentiated set of services to client applications. Chapter 10, "Multicast and NGN," explores these service-aware attributes that are part of the differentiated services architecture. Chapter 2, "The Scope of Service Types," focuses on the MPLS technology as an introductory topic to demonstrate the service creation opportunities. However, factors behind the convergence trend in the industry include a reduction of operating expense, optimizing capital expenditure, and generating new services ultimately to retain profitability. Declining revenues, aging infrastructure, increased competition among service providers, and regulatory condition factors designed to open up the market are additional factors behind the adoption of IP/MPLS by many service providers today. For service providers, we note that aging infrastructure—for example, some PSTN switches—can be ten years or older. Consequently, maintaining such infrastructure becomes cost prohibitive over time. An additional critical factor for such service convergence is to decrease the time to market (TTM) for new services, such as IP-based services, and to facilitate the operating expense reduction (OPeX), such as multiple operations support systems (OSS).

The mid- to long-term strategy characterized over the next three to seven years is for service providers to consolidate these various networks to an all-packet network that supports both existing revenue streams and future new profitable services. Some service providers have already begun this consolidation process. In the long term, the telecommunications industry can no longer support multiple networks to deploy services as these will become cost prohibitive to maintain because they include numerous OSSs, a variety of network operations centers, and so on. Content, broadband, and mobility are drivers for these new profitable services.

An *evolutionary strategy* means a gradual deployment of new services for top-line growth and new customers that require the lowest-cost network architectures. Therefore, migration to IP/MPLS should facilitate this consolidation and the delivery of common services. Figure 1-1 depicts the evolution toward a multiservice-aware IP/MPLS core and highlights the operational inefficiencies with the multiple OSSs. The figure also identifies the opportunity for service automation that can be possible with a converged network using MPLS.

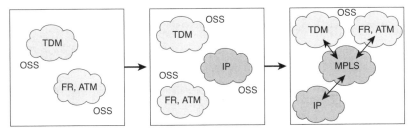

- Create operational efficiencies and increase automation in a highly technology-intensive market.
- Enable competitive differentiation and customer retention through high-margin, bundled services.
- Progressively consolidate disparate networks.
- Sustain existing business while rolling out new services.

Figure 1-1   *Service Provider Network Evolution: Network Consolidation*

One industry dynamic that is a factor for convergence is the merger and acquisitions of service provider companies, such as SBC-AT&T-BellSouth or BT-Infonet. These mergers and acquisitions only highlight the competitive nature of the service market and the trend toward SP industry consolidation.

As mentioned previously, this convergence trend toward a packet-based network, namely IP/MPLS, has often been called the *next-generation network*, a term depicting the evolution from a circuit-switched paradigm to IP/MPLS. The International Telecommunications Union (ITU) has defined the NGN in ITU-T Recommendation Y.2001 as follows:

"Next-generation network (NGN): a packet-based network able to provide telecommunication services and able to make use of multiple broadband, QoS-enabled transport technologies and in which service-related functions are independent from underlying transport-related technologies. It offers unrestricted access by users to different service providers. It supports generalized mobility, which will allow consistent and ubiquitous provision of services to users."

NGNs within service provider companies are also characterized by such factors as:

- Fixed-line-mobile convergence (FMC)

- Use of broadband and cable to deploy triple/quadruple play services, such as voice, data, video, and mobile (add GriD and we have quadruple play plus)

Architecturally, convergence can be depicted by layer simplification, such as IP directly to optics. In fact, converged architectures are no longer a futuristic goal but rather an active pursuit for service providers, such as the following examples: British Telecom's twenty-first century initiative (http://www.btglobalservices.com/business/global/en/business/business_innovations/issue_02century_network. html) and Telecom Italia (http://www.borsaitalia. it/media/borsa/db/pdf/new/2385.pdf).

What About the Enterprise Market?

The enterprise market is evolving from traditional transport services, such as leased line and Frame Relay, to IP VPNs. According to the most recent IDC surveys of corporate WAN managers, IP VPNs are the second most common choice for U.S. companies' "primary WAN technology," trailing only Frame Relay and having surpassed leased lines in late 2002. One-quarter of these enterprise customers subscribing to Frame Relay asserted that they have plans to migrate traffic away from their Frame Relay networks over the next one to two years. In Europe, IP VPN has surpassed Frame Relay but not leased line. One-third of these enterprise customers subscribing to a private line today plan to migrate within a year to IP VPN, with one-third of those migrating to a service provider–managed IP VPN.

Service providers will continue to use IP/MPLS to carry legacy services transparently as part of their evolutionary service strategy. These factors present an opportunity for both service providers and enterprise customers to leverage IP/MPLS as a new service opportunity. For the service provider, IP/MPLS can facilitate quicker time-to-market service delivery to enterprise customers who subscribe to these services. Conversely, the enterprise customer can use IP/MPLS to reduce WAN costs or offer services internally to various departments or subsidiaries. However, enterprise organizations are using MPLS to develop virtualized architectures to scale WAN/LAN, campus, and data center resources.

Service Provider Business Engineering

Service provider business engineering processes can often be complex and cumbersome due to years of supporting multiple OSS platforms. Such complexity affects service creation due to the challenges to reduce OPeX and the requirement by customers (with global subsidiaries) to ensure end-to-end quality of service when transiting multiproviders. Using IP/MPLS for service automation presents an opportunity to reduce such complexity. Work is underway in the industry to explore multiprovider service constructs. Examples include the MPLS and Frame Relay Alliance (MFA) (MPLS Layer Requirements for Inter-carrier Interconnection) and the MIT Futures Communications program for Interprovider QoS (http://cfp.mit.edu/qos/slides.html) to name a few initiatives.

The capability to offer end-to-end quality of service between providers will be pivotal in selling services to multinational enterprise customers. This fact becomes especially true unless one service provider's footprint already meets the multinational enterprise customer's requirements—for instance, Equant with MPLS-based IP VPN offered in 142 countries. Collaboration among service providers and vendors who develop these technologies is required—for example, using IP differentiated class of service to implement a class of service internationally and to ensure that the other provider will honor a class of service designation.

The issue is not so much a technology inhibitor, as it is a requirement to collaborate among providers. However, this requirement for multiprovider collaboration presents competing stresses within service providers, particularly among the global service providers. National and regional providers possess a relatively contained operational and regulatory environment and, therefore, a more containable cost structures. Such providers would benefit greatly by cross-network support from differentiated services that would provide these service providers with greater sales opportunities among multinational enterprise companies.

Global service providers, those with their own infrastructure that spans the globe, might have less to gain by enabling additional "global" service provider competitors except on their own terms. With these dynamics in the background, the questions concerning creating and adopting multiprovider service standards and which providers will drive these standards are still open. Such a standards discussion might be driven by the regional and national providers, therein extending the time for a critical mass of multiprovider services based on differentiated service class constructs. To conclude, we envision more work in this area of multiprovider service standardization. Ultimately, the key word is *service*. End customers subscribe to services based on their relevancy to the customers' business and life, and not to their underlying technology or delivery system.

Business Drivers and Requirements

This section discusses business drivers and requirements that SPs and enterprise organizations use as a framework for service convergence and virtualization via IP/MPLS.

Cost savings and revenue generations are two key drivers that attract service providers to using IP/MPLS as a business opportunity. This business opportunity translates to deploying a global ubiquitous network and to developing services that are based on this technology. Further, as mentioned previously in this chapter, time-to-market deployment possibilities of new services based on MPLS technology are critical for the service provider. Ancillary to this factor is the any-to-any service constructs that one can have with MPLS.

In fact, service providers expect operational savings by deploying new IP/MPLS-based services. Applications once implemented in circuit-based networks, such as voice, are perceived by service providers to be less expensive to deploy over IP. These cost savings come from the opportunity to consolidate multiple infrastructures (PSTN for voice, and video and data over IP). The consolidation can be facilitated by such mechanisms as differentiated class of service (CoS).

Further, service providers are exploring new revenue-generating service offerings based on IP, such as Voice over IP (VoIP), videoconference streaming, video/web data conferencing, mobility management, or follow-me, to name a few potential enhanced services. Chapter 2 describes these service options for both Layer 2 and Layer 3.

Controlling costs while supporting existing and new services, and transitioning multiple networks to a consolidated packet-based service-aware architecture, such as IP/MPLS, are indeed requirements for service providers.

To summarize the key issue, economy of scale with a focus on a multiservice paradigm for multiple customers over a converged IP/MPLS core is an important requirement for a service provider. The service element resides at the edge of the multiservice transport infrastructure.

Fundamentally, the network edge is where the customer access connections come in and where the service is created as shown in Figure 1-2.

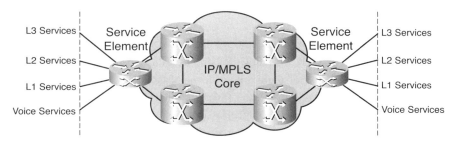

Figure 1-2   *Service-Aware Network Layer Reference Model*

Enterprise Customers

Enterprise customers have invested in applications such as enterprise resource planning (ERP), supply chain management (SCM), and customer relationship management (CRM) that facilitate collaborative workplace processes requiring integration to the corporate LAN. *ERP* is an industry term for the broad set of activities supported by multimodule application software that helps a manufacturer or other business manage the important parts of its business, including product planning, parts purchasing, maintaining inventories, interacting with suppliers, providing customer service, and tracking orders. ERP can also include application modules for the finance and human resources aspects of a business. Typically, an ERP system uses or is integrated with a relational database system.

SCM is the delivery of customer and economic value through integrated management of the flow of physical goods and associated information, from raw materials sourcing to delivery of finished products to consumers.

CRM is an information industry term for methodologies, software, and usually Internet capabilities that help an enterprise manage customer relationships in an organized way. For example, an enterprise might build a database to store information on its customers and that database could describe relationships in detail. The information could be so detailed, in fact, that management, salespeople, people providing service, and perhaps the customer directly could access information, match customer needs with product plans and offerings, remind customers of service requirements, and know which other products a customer has purchased. Applications such as ERP, SCM, and CRM facilitate workflow collaboration across the enterprise organization.

Large enterprises need efficient solutions to provide real-time access of these applications for their customers who might be geographically dispersed throughout the world and where leased lines and Frame Relay might not be readily accessible or even cost effective. Total cost of ownership (TCO) is an important driver for an enterprise customer when comparing various solutions and alternatives. Enterprise customers are exploring the pros and cons of managing disparate networks that can often lead to high operating costs. Additionally, global reach, quality of service, security, and scalability are drivers toward considering an IP VPN solution based on MPLS.

Enterprise Motivations for Migrating to Layer 3 Services

Why are enterprises migrating to Layer 3 services, particularly those that are based on MPLS? Although traditional factors, such as cost and reliability, are significant, there are new challenges for the enterprises, such as distributed applications and business-to-business communications that facilitate workflow collaboration. MPLS provides the any-to-any solution that is requisite for such applications, as opposed to the complex overlay implementations that are common in Layer 2 networks. Moreover, these applications are IP-based, so an opportunity exists for enterprise organizations to mitigate against protocol complexity. They can do so, for example, by executing a strategy that reduces the protocols to IP for applications.

Security is paramount as companies migrate from Layer 2 to Layer 3 services. Detecting and responding to distributed denial-of-service (DDoS) attacks and providing work containment measures without disturbing global services must be part of the overall security policy. MPLS security is specifically discussed in Chapter 8, "Traffic Engineering."

Business separation, mergers and de-mergers, and acquisitions require an extranet implementation coupled with security. Layer 2 implementations can be complex because of the $N*(N-1)/2$ challenge. The $(N*(N-1)/2)$ construct is referred to as an overlay model. With an overlay model, there is the associated complexity of deploying a site because for every connection one needs to reconfigure all other sites correspondingly. In contrast with a peer model for extranet, an organization using Layer 3 (that is, Layer 3 MPLS VPN), simply needs to configure the relevant Provider Edge (PE) for a Virtual Private Network (VPN).

Migrating to Layer 3 services must not negatively impact application performance. For example, in determining bandwidth for streaming services, the amount of bulk data transfer/retrieval and synchronization information is approximately <384 Kb/s. A movie clip, surveillance, or real-time video requires between 20 and 384 Kb/s. Bandwidth requirements for conversational/real-time services, such as audio and video applications, include videophone, which is between 32 and 384 Kb/s; Telnet, which is about <1 KB; and telemetry, which is approximately <28.8 Kb/s. Table 1-1 depicts application performance examples for conversational and real-time services.

Table 1-1 *Evolution of Corporate Applications => WAN Functionality Market Drivers*

Medium	Application	Degree of Symmetry	Typical Data Rates/ Amount of Data	Key Performance Parameters and Target Values		
				End-to-end One-way Delay	Delay Variation Within a Call	Information Loss**
Audio	Conversational voice	Two-way	4–25 kb/s	<150 msec Preferred* <400 msec limit*	< 1 msec	< 3% Packet Loss Ratio
Video	Videophone	Two-way	32–384 kb/s	< 150 msec preferred <400 msec limit Lip-synch: < 100 msec		< 1% Packet Loss Ratio

continues

Table 1-1 *Evolution of Corporate Applications => WAN Functionality Market Drivers (Continued)*

Data	Telemetry two-way control	Two-way	<28.8 kb/s	< 250 msec	N.A	Zero
Data	Interactive games	Two-way	<1 KB	< 250 msec	N.A	Zero
Data	Telnet	Two-way (asymmetric)	<1 KB	< 250 msec	N.A	Zero

* Assumes adequate echo control.
** Exact values depend on specific codec, but assume use of a packet loss concealment algorithm to minimize the effect of packet loss.

Finally, service providers tend to *bundle*, meaning propose multiple services with a target to prevent customer churn. An example is *triple play*, in which voice, data, and video can be offered as a bundle perhaps over a single transport link. Bandwidth requirements for cable modem can be approximately 1 Mb upstream to the provider and 3 Mb downstream to the subscriber. One could additionally have prioritized traffic for VoIP—two VoIP phone lines, per-call charging, and broadcast video MPEG 2—and one half D1, with one channel per set-top.

To summarize, IT managers must continually manage costs and maintain reliable WAN infrastructures to meet their business goals. Success in today's business climate also depends on the ability to overcome a more complex set of challenges to their corporate WANs. Enterprise IT managers are faced with and require a solution that will address the following factors:

- Geographically dispersed sites and teams that must share information across the network and have secure access to networked corporate resources.

- Mission-critical distributed applications that must be deployed and managed on a network-wide basis. Further, IT managers are faced with a combination of centralized, hosted applications and distributed applications, which complicates the management task.

- Security requirements for networked resources and information that must be reliably available but protected from unauthorized access.

- Business-to-business communication needs, both to users within the company as well as extending to partners and customers. QoS features that ensure end-to-end application performance.

- Support for the convergence of previously disparate data, voice, and video networks resulting in cost savings for the enterprise.

- Security and privacy equivalent to Frame Relay and ATM.

- Easier deployment of productivity-enhancing applications, such as enterprise resource planning (ERP), e-learning, and streaming video. (These productivity-enhancing applications are IP-based, and Layer 2 VPNs do not provide the basis to support these applications.)

- Pay-as-you-go scalability as companies expand, merge, or consolidate.

- Flexibility to support thousands of sites.

MPLS provides the any-to-any connectivity, ensures separation of organizations, functions by supporting the concept of VPN, provides security due to its inherent VPN capabilities, and supports QoS mechanisms.

Chapter 15, "The Future of MPLS," examines several case studies with return on investment (ROI) models that explore alternatives to deploying and subscribing to MPLS-based services. For a detailed view of the business implications in deploying IP-based services, please refer to the following book on the topic: *Developing IP-based Services: Solutions for Service Providers and Vendors*, by Monique Morrow et al., ISBN: 155860779X.

Service Providers and Enterprise: The Battle of Outsourcing Versus Do-It-Yourself

An increasing number of organizations is moving toward an outsourced model, or what is commonly referred to as a *managed service*, for IT and/or network operations requirements. An important driver for outsourcing to a service provider or subscribing to a managed service is cost reduction. The main technical motivation for an enterprise to subscribe to a Layer 3 MPLS VPN service has been to better manage hub and spoke topology (common in enterprise networks), where scaling is a major concern and further adds to the management complexity. In fact, an analysis of customer traffic indicates that the vast majority of traffic still flows as hub to spoke in an MPLS network. Most major applications tend to reside in one or two large HQ-operated data centers. The trend toward distributed applications that was in vogue some years ago has now reversed to a centralized operation. MPLS networks are easier to manage and additions/deletions and changes to VPNs are simpler to manage than on traditional point-to-point networks, such as Frame Relay.

Service providers are well placed to address this market using MPLS technology because of the economies of scale. A service provider can use MPLS technology to offer multiple services to multiple customers due to the peer model constructs (as opposed to the expensive overlay model associated with Layer 2 networks). Additionally, the service provider can extend the range of services provided by offering QoS and multicast support. Finally, as customers deploy applications that require an any-to-any topology, and not hub and spoke (for example, VoIP), using MPLS technology enables service providers to support any-to-any topologies.

Secondary benefits are that Layer 3 MPLS VPNs are generally easier to manage, meaning the management is outsourced to the service provider, and that Layer 3 MPLS VPNs provide higher availability (not all-dependant on a hub) as a single source of failure. A Layer 3 MPLS VPN service offering can support CoS options via the implementation of differentiated services, which is further discussed in Chapter 10. Layer 3 MPLS VPNs enable data segregation for security considerations as a result of acquisitions and mergers.

Do-It-Yourself

Total cost of ownership (TCO) is usually more attractive because a DIY deployment typically means that the enterprise customer must invest in capital up front. By employing a managed service based on Layer 3 MPLS VPN, these assets can be reduced resulting in an increase in near-term cash flow. However, some enterprise customers might subscribe to a hybrid service, often packaged by the service provider as an "unbundled" service. An example of a hybrid service is where the enterprise owns and manages the customer edge devices, while the service provider furnishes the Layer 2 transport infrastructure. In the hybrid model, the enterprise customer retains control over its edge domain.

The main motivation to implement or migrate WAN service to Layer 3 MPLS VPN in a DIY model is that the cost of the overall service (equipment and management) is lower than that of Frame Relay.

Some enterprise organizations and government entities have sensitive data security policies that dictate such an internal deployment model. Other large multinational enterprises behave as an internal "service provider" to their own departments, subsidiaries, and third-party partners, therein using MPLS to develop and deploy services. Some large enterprises with global WAN connectivity are considering MPLS to simplify management and provide services, such as via Layer 3 MPLS VPN or traffic engineering, and are challenged to reduce recurring WAN connectivity costs.

One consideration when exploring a DIY implementation versus subscribing to a managed service is to review whether an enterprise customer requires full control and end-to-end security. You also must answer the question, What is the maximum time that an enterprise IT staff needs to detect, diagnose, and restore a network and service problem? How much of the downtime experienced by the enterprise customer is attributed to configuration errors? How much staff is required by the enterprise organization to deploy these services? With pressure to focus on mission-critical applications and demonstrate operating efficiency, enterprise customers might consider a managed service as a viable option.

Enterprise Segmentation

Why segment the enterprise network? The main driver is security—that is, to mitigate against worms and provide virus containment that reduces global service impact. Three types of VPNs for enterprise segmentation are as follows:

- **Server VPNs**—For business-critical applications
- **User VPNs**—For standard production
- **Global VPNs**—For guest access and VoIP

Enterprise virtualized network services include firewalls, intrusion detection, VPN service modules such as IPSec, and load balancers. VLAN "awareness" also comprises an enterprise virtualized network service. So, when exploring enterprise segmentation requirements, it is important to note which capabilities will be applied to the designated service segments, as illustrated in Figure 1-3.

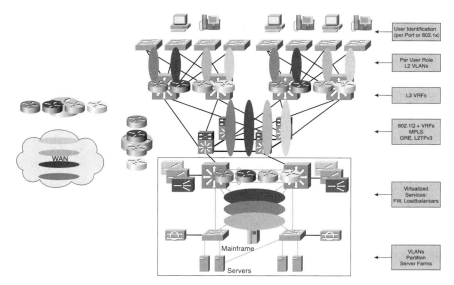

Figure 1-3 *Enterprise Virtualized Network Services*

Traditionally, the most common approach to designing campus networks has been one that is both hierarchical and modular. *Hierarchy* is defined by network roles assigned from the center of the network toward the edge: core, distribution, and access. *Modularity* is defined by grouping distribution switches to provide modular access to the core for the entire physical network areas.

One key element to providing scalability and high availability in a campus network is restraining the reach of Layer 2 failure domains by deploying a Layer 3 (routed) core and distribution, which keeps the surrounding Layer 2 domains isolated from each other in terms of failure propagation. The net result of this type of design is a network that leverages IP routing in its core and bridges toward its edge. The proportion between the size of the Layer 2 and Layer 3 domains is debatable, with some engineers advocating the use of Layer 3 switching everywhere (even in the wiring closet) and others preaching the benefits of using Layer 2 switching over most of the network with the exception of the core.

Central Services with an Enterprise Campus

One of the most important aspects of deploying Layer 3 MPLS VPNs in a campus is that it allows every VPN to utilize services and policies that are centrally available yet private to each VPN. Thus, by defining the VPN routing such that there is a single point of access into and out of the VPN, security policies that used to be distributed across the campus and were therefore hard to manage can now be enforced at this single point of access and are much simpler. The method also allows different VPNs to share a common firewall appliance that provides individualized policies by associating a separate virtual firewall to each VPN.

The key to centralizing services in the campus is to provision the routing within each VPN in such a way that a single, common point of ingress and egress exists among all of them. In service provider terms, this equates to the Internet; in campus terms, this could or could not be associated to the Internet (it generally is).

Thus, the Internet is a transit zone for VPNs to communicate with each other. To reach this transit zone, all traffic must go through a firewall in which security policies are enforced. Services could reside in the transit zone, although if the transit zone is actually the Internet, an extra firewall is required and services should be placed in a services VPN. Note that the firewalls are actually inserted outside each VPN (on the VLAN, which is mapped to the VPN), so at this point the configuration is equivalent to a problem of traditional IP routing between different networks that have a firewall at the head-end.

Subscribing to a Managed Layer 3 MPLS VPN Service

One main goal when considering a managed Layer 3 MPLS VPN-service offering is ensuring that the service is aligned with customer expectations and requirements. The two key aspects to qualifying a service provider are business and technical. For business, contractual factors, such as billing, reporting, and service-level management, highlight discussion points between a service provider and an enterprise customer. Technical discussion points can include setting up a customer edge router that can communicate with an MPLS-enabled service provider core. What role does routing play? Most of the routing protocols—including Routing Information Protocol (RIP), EIGRP, OSPF, eBGP, and static routes—are supported by Cisco. With the exception of EIGRP, these protocols are also supported in the IETF.

If a customer runs a different routing protocol from that which is supported by a service provider, redistribution is required on a customer edge router. Customer edge to customer edge, IPSec, or generic routing encapsulation (GRE) tunnels are also supported. Thus, nothing much changes on a customer edge router, and no additional functionality needs to be enabled on a customer edge router.

For a basic topology, a customer should confirm that a provider supports the following:

- Partial-to-full mesh and hub and spoke implementations.

- Routing protocol supported by the customer's network.

- Whether the service provider has a full MPLS or partial MPLS core and whether the traffic will ever traverse non-MPLS regions. If this is the case, how are SLAs and security guaranteed when traffic traverses a third-party SP network, and/or a non-MPLS network? Additionally, which tools are used for billing, managing, and troubleshooting? Which mechanisms are available to an enterprise customer to validate billing? Order a new service? Check a report? How can an enterprise customer police its SLAs?

Therefore, some key questions to ask the service provider include the following:

- What is the technical know-how of the architecture and engin-eering support staff for the development and deployment of Layer 3 (BGP-VPN) services?

- Which technologies is the service provider using to support critical enterprise applications, such as QoS, multicast, and service description?

- Does a service level agreement description exist? This is often perceived as a marketing paper by enterprises. More specifically, how do service providers implement "tight" SLA guarantees?

- Does the service provider subscribe to its own service? An example of this is the deployment of a service provider's customer care organization as an internal Layer 3 MPLS VPN to the managed service?

- Is the provider relying on a private infrastructure or the public Internet for service deployment?

- What is the number of managed Layer 3 MPLS VPNs (customers and routers, for example)?

- What are the customer references?

- What is the service provider's geographical reach? (This is a concern for multinational corporations.)

- How do service providers implement end-to-end quality of service guarantees while spanning multiple providers internationally?

- What is the Layer 3 MPLS VPN roadmap of the service provider (for example, remote access, Internet access, and so on)?

- Does the service provider support shared services while providing business unit separation? What are the valued services offered (for instance, integrated Internet in the cloud, VoIP, video, IP telephony, messaging, and security)?

- How is IPSec implemented with Layer 3 service based on BGP-VPN, therein providing any-to-any connectivity?

- Is Interior Gateway Protocol (IGP) supported between the PE and CE routers?

- What support does the service provider offer to minimize the renumbering of addresses and parallel implementation of the existing WAN, such as LAN-Interconnect over Frame Relay until a migration from Layer 2 to Layer 3 is completed? How does the service provider manage "backdoor" links?

- What is the migration plan from the service provider?

- For the security implementation, how do service providers detect and diagnose against LSP mismerging? Which mechanisms are in place to ensure that a misconfiguration by the service provider will not expose an end customer (for example, VPN leaking from one customer VPN to another)?

- How does the service provider implement Internet access and security firewalls? Does the managed service include access to multiple service providers?

- What are the service redundancy and recovery mechanisms? How is load-balancing implemented?

- How scalable is the managed service offering? What is the number of supported routes per VPN? What is the maximum number of VPNs supported?

- How is the managed service packaged and priced such that there is beneficial TCO for the enterprise?

- Could the enterprise customer pilot the service?

- Does the service provider offer training workshops with enterprise IT and networking specialists?

- How viable is the service provider's business?

- Finally, does the service provider align its services (present and future) to the enterprise customer's requirements/roadmap (present and future)?

In addition to the previous questions, you need to determine whether the service provider understands the customer business and operational issues. For example, does the service provider inquire about the customer's applications and expectations concerning the user experiences with these applications when deploying over a Layer 3 MPLS VPN? Aligning customer expectations to the new Layer 3 MPLS VPN service offering should be part of the discussion between the service provider and the customer. Also, does the service provider have any awareness of the regulatory issues that might affect the customer? In the United States, for example, Sarbanes-Oxley legislation or the Health Insurance Portability and Accountability Act (HIPAA) and others must be considered. HIPAA has two sections: HIPAA Title I deals with protecting health insurance coverage for people who lose or change jobs. HIPAA Title II includes an administrative simplification section that deals with the standardization of healthcare-related information systems. In the information technology industries, this section is what most people mean when they refer to HIPAA. HIPAA establishes mandatory regulations that require extensive changes to the way that health providers conduct business.

HIPAA seeks to establish standardized mechanisms for electronic data interchange (EDI), security, and confidentiality of all healthcare-related data. The act mandates the following: standardized formats for all patient health, administrative, and financial data; unique identifiers (ID numbers) for each healthcare entity, including individuals, employers, health plans, and healthcare providers; and security mechanisms to ensure confidentiality and data integrity for any information that identifies an individual.

A service provider who can discuss these areas with the customer is more likely to provide a compliant service than one who simply asks, "How much bandwidth do you want?"

The list is not final but certainly represents best practice guidelines toward outsourcing for Layer 3 services.

Overall, the service provider experience in deploying managed Layer 3 MPLS VPN and the service fit to customer requirements are the most critical elements in assessing a service provider. Chapter 15 highlights these key aspects in the case study examples.

The Case for Building VPNs—Layer 2 or Layer 3

VPNs comprise a set of sites that are permitted to communicate with each other privately and securely over a shared infrastructure. VPN types include IPSec, Layer 2 VPN, and Layer 3 (BGP-BGP) VPN. IPSec VPNs are difficult to categorize as either Layer 2 or Layer 3. Specifically, packets are forwarded using Layer 3 information but the service delivered to the customer is a mesh of "connections," just like in a Layer 2 service.

An IPSec VPN is perceived by the customer to be more secure than other VPN types and less reliant upon the service provider. A typical IPSec application is a hub and spoke scenario in which you have a tunnel/circuit mesh mechanism over which you manage a mesh or routing adjacencies. IPSec and MPLS are not competing technologies and, in fact, can be deployed together. This aspect is further discussed in Chapter 8.

Figure 1-4 depicts a basic example of an IPSec implementation. Note the IPSec tunnels (logical) running over the actual physical access technologies (which could be different depending on the local site). This is, of course, another benefit to using a logical Layer 3 MPLS VPN in that a logical Layer 3 MPLS VPN is access agnostic.

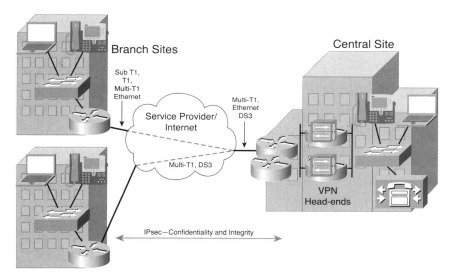

Figure 1-4   *IPSec VPN*

An overlay network is characteristic of the Layer 2 model, in which a customer's IP network is overlaid on top of a provider's network. The provider's transport, such as Frame Relay or ATM, creates a private IP network for the customer and is typically point-to-point. The challenge for the provider is managing scalability because N*(N-1)/2 provisioning is required for each customer connection and can result in inefficient routing. Further, this model lacks scalability and flexibility to support new peer-to-peer applications (any-to-any), as we previously pointed out in this chapter. This model requires complex bandwidth and design layout as it grows.

In a Layer 3 MPLS VPN, the provider exchanges routing information with customer edge routers and the service delivered is a virtual IP cloud per customer. This relationship between provider and customer edge is referred to as the *peer model.* The provider and the customer exchange IP routing information directly. The customer has only one routing peer per site, whereas the provider can have multiple customers. For example, customer A and customer B can possess the same address space, and there is no requirement for these customers to communicate with one another, therein permitting overlapping addresses between two different VPNs.

Layer 3 MPLS VPN deployments are not point-to-point connections. The key benefit of a Layer 3 MPLS VPN is the capability of implementing any-to-any connectivity without a full mesh of circuits and routing adjacencies, therein providing improved scalability for connected VPNs. Chapter 6, "Remote Access and IPSec/MPLS VPN Integration," explores various Layer 3 MPLS VPN service scenarios, such as extranet, Internet access, Carrier Supporting Carrier, and Inter-AS considerations. The Layer 3 MPLS VPN model (peer) is ideal for customers with organic growth or merger and acquisition plans.

Figure 1-5 depicts the general attributes of an overlay versus peer model.

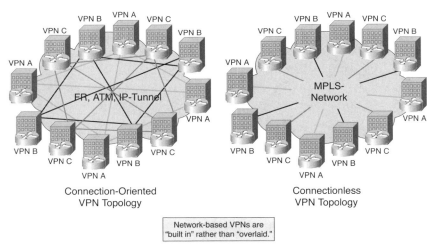

Figure 1-5   Overlay and Peer Networks

In a Layer 2 VPN, a provider forwards customer packets based on Layer 2 information, such as a Frame Relay DLCI or an Ethernet MAC address. For this reason, there is no provider involvement in the customer routing (for example, at

Layer 3) as in a Layer 3 VPN implementation. Layer 2 transport services can be characterized as "wire" and "LAN" services. A virtual private wire service consists of a fixed relationship between an attachment virtual circuit and an emulated virtual circuit (commonly referred to as *pseudowires* or *Martini IETF draft pseudowires*). These services are point-to-point and examples include Frame Relay, ATM, and Ethernet services over IP/MPLS.

A virtual private LAN service comprises a dynamic relationship learned between an attachment virtual circuit and emulated virtual circuits and the relationship determined by the customer's MAC addresses. These service relationships are multipoint services and can be referred to as *Ethernet multipoint service (EMS)*.

Chapter 5, "Layer 3 VPNs," describes these Layer 2 VPN relationships and deployment scenarios. Table 1-2 compares Layer 3 and Layer 2 service characteristics.

Table 1-2   *Layer 3 and Layer 2 VPN Characteristics*

Layer 3 VPNs	Layer 2 VPNs
Provider devices forward customer packets based on Layer 3 information (for example, IP address)	Provider devices forward customer packets based on Layer 2 information (DLCI and MAC)
Provider involvement in customer IP routing; PE is L3 peer to CE	No provider involvement in customer IP routing
RFC 2547bis VPNs (typically MPLS core)	Pseudowire and pseudo-LAN concept (Martini-drafts, L2TPv3 => VPWS, VPLS)

A Layer 3 MPLS VPN service implementation provides the enterprise customer with the following benefits: any-to-any connectivity; integration of data, voice, and video applications; service organizational segregation; ease of provisioning; value-added service extensions, such as quality of service and traffic engineering; and a possible reduction of total cost of ownership. The corresponding service provider benefits include the following: Capex and Opex efficiencies that are achieved by using a single IP/MPLS network for basic IP services, managed Layer 3 MPLS VPN services, Layer 2 transport services, voice services, and a broad portfolio of value-added services that are discussed in Chapter 2.

An enterprise customer might want a Layer 2 VPN to retain control of its Layer 3 policies, such as routing, quality of service, and security. The service provider can offer a simple transport service for customers implementing a DIY model and deliver these services on a common, already deployed IP/MPLS service-aware infrastructure. Layer 2 VPN services are complementary to Layer 3 VPN services, and choosing a VPN is not an either/or decision for an enterprise customer and a service provider because the choice depends on the enterprise customer or the service provider's specific circumstances.

Existing Technologies—Frame Relay, ATM, and IP-Based Networks: What Can They Solve?

Having looked at the case for building VPNs, we are now going to shift gears and examine how to use existing technologies, such as networks based on Frame Relay, ATM, and IP to solve problems. We'll start with Frame Relay.

Frame Relay

Frame Relay is designed as a telecommunications service for cost-efficient data transmissions in which traffic can be intermittent between an enterprise LAN and distributed between WAN locations. As a packet-switching protocol, Frame Relay was developed as a result of WAN requirements for speed and consequently for LAN-LAN, LAN-WAN interworking. Additionally, Frame Relay circuits rarely experience outages.

Frame Relay inserts data in a variable-size unit referred to as a *frame* where the error correction function (retransmission of data) is the responsibility of the end-points. The service provider typically provides a permanent virtual circuit (PVC) for most services, and this results in the customer possessing a dedicated virtual connection without being charged for a full leased line.

An enterprise can select a level of service quality by prioritizing some frames to primarily transport data over Frame Relay. Service providers offer committed information rate (CIR) as an option to a customer that permits an allocated minimum capacity and allows for traffic burst when required. Voice and video applications are not really suited for Frame Relay because these applications require a steady flow of transmission. When transmitting voice traffic over Frame Relay, however, the voice traffic is fragmented and encapsulated (via FRF.12 encapsulation) for transit across the Frame Relay network. The hub and spoke configuration is a common topology used for Frame Relay deployments. Although full mesh implementations are supported, they are rare because of the high price of their individual circuits. Furthermore, operational complexities associated with the maintenance of the connections are in the order of magnitude of N+(N-1)/2 connections; such a configuration also poses significant challenges, as stated earlier in this chapter. Typical applications for Frame Relay include LAN interconnections, client/server, e-mail, terminal-to-host, and host-to-host (such as file transfers between mainframe computers).

Asynchronous Transfer Mode

ATM defines cell switching with a packet adaptation layer that permits the high-speed transmission of data through the use of small, fixed-length packets (cells) rather than frames as used in Frame Relay.

ATM was originally developed to be a key component of Broadband ISDN (B-ISDN) and is a derivative of Frame Relay. ATM was designed to integrate voice, data, and video services by transporting these multiple channels over the same physical connection. A customer can order a private virtual circuit with a specific ATM QoS characteristic, such as voice via constant bit rate (CBR) or transactional applications via variable bit rate (VBR). Available bit rate (ABR) adjusts bandwidth according to the congestion levels in the network, but it is not used for time-critical data, such as real-time voice and video. Unspecified bit rate (UBR) can be used for noncritical applications and is the lowest ATM class.

The class of service elements of ATM provide QoS assurance for the various service types, such as voice and data. ATM benefits include dynamic bandwidth capability and CoS support for multimedia service classes. Typical business applications include videoconferencing, voice, real-time audio, and high-bandwidth data such as medical imagery. Frame Relay and ATM offer connection-oriented services, whereas IP is connectionless.

It should be said that ATM today faces its most serious competition from private leased lines. This is due to the fact that ATM is a point-to-point service and customers with point-to-point requirements often compare the cost of a private leased line with ATM or IP/MPLS and find private leased lines less expensive than ATM and IP/MPLS. However, customers often fail to consider the lack of redundancy in a leased line as compared to a resilient ATM or IP/MPLS service. Therefore, for network requirements that include resiliency or more than a few point-to-point connections, scaling and resiliency factors usually render this option unviable.

The Internet Protocol

IP has become the world's most popular open system because it is used to communicate across any set of interconnected networks. The IP suite consists of IP and the Transmission Control Protocol (TCP) and specifies common applications, such as e-mail, file transfer, and terminal emulation. The User Data Protocol (UDP) is a lightweight transport built on top of IP, and it squeezes extra performance from IP by not implementing some of the features that a more heavyweight protocol such as TCP offers. Specifically, UDP allows individual packets to be dropped (with no retries) and UDP packets to be received in a different order than the one in which they were sent. UDP is often used in videoconferencing applications or games where optimal performance is preferred over guaranteed message delivery.

Data traverses an IP-based network in the form of packets, where each packet consists of a header that specifies the source, the destination, and the message itself. The IP addressing scheme uses either IPv4 or IPv6 to address computers on the Internet. IPv4 uses 32 bits for addressing, whereas IPv6 has a 128-bit source and destination address scheme that provides more addresses than IPv4. IP permits connectivity via a variety of physical media and provides a best-effort datagram service. Therefore, no hard packet delivery guarantees exist. TCP is often used where reliability is a concern because it guarantees the delivery and ordering of transmitted data. IP provides any-to-any connectivity, as demonstrated by the Internet. Common applications that are used today by companies include e-mail, web hosting, electronic commerce, corporate intranets and extranets, and emerging VoIP. Moreover, enterprise applications, such as enterprise resource planning (ERP) and supply chain management (SCM), use IP as the key transport protocol. Business engineering processes, such as order entry, billing, and reporting, also implement IP-based applications that automate these processes.

Real-Time Transport Protocol (RTP) is one of the IPv6 protocols. It is designed to provide end-to-end network transport functions for applications transmitting real-time data, such as audio, video, or simulation data, over multicast or unicast network services. RTP provides services that include payload-type identification, sequence numbering, time-stamping, and delivery monitoring to real-time applications.

As service providers and enterprise customers converge on IP-based solutions, providing QoS and CoS guarantees such as ATM are requirements for SLA contractual adherence. Further, service interworking between access technologies, such as Frame Relay, ATM, and Ethernet, offer benefits for the customer, including nondisruptive service migration with service enhancements for a cost that is as good or better than what customers are receiving with their existing service. For the service provider, this opportunity translates to customer churn avoidance and economies of scale by eliminating stove-pipe networks, while simultaneously providing service continuity. The main goal for service convergence, therefore, is to provide common Layer 2 transport capabilities, such as QoS; SLA; operations, administration, and maintenance (OAM); and security, while retaining the ubiquity and flexibility of IP-based services. Revenue migration rather than cannibalization is the real benefit for the service provider, and this factor is discussed further in Chapter 15.

Service Examples

Customers generally desire the lowest-cost portfolio of WAN services that meet their quality objectives and connectivity requirements. Total cost of ownership factors include staff training, equipment, service charges, and service exit fees, such as those incurred when subscribing to an alternative service. For these customers, WAN connectivity costs are high due to the multiplicity of protocols implemented by the service providers. Because legacy services are expected to be matched by new service offerings, an Ethernet interface for WAN connectivity is attractive for customers because of the potential cost savings that is attributed to the removal of the protocol. Transparent LAN service (TLS) originates from metro-Ethernet at the access. Multicast-aware, VPN-based service is an example of an enhanced service offering that is needed to support IP-TV, videoconferencing, and push applications, such as stock market quotations. Internet access and secure firewall services broaden the service provider's portfolio for enhanced services, all of which can be deployed over IP/MPLS. Layer 2 MPLS services can lower transmission division multiplexing (TDM) switching costs by emulating existing Frame Relay and ATM services. MPLS traffic engineering (TE) and fast reroute (FRR) can replace synchronous digital hierarchy (SDH) for network resilience under failure scenarios. Layer 3 MPLS VPNs offer any-to-any connectivity, with support of data, voice, and video intranet applications via differentiated CoS mechanisms. Chapter 2 discusses these services in more detail.

Summary

IP/MPLS presents an opportunity for service providers to evolve their networks and services toward convergence, where intelligence and the service creation function exist at the network edge therein resulting in a multiservice architecture. This potential for service providers means optimizing economies of scale by creating new services and reducing operating expense. For the customer of a managed service, enhanced services and a reduction of total cost of ownership are possible benefits. For the enterprise, reducing operating cost and increasing WAN efficiency are motivators for deploying IP/MPLS.

CHAPTER 2

THE SCOPE OF SERVICE TYPES

This chapter discusses the breadth and depth of services available to the service provider and the enterprise customer. It provides an overview of Layer 2; Layer 3; remote access; and value-added services, such as managed VPN, web hosting, and managed shared services, as well as their applicability in the current environment. Subsequent chapters cover more detailed service descriptions; for example, Chapter 4, "Layer 2 VPNs," covers Layer 2; Chapter 5, "Layer 3 VPNS," examines Layer 3 MPLS VPN; and Chapter 6, "Remote Access and IPSec/MPLS VPN Integration," discusses remote access and IPSec integration.

Although enterprise IT managers must continually manage costs and maintain reliable wide area network (WAN) infrastructures to meet their business goals, success in today's business climate also depends on the ability to overcome a more complex set of challenges to their corporate-wide area networks. Enterprise IT managers are faced with:

- Geographically dispersed sites and teams that must share information across the network and have secure access to networked corporate resources.

- Mission-critical, distributed applications that must be deployed and managed on a network-wide basis. Most IT managers additionally must confront a combination of centralized hosted applications and distributed applications that further complicate the management and operations tasks.

- Security requirements for networked resources and information that must be reliably available but protected from unauthorized access.

- Business-to-business communication needs, both to users within the company as well as extending to partners and customers.

Layer 3 MPLS VPNs provide enterprise IT managers with a variety of opportunities for meeting these challenges, including:

- Enhanced ability to deliver a wide range of connectivity options to geographically dispersed branch offices, remote users, and teleworkers (who are viewed somewhat differently from remote users). Remote users are generally considered to be in a fixed location for at least some period of time. Traveling users or teleworkers are usually in a variety of locations and often cross several geographical borders in a day. Layer 3 MPLS VPNs also serve as foundations for extranets, such as business partners, subsidiaries, and Internet access, which are Q-quality of service (QoS) features that ensure end-to-end application performance.

- Support for the convergence of previously disparate data, voice, and video networks resulting in cost savings for the enterprise.

- Security and privacy equivalent to Frame Relay and ATM.

- Easier deployment of productivity-enhancing applications, such as enterprise resource planning (ERP), e-learning, and streaming video. (These productivity-enhancing applications are IP based, and Layer 2 VPNs do not provide the basis to support these applications.)

- Pay-as-you-go scalability as companies expand, merge, or consolidate.

- Flexibility to support thousands of sites and tens of thousands of users.

New challenges arise when extending a network footprint globally. Large enterprises with a global reach have a few options for handling these issues when working with service providers that supply global services. The preferred option is to work with a service provider that already has a global presence. Alternatively, enterprises might choose to work with multiple service providers to achieve the same global network presence. When working with multiple service providers, enterprises can choose to self-manage the interconnection between the two networks or require the service providers to manage the interconnection. In the case of self-managing the interconnection, the enterprise purchases and installs the appropriate network devices, provides the necessary support and management, and determines how to handle the routing policies between the two networks.

In the second case—when service providers manage the interconnection—the two service providers might cooperate and work out the interoperability and interconnect service issues without active participation from the enterprise. The two service providers might even implement mechanisms to maintain service quality consistently across the two networks.

Building such VPNs requires the use of Inter-Autonomous Systems (Inter-AS) VPNs. Providing seamless Layer 3 MPLS VPNs requires Inter-AS; however, networks can also be connected using other methods for which VRFs are not exchanged. Some examples of non-Layer 3 MPLS VPNs constructs are at Layer 2—for example, peering at Layer 2. Additionally, there is emerging work in the industry: Some customers are implementing Inter-AS traffic at Layer 3. IETF RFC2547bis describes alternatives for Inter-AS Layer 3 connectivity options. Additionally, Chapter 5 provides an overview of the three Layer 3 Inter-as options along with their benefits and limitations. Finally, we examine Inter-as traffic in Chapter 8, "Traffic Engineering."

Whichever situation arises, the enterprise IT managers must address interconnect issues with the service providers and be prepared to address future issues as the networks and services scale and as new services are introduced onto the MPLS-based VPNs. We explore the migration scenarios and alternatives in the Chapter 14 case study "MPLS Case Studies."

This chapter examines Layer 2, Layer 3, remote access, and value-added services as input for an IT manager and a service provider business development manager.

Overview of Layer 2 Services

Layer 2 service types include private circuit constructs: Frame Relay/ATM and emerging Ethernet. However, the use of XoverMPLS, where X is a Layer 2 construct such as Frame Relay, ATM, or Ethernet that is used to create Layer 2 VPNs for like-to-like or any-to-any implementations, is growing. This section describes various Layer 2 services available to customers.

Private circuit mechanisms typically are delivered over SONET/SDH and have been popular for the past several years. The reliability inherent in SONET/SDH is due to the automatic protection switching (APS) element, which provides recovery within 50 milliseconds. The lack of bandwidth flexibility actually makes a private circuit service less interesting for customers today because they must select between a fixed bandwidth rate, such as T1 (1.5 Mbit/s) and T3 (45 Mbit/s) in North America and E1 (2 Mbit/s and E3 (34 Mbit/s) in Europe and elsewhere internationally. The bandwidth and price differences are so significant between

T1/T3 and E1/E3 that customers tend to remain with their T1/E1 links and seek ways to reduce usage on these links. More important is that an equipment upgrade is required for both the service provider and the customer to increase from one rate to another. In a Layer 3 MPLS VPN environment, the average port speed can be less than 1 Mbps and most leased line access is purchased as fractional T1/E1.

This is where the so-called Next-Generation SDH/SONET service becomes interesting for both the service provider and the customer to deliver what the Metro Ethernet Forum (MEF) has termed *Ethernet Private Line* capability. This involves circuits with Ethernet interfaces by which a customer can subscribe to high bandwidth at rates of 1 Gbit/s or higher; additionally, an upgrade can be implemented via software instead of hardware.

Ethernet Services

Three types of Ethernet services are relevant to our discussion: Ethernet Private Line (EPL) is a point-to-point dedicated bandwidth service for customers; Ethernet Wire Service (EWS) is a point-to-point shared bandwidth service; and Ethernet Relay Service (ERS) is a point-to-multipoint service delivery that can integrate very well with Ethernet Access and Layer 3 services. Figure 2-1 depicts ERS, which fundamentally emulates Frame Relay. Frame Relay works on the principle of a permanent virtual circuit (PVC) being a logical connection, where the end points and a stated bandwidth called a *committed information rate (CIR)* are defined to the Frame Relay network devices. The bandwidth can not exceed the possible physical bandwidth. The equivalent attribute in an ERS is a VLAN-CIR-burst where the service provider specifies a VLAN ID that is similar to a Frame Relay data link connection identifier (DLCI), which is used to identify a unique virtual point-to-point connection. The customer premise equipment (CPE) is a router that could be provisioned by the service provider. The bandwidth can be complementary to Frame Relay or ATM and priced on a per–virtual circuit basis (origin-destination). Service interworking capability—for example, Ethernet to Frame Relay or ATM—can be implemented by the service provider.

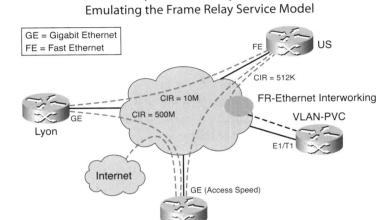

ERS (Ethernet Relay Service)
Emulating the Frame Relay Service Model

GE = Gigabit Ethernet
FE = Fast Ethernet

FE — US

CIR = 512K

CIR = 10M   FR-Ethernet Interworking

GE — CIR = 500M   VLAN-PVC

Lyon

E1/T1

Internet

GE (Access Speed)

Paris

Possible Application
• Nationwide WAN between Key Sites

Figure 2-1   *Ethernet Relay Service*

A multipoint-to-multipoint service is possible via Ethernet Private Ring (EPR), which integrates well with Ethernet Access and Layer 3 services such as ERS. EPR provides dedicated bandwidth similar to EPL. Figure 2-2 summarizes the EPR service attributes, such as dedicated bandwidth for a single customer's site, which can be based on combined time-division multiplexer (TDM) ring processor recovery (RPR) mechanisms. A single physical interface reaches all sites, and the customer assigns the VLAN IDs. The CPE is a router or bridge, and the pricing can be per site and per circuit speed. The service price can be lower than a point-to-point SDH private line and Ethernet private line.

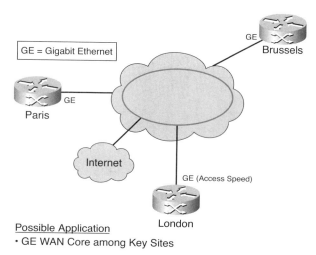

GE = Gigabit Ethernet

Possible Application
• GE WAN Core among Key Sites

Figure 2-2   *Ethernet Private Ring*

Ethernet Multipoint Service (EMS) is commonly referred to as a virtual private LAN service (VPLS) and extends service to shared bandwidth. Ethernet Relay Multipoint Service (ERMS) provides similar capability, but like EWS and EPR, it integrates well with Ethernet Access and Layer 3 services. Figure 2-3 details the EMS service attributes that are common in this service deployment. Key attributes of ERMS include any-to-any connectivity at Layer 2. The service provider network learns the customer MAC addresses, the customer assigns VLAN IDs, and the CPE can be a router or a bridge. The service pricing is per access and might require MAN-WAN rate limiting. Interworking is via Ethernet over X, where X can be Frame Relay or xDSL, for example.

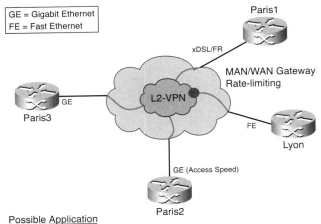

EMS (Ethernet Multipoint Service)
Any-to-Any VPN at Layer2 (=VPLS)

GE = Gigabit Ethernet
FE = Fast Ethernet

Paris1

xDSL/FR

MAN/WAN Gateway
Rate-limiting

L2-VPN

GE

Paris3

FE

Lyon

GE (Access Speed)

Paris2

Possible Application
• City LAN-Interconnect between Key Sites

Figure 2-3 *Ethernet Multipoint Service*

Figure 2-4 summarizes these service constructs.

Ethernet-Based VPN Services
Layer1 & Layer2 Services + Layer3 Access

	Dedicated Bandwidth	Shared Bandwidth
Point-to-Point	EPL (Ethernet Private Line)	EWS (Ethernet Wire Service)
Point-to-Multipoint		ERS* (Ethernet Relay Service)
Multipoint-to-Multipoint	EPR* (Ethernet Private Ring)	EMS, ERMS* (Ethernet Relay Multipoint Svc)

*Integrates well with Ethernet Access to Layer 3 Services.

Figure 2-4 *Ethernet-Based VPN Services: Layer 1 and Layer 2 Services + Layer 3 Access*

Next-Generation Network Overview and Interworking Functions

Traditionally, service providers have deployed L2VPNs over Frame Relay and ATM, which has resulted in supporting multiple service networks as described in Chapter 1, "The Dynamics of Service Creation and Deployment." Similar to traditional private circuits, Frame Relay also has limitations, such as low bandwidth capacity, and deploying or modifying Frame Relay VPNs can be cumbersome because each individual circuit must be configured manually.

A typical Frame Relay topology is hub and spoke, often burdening the hub with unnecessary transit traffic that impacts overall service efficiency, resiliency, and performance. For some carriers, Frame Relay still represents significant revenue for their business; however, the trend toward reducing operating expenses and offering customers better services (as described in Chapter 1) cannot be ignored by service providers.

IP/MPLS offers a service provider the opportunity to converge such services onto a single network infrastructure and create additional value-added services, as is described later in this chapter. Figure 2-5 summarizes these service opportunities.

The International Telecommunications Union-Telecom (ITU-T) standards body defines "NGN" (http://mailcenter.comcast.net/wm/toolbar/notheme .html#_ftn1) as "a packet-based network able to provide telecommunication services and able to make use of multiple broadband, QoS-enabled transport technologies and in which service-related functions are independent from underlying transport-related technologies. NGN enables unfettered access for users to networks and to competing service providers and/or services of their choice. It supports generalized mobility which will allow consistent and ubiquitous provision of services to users." The Cisco vision focuses on NGN convergence by the service provider of multiple services, where the converged platform could be IP/MPLS.

NGN = A Common IP/MPLS Network
Supporting ALL Services

Figure 2-5   NGN = A Common IP/MPLS Network Supporting All Services

A Layer 2 MPLS network using pseudowire technology enables the transport of various types of traffic across the IP/MPLS network as if it were a virtual wire. The IETF Pseudowire Edge (PWE) Working Group defines pseudowire mechanisms. Each of the ends of a pseudowire can possess the same Layer 2 encapsulation, such as ATM and Frame Relay. The connection between a CPE and a provider edge (PE) is referred to as an *attachment circuit (AC)*. When both ACs of a pseudowire belong to the same encapsulation type at both ends of a pseudowire, this relationship is called *like to like*.

In this case, because the data plane is still homogeneous (like to like) and both end points are of the same Layer 2 encapsulation even though there is no data plane interworking, the interworking function might involve some kind of network interworking at the control plane during the establishment of the pseudowire. Control plane interworking might be required when one attachment circuit is connected to a legacy ATM network (non-IP network) and the other end of the pseudowire attachment circuit might or might not be connected to the legacy network.

The following are the various types of L2VPN:

- ATM over MPLS (ATMoMPLS)
- Frame Relay over MPLS (FRoMPLS)
- Ethernet over MPLS (EoMPLS)

Any-to-any L2VPN is formed when both end points of the attachment circuit are not homogeneous. In this case, both end points of an AC can belong to different Layer 2 services, such as ATM, Frame Relay, Ethernet, and so on. The service interworking conversion from one type to another can be performed at either of the end points and can be either signaled or provisioned at the corresponding end points.

The following are common any-to-any configurations:

- ATM to Frame Relay
- Frame Relay to Ethernet
- ATM to Ethernet

This deployment is called XoverMPLS for Layer 2 VPNs over MPLS. Some carriers might be reluctant to deploy such services because private circuits still represent a significant revenue for their business. However, Layer 2 VPNs over MPLS present an opportunity for carriers to generate new revenue opportunities for enterprise customers who might accept risk in service quality as a tradeoff for lower costs.

For example, carriers can offer Frame Relay services over Layer 2 MPLS VPNs by encapsulating Frame Relay in MPLS frames. One motivation to migrate to a Layer 2 over MPLS business model can be depicted by the example of a global service provider offering the following types of services to enterprises and carriers: IP, Internet access, IP transit, IP-VPN and legacy voice, FR, ATM, and X25 where the majority of traffic is IP based. Further, one can observe that IP is becoming a larger part of the transport traffic mix.

The current transport traffic mix is approximately:

- 90 percent of traffic is IP.
- 10 percent of traffic is legacy, such as Frame Relay or ATM.

Up to now, all this IP and legacy traffic had been consolidated over the service provider's Layer 2 ATM backbone. The service provider seeks opportunities and alternatives for cost reduction by migrating the backbone from ATM to IP/MPLS. On a site-by-site basis, a service provider's wide range of connectivity offerings—such as ATM, Frame Relay, Ethernet, or DSL—must be considered and matched to the networking requirements for that site. If a Layer 2 connectivity option is being considered for some sites, the factors for making the decision include:

- **Existing equipment and interfaces**—Will the service provider be able to offer a connectivity option that can leverage existing equipment investments at those sites?

- **Speeds and feeds**—How much bandwidth must be provided by the service provider for those sites?

- **Ethernet availability**—Many service providers are now offering metro Ethernet services, and some sites might want to take advantage of this option. Many service providers are taking full advantage of the inherent capability of MPLS to deliver multiple services over the same device, including the delivery of metro Ethernet services.

- **Managed or self-managed customer equipment (CE)**—Consider the installation, provisioning, management, and support responsibilities for CE at each site, and factor the cost into the overall connectivity choice.

Chapter 4 describes the technology details for Layer 2 VPN constructs over MPLS.

Layer 3 Services

Common Layer 3 MPLS VPN services include the following:

- Layer 3 MPLS VPN
- Traffic engineering and differentiated services for QoS deployments
- Internet access
- Extranet service constructs

- Remote access
- Value-added services such as IP telephony, web services, and so on, which are discussed further in this chapter

A VPN is a set of sites that are allowed to communicate with each other over a shared infrastructure. Examples of VPNs are IPSec VPNs, Layer 3 MPLS VPNs, and Layer 2 VPNS. IPSec VPNs are difficult to categorize as either Layer 2 or Layer 3. Specifically, packets are forwarded using Layer 3 information but the service delivered to the customer is a mesh of "connections" just like a Layer 2 service. IPSec VPNs are perceived by customers as very secure and as less reliant on the service provider for actual implementation. IPSec VPNs are a carry-over experience from the remote access VPN where a typical application is hub and spoke via the tunnel/circuit mesh mechanism over which you manage a mesh of routing adjacencies.

At the Layer 3 MPLS VPN, a provider exchanges routing information with customer edge routers and the service delivered is a (virtual) private IP cloud per customer. This service can provide any-to-any connectivity without a full mesh of circuits and routing adjacencies, thus resulting in improved scalability for richly connected VPNs. Layer 3 MPLS VPNs have been deployed by service providers since 1999. Enterprise customer benefits include any-to-any connectivity as opposed to an expensive full-meshed Layer 2 overlay deployment and data/voice/video intranet applications for so called triple-play services.

Additionally, service and organizational segregation, ease of provisioning, quality of service and traffic engineering as value-added attributes are available via Layer 3 constructs. This results in a potential total cost of ownership reduction (TCO) for the enterprise customer and an extension of benefits to the service provider, such as the following: Capex/Opex efficiencies obtained by using a single IP/MPLS network for basic IP services, managed BGP-VPN services, Layer 2 transport services, voice services, and a broad portfolio of value-added services.

The business models are further discussed in Chapter 14, which presents a case study. Layer 3 MPLS VPNs are applicable for an enterprise customer who wants to subscribe to a managed Layer 3 service offering and are not in competition to IPSec VPN services because both can be offered as a service package to customers. For enterprise customers deploying MPLS technology, reasons for not subscribing to a managed Layer 3 service can include the following:

- Data segregation is the main goal for the enterprise organization.

- An enterprise can possess sensitive data and security concerns that dictate implementation by the enterprise customer.

- The business motivation might be to be an internal service provider to company subsidiaries and other enterprises.

- Large multinational firms with global WANs want to simplify and provide intelligent services.

- Easier modular integration for acquisitions is possible.

- Managing overlapping addresses is a potential issue due to mergers and acquisitions.

- Some customers simply do not trust service providers to manage their networks. Some customers might invest in skills or staff to deploy WAN services (for instance, technology companies).

- Some customers might want to direct access to routers to expedite the configuration change process and thereby avoid going through a service provider.

In summary, enterprise customer benefits for not subscribing to a managed service offering include fulfilling the enterprise customer's desire to retain control of Layer 3 policies (routing, Qos, and security) and to manage its own customer provider edge. However, a service provider can provide simple transport service for such customers and further deliver these services on a common, already deployed IP/MPLS infrastructure. Although Layer 2 services permit customers to retain Layer 3 visibility and control of the routers, the control can result in complexity in terms of resource management (such as operating expenditure and capital expenditure). This is because managed Layer 3 MPLS VPN services offer full outsourcing benefits (reallocation of critical staff from WAN management and troubleshooting).

However, Layer 2 VPN services are complementary to Layer 3 MPLS VPN services.

Remote Access

Enterprise telecommuters and mobile workers require secure, remote access to corporate resources from any location. In parallel to the increase of remote users, service provider offerings for broadband access over cable, DSL, and wireless technologies are becoming increasingly available. Combined with the use of VPN, these broadband services provide telecommuters and mobile workers with high-speed access (including wireless) to corporate networks from airports, hotel rooms, coffee shops, and small offices previously limited to low-speed dialup lines. Two market factors can be attributed to the growth of remote access VPN services: the geographical diversity of the workplace and the mobility of the worker. These factors drive the requirement for secure, reliable, and ubiquitous access to corporate intranets.

From a service provider's perspective, a remote access service must operate "on-net," (over the service provider's share network) and "off-net" (over the Internet or a third-party partner's network). The second market factor is due to the availability, affordability, and capability of broadband cable, DSL, and wireless technologies that motivate both enterprise customers and service providers to adopt a remote access deployment that operates over the Internet. Some reasons for such an adoption are faster network performance; increased productivity; and improved access to value-added corporate applications, such as Voice over IP (VoIP), managed security, workforce collaboration, distance learning, enterprise resource planning (ERP), videoconferencing, multicast, and secure content delivery. Applications, such as Citrix, which enables critical enterprise applications to be accessed via any enterprise device, drive a requirement for remote access capabilities with low latency to ensure effective communications—particularly for remote workers. ERP is used for a majority of business functions, such as financial planning, order management, manufacturing processes, and procurement planning deployed across various enterprise departments.

Examples of remote access to Layer 3 MPLS VPN include dial, IPSec to Layer 3 MPLS VPN, and ISDN backup. Wireless access to VPNs via Wireless Fidelity (Wi-Fi) using Secure Socket Layer (SSL) or IPSec is also growing rapidly. In terms of target market positioning, a managed low-end VPN leverages access for DSL cost-efficiency with a target market of small to medium enterprises. Figure 2-6 depicts on-net remote access via PSTN, ISDN, cable, and DSL. Remote access details are further discussed in Chapter 6.

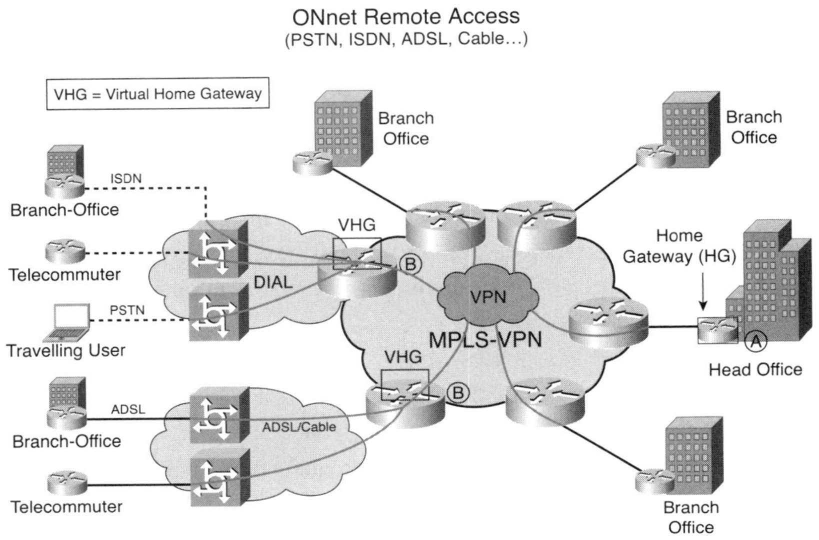

Figure 2-6 *On-Net Remote Access: PSTN, ISDN, ADSL, and Cable*

NOTE	To provide a secure off-net service via the Internet or a third-party partner network, the connection is encrypted to the corporate VPN for security. Figure 2-7 shows an off-net service construct.

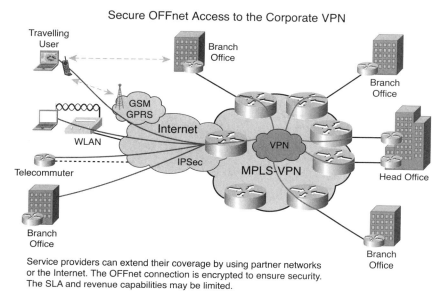

Secure OFFnet Access to the Corporate VPN

Service providers can extend their coverage by using partner networks or the Internet. The OFFnet connection is encrypted to ensure security. The SLA and revenue capabilities may be limited.

Figure 2-7 *Secure Off-Net Access to the Corporate VPN*

Finally, an enterprise customer can select site backup and resilience options from a service provider using Layer 3 MPLS VPN technology and select the appropriate service level agreement (for example, dual-leased lines to different provider edge devices with a backup for resiliency) via dial or DSL. Figure 2-8 portrays some examples of such options. Additionally, customers are also requesting the use of the Internet for backup and are willing to risk performance for the low cost of the service because they assume that the backup will be in operation for short and infrequent durations.

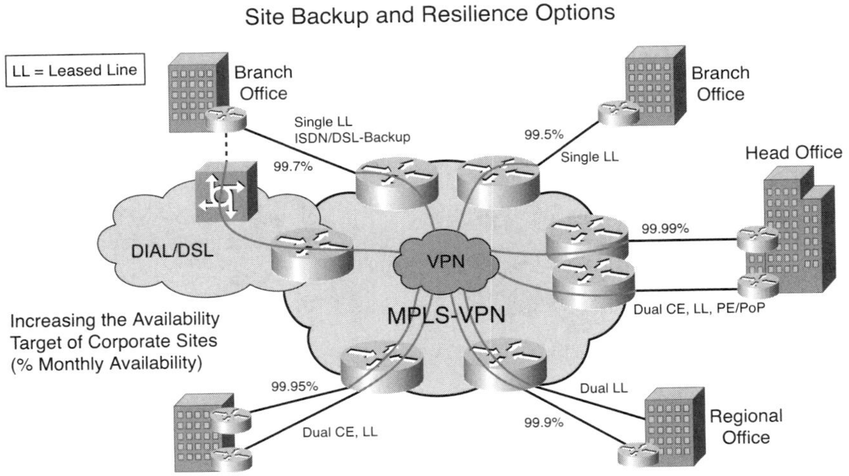

Site Backup and Resilience Options

Figure 2-8 *Site Backup and Resilience Options*

Value-Added Services

IP VPN, web, and content hosting are examples of services that service providers offer today and that can be offered via Layer 3 MPLS VPN technology. Additionally, managed security and firewall services, Internet access, VoIP with voice VPNs, and video services can be deployed using Layer 3 MPLS VPN technology. The opportunity to move up the value-added service chain via developing and deploying services based on Layer 3 MPLS VPN technology exists. A service provider can implement managed central services, such as VPN-aware HSRP/VRRP for server redundancy, VPN-aware NAT, and multicast VPNs. For secure Internet access, a firewall can be CPE or network-based, dedicated or shared, and managed by the service provider or by the enterprise itself. Figure 2-9 shows an example of a secure Internet access service.

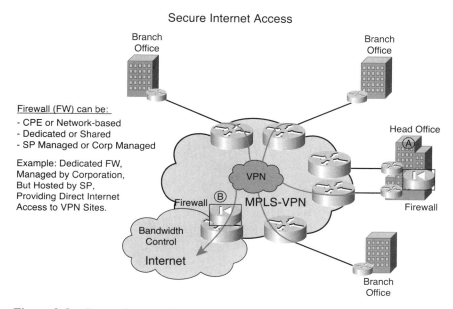

Figure 2-9 *Secure Internet Access*

Building on these service blocks, the service provider can also develop a managed intrusion detection service (IDS) with antivirus scanning, URL filtering, and denial-of-service (DoS) protection services for the enterprise customer. An example of dedicated and shared server hosting for an intranet VPN using Layer 3 MPLS VPN technology is shown in Figure 2-10.

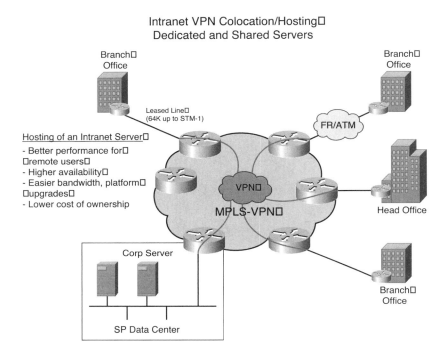

Intranet VPN Colocation/Hosting
Dedicated and Shared Servers

Figure 2-10   *Intranet VPN Colocation/Hosting: Dedicated and Shared Servers*

IP videoconferencing in the VPN can be implemented by the service provider via either a site-based or service provider–hosted model, which is depicted in Figure 2-11.

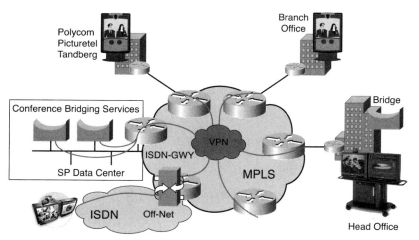

Figure 2-11 *IP Video in the VPN: Site-Based or SP-Hosted Bridges*

The use of content engines and content distribution managers permits full-screen video services to small and mid-size VPN sites. Content engines can also cache Internet content, and for further efficiency, private content can be hosted. Applications, such as e-learning, broadcast streaming, and file/software distribution, are supported by such a capability. An example is show in Figure 2-12.

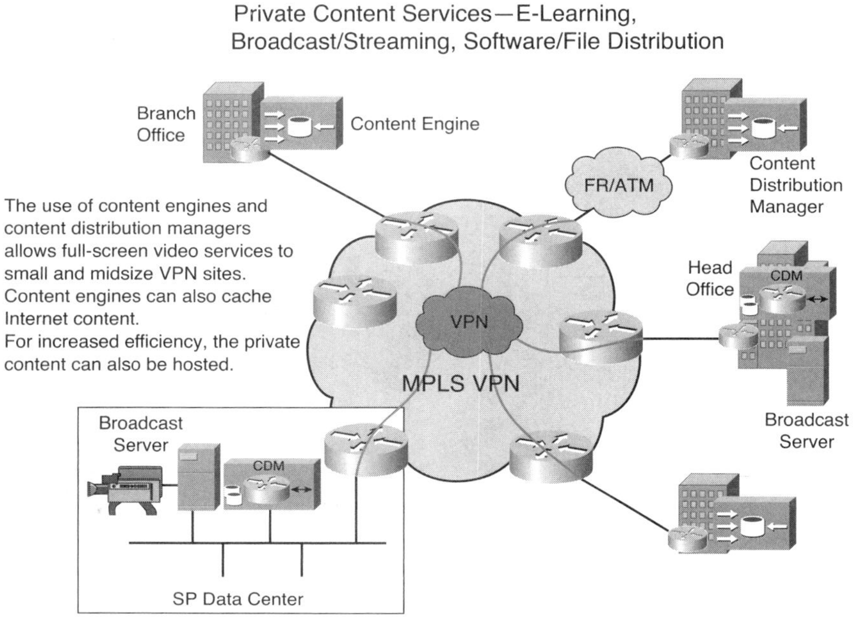

Private Content Services—E-Learning,
Broadcast/Streaming, Software/File Distribution

Branch
Office

Content Engine

FR/ATM

Content
Distribution
Manager

The use of content engines and
content distribution managers
allows full-screen video services to
small and midsize VPN sites.
Content engines can also cache
Internet content.
For increased efficiency, the private
content can also be hosted.

Head
Office

CDM

VPN

MPLS VPN

Broadcast
Server

CDM

Broadcast
Server

SP Data Center

Figure 2-12   *Private Content Services: E-learning, Broadcast/Streaming,*
Software/File Distribution

Multicast supports company video broadcasts, software distribution, music
on hold for IP telephony, and e-learning applications (just to name a few). Via
Layer 3 MPLS VPN technology, a service provider can develop and deploy a
multicast VPN for enterprise customers. Figure 2-13 depicts a multicast VPN
implementation.

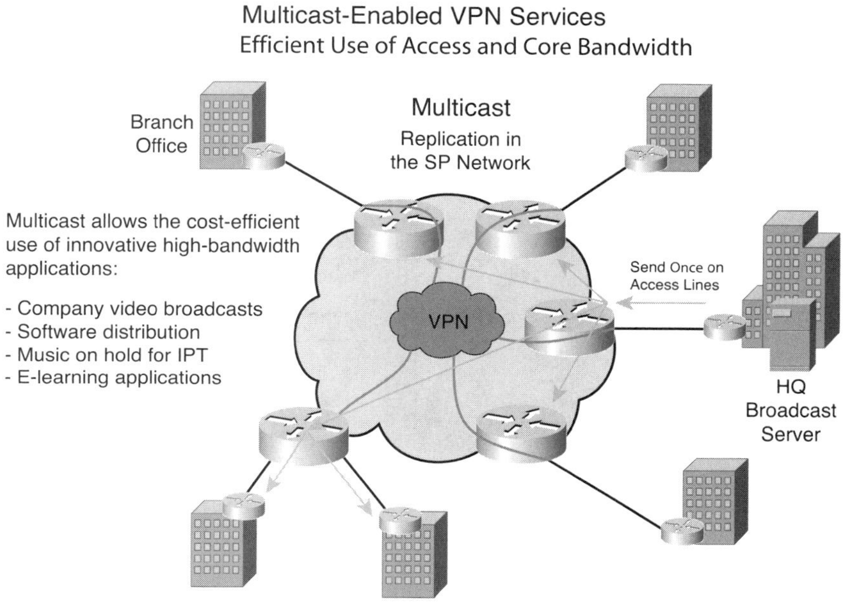

Multicast-Enabled VPN Services
Efficient Use of Access and Core Bandwidth

Branch Office

Multicast
Replication in
the SP Network

Multicast allows the cost-efficient
use of innovative high-bandwidth
applications:

- Company video broadcasts
- Software distribution
- Music on hold for IPT
- E-learning applications

Send Once on
Access Lines

VPN

HQ
Broadcast
Server

Figure 2-13 *Multicast-Enabled VPN Services: Efficient Use of Access and Core Bandwidth*

Both service providers and enterprise customers can use Layer 3 MPLS VPN technology to develop, deploy, and subscribe to a range of value-added services. As IP VPNs become commoditized, the opportunity to provide differentiated services is excellent for both the service provider and enterprise customer. Finally, the service provider can provide end-to-end SLAs via the use of differentiated services to define service classes for various services such as voice, video, and data. Differentiated service (class of service) is discussed in Chapter 9, "Quality of Service."

Figure 2-14 summarizes these value-added services. Figure 2-15 depicts the service expansion evolution for the service provider.

Summary of Value-Added Services for IP-VPNs

Managed CE	Voice VPNs
Site backup and resilience	IP telephony integration
Classes of service	Private content services
Telecommuter services	Video services (multicast)
Traveling user services	Managed extranet services
Internet access integration	ASP services
Firewall services	Virtual ISP services
Secure off-net access	Unified communications
Intranet hosting services	E-commerce
Site-to-site encryption services	End-to-end SLAs

Figure 2-14 *Summary of Value-Added Services for IP VPNs*

Extend the Scope of SP Services
Complementing Connectivity with Value-Added Services

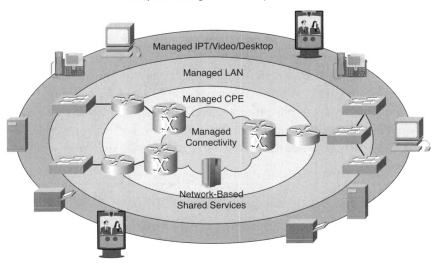

Figure 2-15 *Extend the Scope of SP Services: Complementing Connectivity with Value-Added Services*

Summary

Services can indeed be developed using MPLS technology for Layer 2, Layer 3, and an enhanced portfolio of value-added service options. Service providers can use MPLS technology to differentiate themselves in the market by evolving service blocks and service bundles to enterprise customers. Further, IP/MPLS technology can be a foundation for service convergence as specific to next-generation networks. Enterprise customers can further drive the service opportunities as per their own requirements and use IP/MPLS as a mechanism to deploy architectures that facilitate segmentation and resource virtualization.

PART 2

THE
TECHNICAL
CASE FOR
MPLS

CHAPTER 3

TECHNOLOGY OVERVIEW: MAKING THE TECHNOLOGY CASE FOR MPLS AND TECHNOLOGY DETAILS

This chapter highlights all the available technologies for creating the services described in the previous chapters. It provides pros and cons for each option and builds a case for multiprotocol label switching (MPLS) as a baseline technology for service creation. It also discusses the MPLS technology details. From a service provider perspective, it is pivotal that MPLS as a technology has been adopted by service providers as a key architectural component for next-generation networks (NGNs) because it is an enabler for services based on IP. For enterprise organizations, the virtualization capabilities inherent in MPLS facilitate LAN/ WAN segmentation rather than the implementation of static circuits and mechanisms that can be costly in the end.

Available Technologies and Options

Layer 2 technologies, such as Frame Relay and ATM, have long been deployed to provide a VPN-like service. The attributes of both technologies are quite similar, as follows:

- A virtual circuit has bi-directionality.
- A virtual circuit is established via signaling.
- A fixed hierarchy exists of a virtual path or virtual circuit.
- The virtual circuit is connection oriented and not tied to an IP control plane.
- A single route exists between the source and destination.
- A full-mesh of VCs is required to have any-to-any connectivity.

A typical topology for Layer 2 implementations has been hub and spoke, in which all VCs terminate at a central location—for example, at the enterprise headquarters. Hub and spoke topologies are depicted in Figure 3-1.

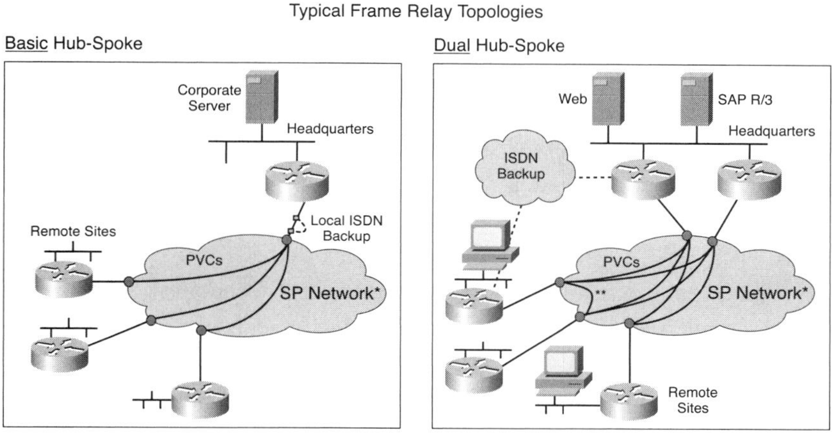

Typical Frame Relay Topologies

Basic Hub-Spoke

Dual Hub-Spoke

Figure 3-1   *Typical Frame Relay Topologies*

The attributes of a Layer 2 technology, such as Frame Relay, include the following:

- Secure, closed user group connectivity exists amongst corporate sites.

- Statistical performance guarantees throughput via permanent virtual circuit (PVC) constructs with a committed information rate (CIR) and excess information rate (EIR).

- Approximately 80% of the traffic over a Frame Relay network is IP.

As an *unbundled* service, Frame Relay is Layer 2–centric where the target market consists of enterprise customers who implement their own corporate virtual private networks (VPNs). The enterprise purchases a PVC from a service provider; consequently the enterprise is responsible for designing the VPN topology and managing the customer edge router (CE) IP routing, quality of service (QoS) policies, and application prioritization. For a service provider, Layer 2 virtual circuits are easy to sell, manage, and bill.

Another type of service using Frame Relay technology (there is a similar service in ATM service) is a *bundled* Frame Relay managed router service, which has a look and feel similar to that of an IP VPN. The target market is customers who want to outsource a VPN (Layer 2-based) to a service provider. The enterprise customer subscribes to Layer 2-based VPN services and is not involved in the PVC complexity discussions. The service provider must manage the PVC complexity, the corresponding topology, and the CE and address customer routing, application prioritization, and service level agreement management issues.

What are the possible limitations of a Layer 2 technology, such as Frame Relay, as customers request value-added services, such as a service provider–hosted IP telephony? The service provider must provision a full mesh of PVCs among all sites—for example, a VPN with 50 sites would require 1225 PVCs. Due to the requirement to prioritize Voice over IP (VoIP), the service provider must deploy separate voice and data PVCs. With shared service provider–hosted PBXs and offnet gateways, the service provider must provision PVCs from each customer site to the service provider data center. As a result, enterprise customers often do not accept a bill for the cost-prohibitive PVC mesh and the service provider consequently bears the cost itself. So, scalable value-added service architecture is needed, and MPLS technology possesses attributes that contribute to a scalable architecture for managed VPNs with value-added service elements.

Why MPLS? (High-Level Detail)

Multiprotocol label switching architecture, as discussed in IETF RFC 3031, combines the benefits of the hardware packet switching approach of ATM and the Layer 3 approach of IP. The MPLS architecture separates the control information for packets required for packet transfer itself; that is, it separates the control and data planes. In traditional IP routing, a packet is assigned in each router to a particular flow corresponding to a class of routing or a forward equivalence class (FEC). In contrast, in MPLS this assignment is performed once at the entry, or *ingress*, to the MPLS network. In an MPLS network, the FEC is identified by the network exit destination, or *egress*, and by the ingress label-switched router (LSR).

The FEC consists of a simple group of IP destinations for which a transfer can be managed in the same manner and which is assigned a fixed-length identifier called a *label.* The path corresponding to each FEC between the ingress and egress LSRs is called a *label-switched path (LSP).* An FEC, therefore, determines how packets are mapped to an LSP. This means that a packet entering at the egress LSR of an MPLS domain is assigned to an FEC following the analysis of the IP header.

A label is assigned to the FEC imposition operation either by tagging an existing field or as a complement in the packet header. The label is pivotal to the establishment of the LSP through all the routers or switches in the MPLS domain. Each LSR analyzes the incoming packet label. Then after consulting a label table that permits it to recognize the LSP, the LSR switches the packet to the next LSR after changing the value of the label. The label is removed at the egress LSR or a disposition operation is performed. By definition, an LSP is *unidirectional*—that is, two LSPs are required to support bi-directional traffic. We can compare the MPLS behavior as a Layer 2 switching approach to ATM and a Layer 3 routing approach to IP. Figure 3-2 depicts the actual MPLS label.

Label Header for Packet Media

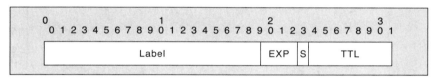

Label = 20 bits
COS/EXP = Class of Service, 3 bits
S = Bottom of Stack, 1 bit
TTL = Time to Live, 8 bits

- Can be used over Ethernet, 802.3, or PPP links
- Uses two new Ethertypes/PPP PIDs
- Contains everything needed at forwarding time
- One word per label

Figure 3-2   *Label Header for Packet Media*

The tag frame encapsulation uses a *shim header.* The shim is a header that sits between a transport header and the Layer 3 header in the packet. The label format is generic because it can be used on link layers, such as Ethernet 802.3, PPP, Frame Relay, ATM PVC, and so on. The label value consists of four octets, although several labels can be assigned to a packet, because of a concept called *label stacking*. The label can be tagged in AM in the virtual circuit identifier (VCI) and virtual path identifier (VPI) fields of the cell headers. For Ethernet, PPP, FDDI, and other technologies, an interposed header (shim) is located between the link and network headers and is used to transport the label. The LSR performs the control and transfer functions, and the transfer element uses fixed-length labels. These labels are memorized in a table with a path indication for outgoing packets. The control element consists of network-layer routing protocols and one or more label allocation mechanisms. Figure 3-3 summarizes the fundamental MPLS operation.

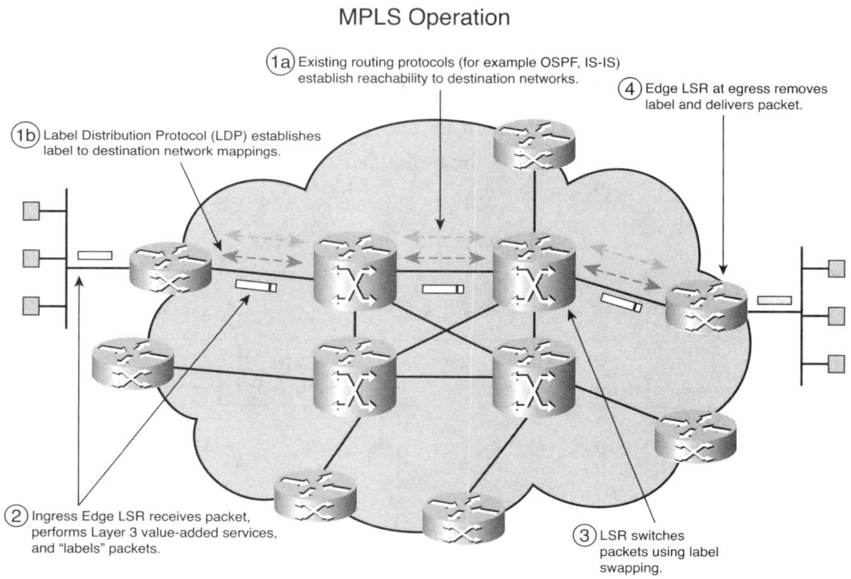

MPLS Operation

(1a) Existing routing protocols (for example OSPF, IS-IS) establish reachability to destination networks.

(4) Edge LSR at egress removes label and delivers packet.

(1b) Label Distribution Protocol (LDP) establishes label to destination network mappings.

(2) Ingress Edge LSR receives packet, performs Layer 3 value-added services, and "labels" packets.

(3) LSR switches packets using label swapping.

Figure 3-3 *MPLS Operation*

As previously mentioned, one of the key advantages of the MPLS architecture is the separation into two planes—the data plane that contains the information required to transfer a packet and a control/signaling plane that allocates the transfer information. The data plane is used for the transport of packets (or label swapping algorithm), and the control plane is analogous to routing information (for example, the location to which to send the packet). This capability is programmed into hardware by the control plane. This separation permits applications to be developed and deployed in a scalable and flexible manner. Examples of applications that are facilitated by MPLS technology include the following:

- **MPLS QoS**—This implements a quality-of-service mechanism that enables the creation of LSPs with guaranteed bandwidth.

- **BGP VPNs**—Border Gateway Protocol (BGP) is used to exchange FEC-label binding. Further, a service provider can use BGP in its network with IP routing protocols or static routing between the service provider and the customer to create a Layer 3 VPN service.

- **Traffic engineering**—Traffic engineering enables one to control traffic routing via constraint-based routing. Constraint-based routing enables a demand-driven, resource-reservation aware, routing paradigm to co-exist with current topology-driven hop-by-hop Internet interior gateway protocols.

- **Multicast routing**—Protocol Independent Multicast (PIM) is the control protocol used to create FEC tables; extensions of version 2 of the PIM protocol are used to exchange FEC-label binding.

- **Pseudowires**—These can be used to evolve legacy networks and services, such as Frame Relay, ATM, PPP, High-Level Data Link Control (HDLC), and Ethernet. Traffic is accepted into the network via a variety of access technologies, labeled at the edge, and transported over a common MPLS core. At the network egress, the label is removed and delivered in a manner similar to the ingress implementation.

- **Generalized MPLS (GMPLS)**—The goal of GMPLS is to integrate control of the routing layer with that of the optical transmission layer, thus facilitating the implementation of traffic engineering across the network. Optical cross-connect platforms do not examine traffic passing through them—in contrast to routers, for example. GMPLS deployment links capacity provisioning in the optical layer for an automated execution of resource reservation (for example, bandwidth brokering and provisioning).

As an overview, MPLS uses label swapping rather than conventional IP routing. IP routing defaults might appear, such as in traffic engineering, where the establishment of optimal routes and the analysis of available bandwidth on the various links are necessary to optimize the use of network resources. Although conventional IP routing can examine the optimal route by applying metrics, it cannot analyze the available bandwidth on the individual links.

The term *traffic engineering* refers to the specific actions performed to ensure that the express demand remains within the available capacity of network resources. These actions include routing, dimensioning procedures, and demand estimation. Current routing on IP networks is based on computing the shortest paths, where the "length" of the link is determined by an administrative assigned weight. If the traffic matrix (defining expected demand between all network end points) is known, then by appropriately setting the value of these weights, you can ensure that traffic flows are routed optimally. For example, you can ensure that available capacity is used to its maximal effect.

MPLS offers additional possibilities for routing traffic over links with sufficient capacity. LSPs completely specify the path for broadly defined traffic aggregates (defined by source and destination addresses, for instance). These attributes can be constructed in real time as required or by network management procedures by using an estimated traffic matrix. Route selection can be performed end-to-end by the edge routers or on a hop-by-hop basis.

MPLS and Quality of Service

For QoS, the integrated services model (InServ) specifies two classes of services—controlled load (CL) and guaranteed service (GS)—and uses a signaling protocol known as Resource Reservation Protocol (RSVP). Briefly, the quality of CL end-to-end connections (IETF RFC 2211) is intended to be equivalent to that provided by the traditional best effort service in a lightly loaded network. Here is an example: A large percentage of packets is successfully transmitted to the recipient and latency is no greater than the minimum delay for packets circulating in a lightly loaded network. To ensure compliance with these conditions, applications addressing CL requests (via RSVP) supply the network with an estimate of the traffic they are likely to generate via the parameters of a "leaky-bucket." This so-called *traffic specification (Tspec)* is used by each network node on the flow path to carry out admission control. The following are possible mechanisms for implementing CL:

- **Priority queuing**—It uses two queues, a high priority queue subject to CL traffic admission control and a best-effort queue.

- **Weighted fair queuing (WFQ)**—It enables you to regulate the way link capacity is shared between various traffic flows. All flows have access to the full connection bandwidth, but when several flows have packets in the queue, the service rate of each flow is proportional to its assigned "weight." By selecting the appropriate weights, you can therefore reserve capacity for CL more efficiently.

  - **Class-based queuing (CBQ)**—This is an alternative algorithm that also permits rate control for various classes of traffic.

  - **Random early detection (RED)**—This protects CL traffic to some extent from any unresponsive best-effort flows.

    RED is an active queue management mechanism that tends to ensure a fairer distribution of bandwidth between contending flows. Additionally, low latency queuing (LLQ), which is in fact Class Based Weighted Fair Queuing with a Priority Queue (know as PQCBWF), is a critical mechanism that supports both data class of service and VoIP.

- **Weighted random early detection (WRED)**—This combines the capabilities of the RED algorithm with IP precedence. This combination provides for preferential traffic handling for higher-priority packets. It can selectively discard lower-priority traffic when the interface starts to get congested and can provide differentiated performance characteristics for different classes of service. WRED is also RSVP aware and can provide an integrated services controlled-load QoS.

The guaranteed service (IETF RFC 2212) permits applications with strict requirements for both assigned bandwidth and packet delay. It ensures that all packets are delivered within a given time and not lost as a result of queue overflow. This service is first invoked by the sender, who specifies the Tspec and QoS requirements. Resource reservation is performed in the reverse direction with the receiver specifying the desired level of service (Rspec). As for CL, Tspec corresponds to the parameters of the leaky-bucket.

The InServ model did not achieve the success anticipated because its implementation is much more complex than the best-effort model. The fact that all routers must be RSVP-capable and able to store the details of every reserved CS and GS flow, although feasible on small networks, makes it unwieldy when applied to large backbones. Additionally, the guarantees defined in the two service classes tend to be either too strict (GS) or too vague (CL) for most applications.

The differentiated services model (DiffServ) relies on a broad differentiation between a small number of service classes. DiffServ support over MPLS is documented in IETF RFC 3270. Packets are identified as belonging to one class or another via the content of the differentiated services (DS) field in the IP header. Packets are generally classified and marked at the network edge depending on the type of service contract or service level agreement (SLA) between the customer and the service provider. The different classes of packet then receive different per-hop behaviors (PHBs) in the network core nodes. Service differentiation, therefore, implies differential tariffs depending on the QoS offered to flows and packets belonging to different classes. The DiffServ architecture consists of a set of functional elements embodied in the network nodes, as follows:

- The allocation of buffering and bandwidth to packet aggregates corresponding to each PHB

- Packet classification (FEC)

- Traffic conditioning, metering, and shaping

The DiffServ architecture avoids the requirement to maintain per-flow or per-user state within the network core, as is the case of InServ. The DS field (IETF RFC 2474) replaces existing definitions in the type of service (TOS) byte in IPV4 and the traffic class byte in IPv6. Six bits of the DS field are used in the form of the DS code point (DSCP) to identify the PHB to be received by a packet to each node.

Packets must first be classified according to the content of certain header fields that determine the aggregates defined in the user's SLA. Each aggregate is checked for conformity against SLA traffic parameters, and the contents of the DSC field are suitably marked to indicate the appropriate level of priority and PHB. The flow produced by certain aggregates can be reshaped to make these conform to the SLA.

In addition to best effort, considered to be the default PHB, two other PHBs have been defined by the IETF: expedited forwarding (EF) (IETF RFC 2598) and assured forwarding (AF) (IETF RFC 2597). These attributes are further discussed in Chapter 9, "Quality of Service." Service implementations using DiffServ include a virtual leased line for Vo IP via EF PHB and a so-called Olympic service using the AF PHB group where the four AF classes are used to create four service qualities referred to as platinum, gold, silver, and bronze.

Differentiating Service with Traffic Engineering

Deploying different tunnels satisfying a variety of engineering constraints can be done via DiffServ traffic engineering (DS-TE). Figure 3-4 depicts the implementation of DiffServ traffic engineering.

Different Tunnels Satisfying Different Engineering Constraints

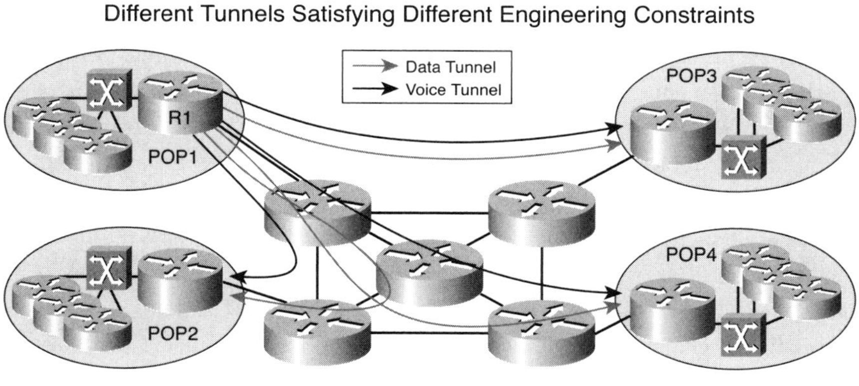

Figure 3-4   *Different Tunnels Satisfying Different Engineering Constraints*

For example, with DS-TE in Figure 3-4:

- R1 can build a voice tunnel and a data tunnel to every POP.

- If R1 sends a data packet in a data tunnel (with EXP = Data), it gets the correct QoS for data.

- If R1 sends a voice packet in a voice tunnel (with EXP = Voice), it gets the correct QoS for voice.

Class of service–based traffic engineering tunnel selection (CBTS) provides a mechanism for dynamically using different tunnels—that is, dynamically steering packets to the designated DS-TE tunnel depending on the destination or class of service (CoS). Therefore, CBTS involves minimum configuration and automatic routing and rerouting when required. CBTS complements DS-TE to achieve dynamic QoS-based routing over an MPLS core where each CoS is transported over a tunnel engineered for its specific requirements; finally, CBTS achieves strict QoS with "right-provisioning" using the mechanism available with this technology, instead of wasteful "over-provisioning."

Multicast

For multicast VPN (MVPN) implementation, the VPN multicast flow is encapsulated inside an IP multicast GRE packet at the provider edge (PE) replicated inside the MPLS cloud. This encapsulation and replication are performed via regular IP multicast methods toward the far PE, which unwraps the GRE packet to obtain the customer multicast packet. The multicast destination of the GRE packet is unique per multicast domain (that is MPLS VPN). Two kinds of multicast trees can be created in the core: default-mdt and data-mdt. The default-mdt is the basic vehicle that allows the VPN routing and forwarding (VRFs) in the PEs to establish PIM neighbor relationships and pass multicast data between the PEs. All the multicast-enabled PEs of a VRF are members of the default-mdt. The "all" requirement means that PEs that are not interested in particular (S,G) flow still get it. The data-mdt is a traffic-triggered multicast tree created separately from the default-mdt that consists only of the PEs that want to get a particular customer (S,G). Figure 3-5 summarizes the multicast VPN implementation.

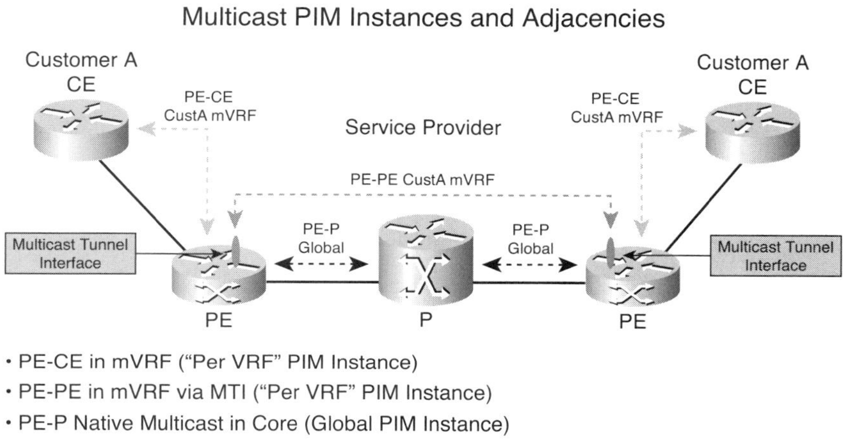

Multicast PIM Instances and Adjacencies

Figure 3-5   Multicast PIM Instances and Adjacencies

We have provided an overview of the MPLS operation with traffic engineering, quality of service, and multicast descriptions for use in an MPLS-based network. The next section discusses the benefits of MPLS as a technology foundation for service development and deployment.

Benefits

This section focuses on MPLS technology as a service building block and foundation for enterprise virtualization implementation.

MPLS offers the following benefits for service providers and enterprises:

- Flexible classification of packets and the optimization of network resources.

- Label distribution through various protocols such as BGP, LDP, RSVP, and PIM.

- The coexistence of different distribution protocols in the same LSR.

- The redundancy of numbering and global label allocation, as labels that have only a local significance.

- The introduction of modular value-added applications such as traffic engineering, quality of service, multicast, and VPN.

- Facilitation of the evolution of legacy services via Any Transport over Multiprotocol Label Switching (AToM) and even the introduction of Layer 2 VPNs as the cost of retaining Frame Relay and ATM infrastructures becomes prohibitive.

- Unification of optical and routing control planes in GMPLS to evolve SDH and Sonet services. Also, GMPLS is used to generalize the MPLS control plane over many types of transports, including packet-type networks.

MPLS, therefore, provides the predictability of routing performance required to support differentiated services and the capability to offer tight SLAs associated with these differentiated service constructs. MPLS facilitates the integration of multiple services over a common switching platform, therein contributing to the reduction of operating expense. MPLS traffic engineering can reduce the management burden for IP-based services via the creation of backup paths and by facilitating the deployment of VoIP VPNs.

Path diversity can result in unpredictability in end-to-end delay because the number of links and routers by successive packets can be varied. With path diversity, each router must perform a full routing table lookup to determine the next-hop router along the path. This process is time-consuming and produces difficulties in attaining end-to-end delay within acceptable bounds for voice and video applications.

MPLS addresses the problem in several ways. Label-switched networks fundamentally implement a simpler procedure to determine the exit path for any incoming packet (as previously discussed). In addition, traffic can be fixed to certain paths (constrained routing) via traffic engineering, which allows the service provider to exert more control over traffic congestion. For resiliency, the service provider can create backup paths such that in the event of a link or node failure, the alternative path can be activated to reduce service failure. Therefore, MPLS opens up new possibilities for traffic engineering. The definition of LSPs and their FECs allows specific traffic flows to follow paths that deviate from the shortest path designated by classical IP routing protocols.

Implementing the DiffServ architecture with MPLS can provide traffic CoS capabilities over a packet-based network, therein providing the capability to deploy voice and multimedia applications marked with a service priority. Service providers can also deploy MVPNs to support applications using streaming, such as IPTV, Windows Media Player, Real Player, Quick-Time Video Conferencing, and Netmeeting.

Service providers are deploying Layer 2 VPNS to reduce TDM switching and transmission costs as AToM technology emulates Layer 2 services, such as Frame Relay, ATM, PPP, HDLC, and Ethernet. Further, Fast Reroute is used to provide network resilience in place of SDH. Finally, GMPLS can be deployed by organizations with mixed networks and services that require control of multiple technologies, including the optical domain with rapid bandwidth allocation as a key driver to GMPLS implementation. Some current issues with GMPLS include a lack of standards for interdomain routing, integration across nonGMPLS networks, and end-to-end instantiation.

In summary, MPLS technology offers service providers the capability to develop and deploy value-added services and to implement these services in an evolutionary manner. The service architecture is depicted in Figure 3-6.

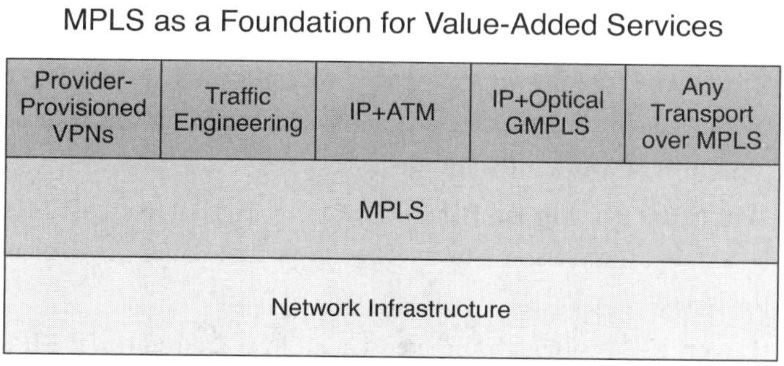

MPLS as a Foundation for Value-Added Services

Provider-Provisioned VPNs	Traffic Engineering	IP+ATM	IP+Optical GMPLS	Any Transport over MPLS
MPLS				
Network Infrastructure				

Figure 3-6   *MPLS as a Foundation for Value-Added Services*

MPLS Technology Details

This section examines how MPLS facilitates the development of service types, such as Layer 3 VPNs and traffic engineering. Figure 3-7 depicts the MPLS advanced service architectural components that include Layer 3; traffic engineering; differentiated services; Layer 2 VPNs; Virtual Private LAN Service (VPLS); IPv6, multicast GMPLS; and the key control protocols, such as Label Distribution Protocol (LDP), BGP, RSVP, and so on, that activate these service functions. As mentioned previously in this chapter, one of the key benefits of the MPLS architecture is the separation into two planes—one containing information required to transfer a packet (the data plane) and the other allocating the transfer information (the control plane). This separation permits applications to be developed and deployed in a scalable and flexible manner.

Several applications that are facilitated by the implementation of MPLS include:

- **MPLS QoS**—Implements quality of service mechanisms, such as differentiated service, which enables the creation of LSPs with guaranteed bandwidth.

- **Layer 3 VPN**—Uses BGP in the service provider's network with IP routing protocols or static routing between the service provider and the customer. The BGP protocol is used to exchange the FEC-label binding.

- **Traffic engineering**—Uses extensions of IS-IS or OSPF to distribute attributes in the network. Control processes the FEC-binding through RSVP. Traffic engineering enables you to control traffic routing and thus optimize network utilization.

- **Multicast routing via PIM**—The protocol used to create FEC tables; extensions of version 2 of the PIM protocol are used to exchange FEC–label binding.

- **Layer 2 VPN**—Can be created via a Layer 2 circuit over MPLS, commonly referred to as *Any Transport over MPLS*. Layer 2 VPNs, therefore, use Layer 2 transport as a building block to construct a Layer 2 VPN service that includes auto configuration, management, QoS, and so on.

The sections that follow focus on the technology details for a base of these services, such as Layer 3 VPNs, traffic engineering, differentiated services, and Layer 2 VPNs. Multicast, IPv6, and GMPLS are discussed in later chapters.

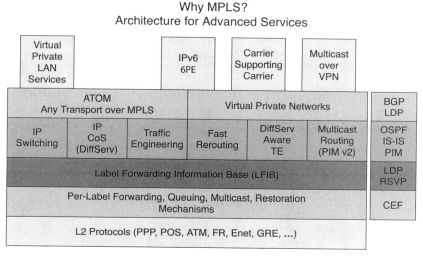

Figure 3-7 *Architecture for Advanced Services*

Layer 3 VPNs

A virtual private network can be defined as a network shared between organizations, each one with its own individual policy concerning addressing, routing, and security. A VPN thus offers significant savings to organizations because the network investment and operating costs are shared between all users. As long as the service provider ensures that traffic belonging to the various companies is isolated and the preceding policies are respected, the VPN can be considered *transparent*. Because the VPN is managed by an operator external to the company, service provision is subject to a contract in which the operator agrees to respect the terms of an SLA. This specifies, for example, the degree of network availability (number of outages, average time to repair, and so on), the minimum transmission rate between sites, packet loss, jitter, and the maximum latency between sites.

Until the introduction of MPLS architecture, private networks were deployed by using one of two basic techniques: the *overlay* and the *peer-to-peer* models. The overlay model typically uses the virtual circuits of a Frame Relay or ATM service, which means that sites can be interconnected by stacking the IP layer above a Layer 2 connectivity service. The overlay model has advantages such as permitting the duplication of addresses and the isolation of the control and security planes. The overlay model, however, also has drawbacks, including the difficulty in optimizing the size of the virtual circuits between sites, the requirement for meshed circuits that optimize routing, and the obligation to manage Layer 3 adjacencies for all circuits. Conversely, implementing IPSec over the Internet or via general routing encapsulation (GRE) tunnels are examples of Layer 3 overlay over IP for private or public network constructs.

An example of the overlay model is shown in Figure 3-8.

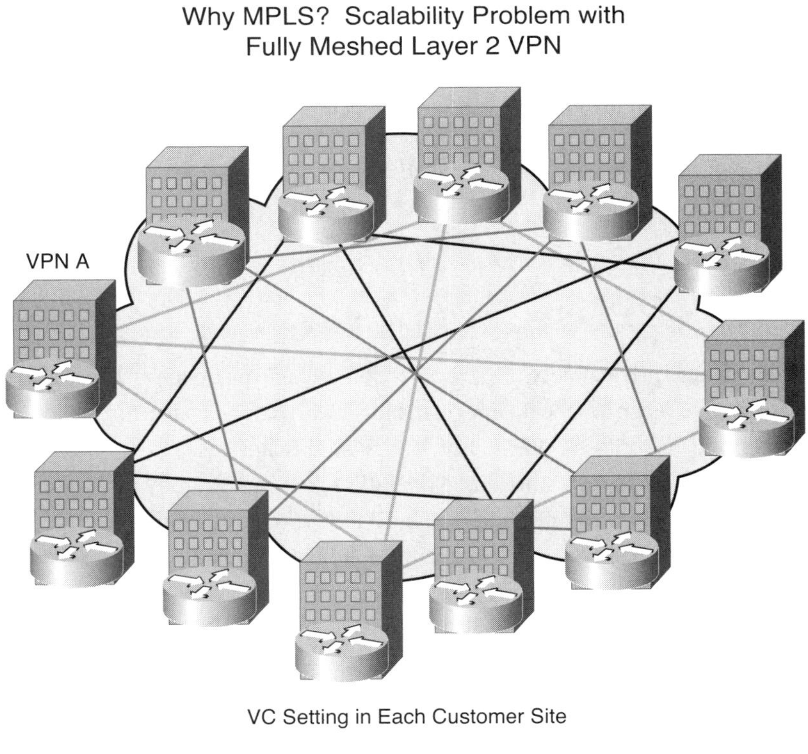

Why MPLS? Scalability Problem with
Fully Meshed Layer 2 VPN

VPN A

VC Setting in Each Customer Site

Figure 3-8   *Scalability Problem with Fully Meshed Layer 2 VPN*

Peer-to-Peer Model

In the peer-to-peer model, certain limitations of the overlay model are overcome by replacing the use of multiple virtual circuits with a direct exchange of routing information between the service provider and the customer's equipment. The main advantage of this model is the simplification of routing as it appears from the CE installation, thanks to the elimination of multiple virtual circuits. Moreover, the size of the circuits is no longer problematic, and intersite routing is optimal from the moment the service starts up. The main disadvantages of the model are the requirement for the service provider's IGP protocol to manage all the customer VPN routes and the fact that duplication of addressing between clients is impossible.

The VPN service defined over the MPLS architecture allows a group of customers to share common routing information. Thus, a site can belong to one or more VPNs. An MPLS VPN operates at Layer 3 and is also referred to as a *BGP-VPN* because multiprotocol BGP is used to transport the VPN constructs, as is discussed later in this section. The MPLS VPN architecture is based on a VPN router from the customer site (CE) and a provider edge router (PE). The service provider's backbone—specifically the provider (P) routers—have no knowledge of the routing information specific to the various customer VPNs. The PE performs the most important function in the MPLS VPN architecture; the VPN's intelligence is located on the PE, but only for VPNs directly attached to it. The PE manages two or more separate tables for storing routing information.

- **Global table**—Contains all the service provider's internal routes as well as the interface addresses of routers not linked to the VPN (P routers) and the PEs. The global table can contain external IPv4 routes that are useful for providing Internet access for example.

- **VPN routing and forwarding instances (VRF) table**—Includes the customer VPN routes associated with one or more directly connected sites (CE routers). The notion of a VRF is similar to a virtual router.

MPLS-VPN is an example of a peer-to-peer model and is depicted in Figure 3-9.

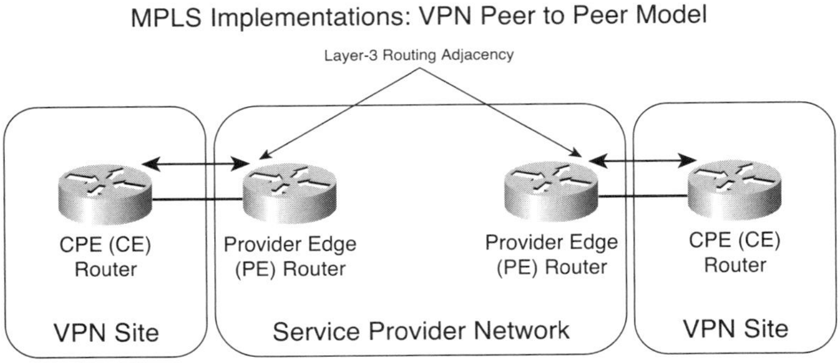

MPLS Implementations: VPN Peer to Peer Model

Layer-3 Routing Adjacency

CPE (CE) Router | Provider Edge (PE) Router | Provider Edge (PE) Router | CPE (CE) Router

VPN Site | Service Provider Network | VPN Site

Figure 3-9   *MPLS Implementations: VPN Peer-to-Peer Model*

VRF and its Function

A VRF table can be associated with all types of interfaces, logical or physical, and these interfaces can share the same routing information. Whenever a route is defined for a VPN site, the corresponding VRF is informed thanks to the routing context associated with the incoming interface. A routing context can be thought of as the capacity to manage several instances of a given routing protocol, but with a total separation of routing information between the contexts, as summarized in Figure 3-10.

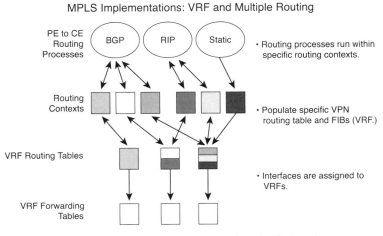

Figure 3-10   *MPLS Implementations: VRF and Multiple Routing*

To allow the duplication of addressing between VPN clients, a single identifier is required: the *route distinguisher (RD)*. The RD is added to the beginning of an IPv4 route before the route is distributed in BGP and is used for exchanging VPN routes between the PE routers. The combination of the RD and the IPv4 prefix constitutes the VPNv4 prefix. The exchange of routing information for MPLS-VPN or Layer 3 VPN is carried out using the dynamic routing protocols (BGP-4, OSPF, RIPv2, and EIGRP), one the PE-CE links, (or by static routing), and by using multiprotocol BGP between the PE routers. The multiprotocol extension of BGP is necessary because BGP does not carry simple IPv4 prefixes in the MPLS-VPN architecture. In fact, with the creation of the VPNv4 prefix through the addition of the RD to the IPv4 prefix, BGP should be able to transport prefixes that are no longer IPv4. After the route is memorized in the VRF, it is redistributed through the backbone as a VPNv4 prefix via multiprotcol BGP to the other PE routers, as shown in Figure 3-11.

MPLS Implementations: VRF Route Distribution

- PE routers distribute local VPN information across the MPLS/VPN backbone through the use of MP-iBGP and redistribution from VRF receiving PE imports routes into attached VRFs.

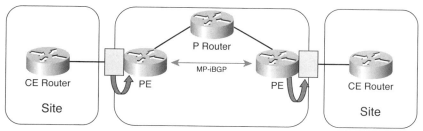

Figure 3-11   MPLS Implementations: VRF Route Distribution

Clearly, a mechanism must exist to permit the receiving PE to distribute the information on the input routes to all VPN sites concerned. The PE router must be able to obtain the suitable routes from the appropriate VRF table and then inform the affected VPN sites. To do this, the sending PE router inserts an extended community attribute called a *route target (RT)* in the BGP message. The route target is used by the receiving PE to identify which of its various VRF tables should receive the route. This function is entirely managed by configuration. Each VRF of the receiving PE must be configured with the acceptable RT values that allow it to import the appropriate routes. After the routes are imported into VRFs, the PE router can transmit them to the affected VPN sites, providing the routing information that ensures connectivity between the VPN sites. Figure 3-12 depicts the RT operation.

MPLS Implementations: Basic VPN Model

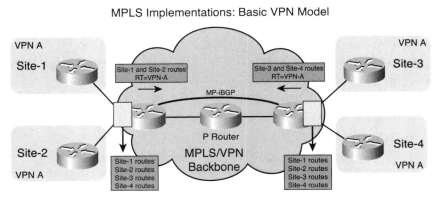

Figure 3-12 *MPLS Implementations: Basic VPN Model*

MPLS Label Stack Role

To permit label switching in the MPLS backbone, an MPLS label used by the receiving PE as an index in the transfer table is associated with each VPN route communicated via multiprotocol BGP. An additional label is then used to switch the packet to the source PE. To make the MPLS network transparent for the transmitted and received data on a VPN link, a stack or hierarchy of labels allows the transfer of information between the two PEs, while a second level (announced via multiprotocol BGP) informs the exit or egress PE on which VPN interface to send the packet. In this way, a two-level stack of labels is used for end-to-end transfer, as shown in Figure 3-13.

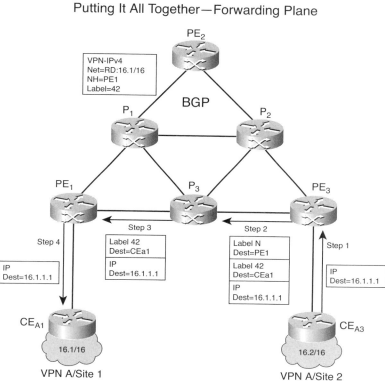

Figure 3-13 *Putting it All Together: Forwarding Plane*

Topologies

We have discussed building a basic VPN or an intranet. Via the manipulation of RTs, so-called *extranets* can also be deployed; additionally, hub and spoke topologies can be supported. The next section discusses advanced services, such as Carriers Carrier (CsC) and Inter-Provider Autonomous System (Inter-AS). CsC and Inter-AS are described in detail in the book *MPLS and VPN Architectures*, Vol 2, J. Guichard, et al., Cisco Press.

Finally, you could use a subset of the MPLS-VPN architecture. For example, you could use virtual routing forwarding instances to support multiple (overlapping and independent) routing tables (and forwarding tables) per customer, which is referred to as *Multi-Lite VRF.* The CE supports traffic separation between customer networks. In addition, no MPLS functionality exists on the CE and no label exchange exists between the CE and PE.

A customer could implement Multi-Lite CE in an enhanced branch office capability where CE routers use VRF interfaces. VLAN-like configuration on the customer side and the CE router can only configure VRF interfaces and support VRF routing tables. An alternative to Multi-Lite VRF is to use separate CE routers per each client's organization.

NOTE	When deploying Multi-Lite VRF in a multiclass configuration that has different class treatments per VRF, certain complexities are introduced that require careful rule sets to preserve traffic characteristics for each class or QoS set.

Figure 3-14 shows an example of Multi-VRF deployment.

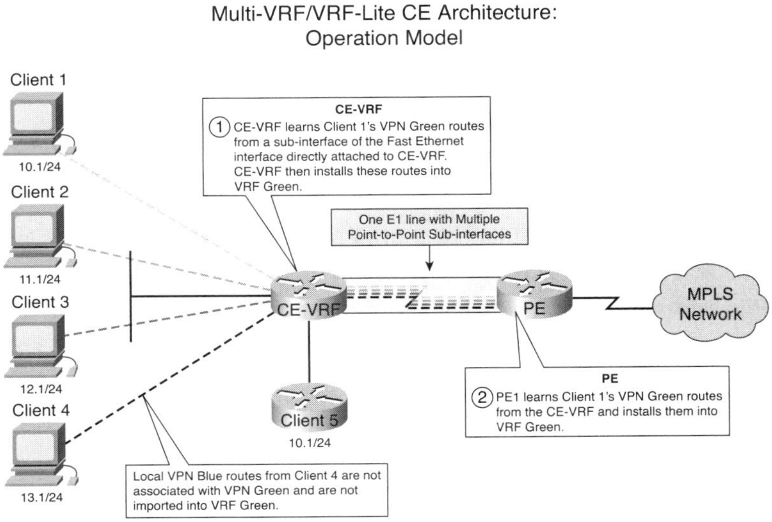

Multi-VRF/VRF-Lite CE Architecture:
Operation Model

Figure 3-14   *Multi-VRF/VRF-Lite CE Architecture: Operational Model*

(82)

We have discussed the Layer 3–centric examples of MPLS used to build VPNs or BGP-based VPNs. We have also highlighted VRF's attributes and the types of topologies that can be supported.

In the next section, we explore advanced MPLS VPN implementations, such as Carrier Supporting Carrier and Inter-AS constructs, specifically used across multiple operator domains.

Carrier Supporting Carrier and Inter-Provider Autonomous Systems

MPLS-VPN architecture can be further extended to implement advanced services, such as CsC or Inter-AS. For example, VPN sites might be geographically dispersed, requiring connectivity to different MPLS VPN service providers. That is, the transit between VPN sites might pass through multiple providers' MPLS backbones implying an exchange of VPN routing information between providers and the provider backbones might or might not provide VPN service directly. Figures 3-15 and 3-16 summarize the Inter-AS service problem and available options.

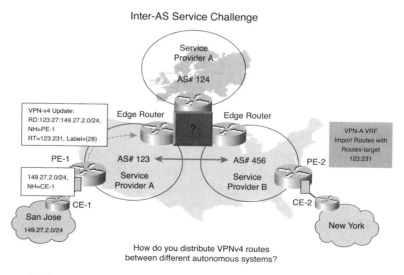

Figure 3-15 *Inter-AS Service Challenge*

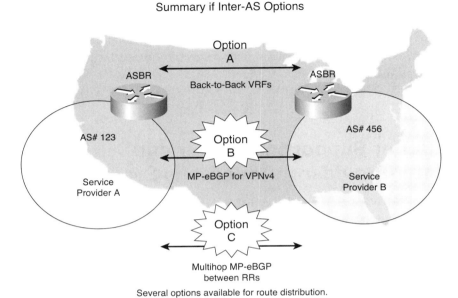

Summary if Inter-AS Options

Figure 3-16   *Summary of Inter-AS Options*

In the next section, we examine traffic engineering implementations as a service building block for MPLS-based networks.

Traffic Engineering

Traffic engineering is the process of routing data traffic to balance the traffic load on the various links, routers, and switches in the network and is most applicable in networks where multiple parallel or alternate paths are available. Fundamentally, traffic engineering involves provisioning the network to ensure sufficient capacity exists to handle the forecast demand from the different service classes while meeting their respective QoS objectives. Current routing on IP networks is based on computing the shortest path where the "length" of a link is determined by an administratively assigned weight. Reasons to deploy traffic engineering include the following:

- Congestion in the network due to changing traffic patterns

- Election news, online trading, or major sports events

- Better utilization of available bandwidth

- Route on the path that is not the shortest

- Route around failed links/nodes; fast rerouting around failures, transparently to users like SONET Automatic Protection Switching (APS)

- Building of new services—virtual leased-line services

- VoIP Toll-Bypass applications, point-to-point bandwidth guarantees

- Capacity planning traffic engineering improves aggregate availability of the network

Additional reasons to consider traffic engineering are that IP networks route based only on destination (route) and ATM/FR networks switch based on both source and destination (PVC and so on). Some large IP networks were built on ATM or FR to take advantage of source and destination routing, and overlay networks inherently hinder scaling (see "The Fish Problem" in Figure 3-17). MPLS-TE allows you to do source and destination routing while removing the major scaling limitation of overlay networks. Finally, MPLS-TE has since evolved to do things other than bandwidth optimization, which is discussed in detail in Chapter 8, "Traffic Engineering."

The challenge with destination leased cost routing is that alternate links are often underutilized, as shown in Figure 3-17.

IP Routing and the Fish

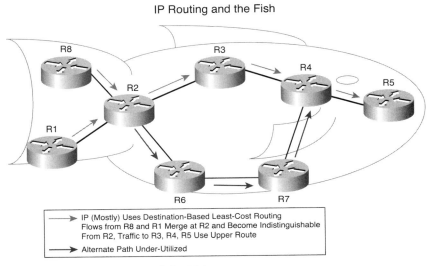

Figure 3-17   *IP Routing and the Fish*

To demonstrate how traffic engineering addresses the problem of underutilized links, we will take an example in Figure 3-18 by first defining the traffic engineer terminology:

- **Head-End**—A router on which a TE tunnel is configured (R1)
- **Tail-End**—The router on which the TE tunnel terminates (R3)
- **Mid-point**—A router through which the TE tunnel passes (R2)
- **LSP**—The label-switched path taken by the TE tunnel; here it's R1-R2-R3
- **Downstream router**—A router closer to the tunnel tail
- **Upstream router**—A router farther from the tunnel tail (so R2 is upstream to R3's downstream, and R1 is upstream from R2's downstream)

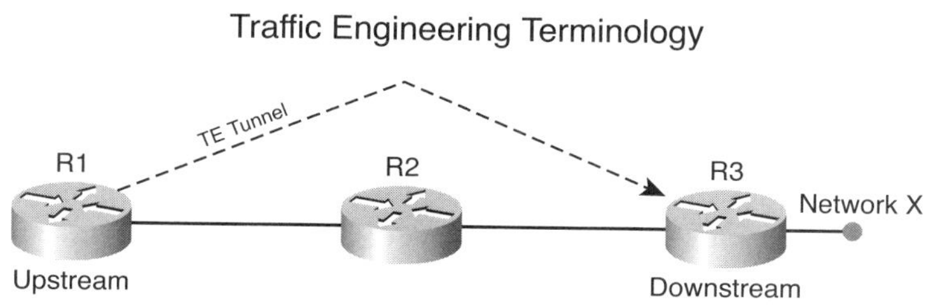

Traffic Engineering Terminology

Figure 3-18   *Traffic Engineering Terminology*

Continuing the traffic engineering building block, information distribution is done via a link state protocol, such as IS-IS or OSPF. The link state protocol is required only for traffic engineering, not for the implementation of Layer 3 VPNs. A link state protocol is required to ensure that information gets flooded and to build a topology of the entire network.

Information that is flooded includes link, bandwidth, and attributes. After available bandwidth information is flooded, a router can calculate a path from head to tail. The TE head-end performs a constrained SPF (CSPF) calculation to find the best path. CSPF is just like regular IGP SPF, except that it takes required bandwidth into account and looks for the best path from a head to a single tail, not to all devices.

Note that control capabilities offered by existing Internet Gateway Protocols (IGPs) are adequate for traffic engineering. This makes actualizing effective policies to address network performance problems difficult. IGPs that are based on shortest path algorithms contribute to congestion problems in autonomous systems within the Internet. SPF algorithms generally optimize based on a simple additive metric. These protocols are topology driven so bandwidth availability and traffic characteristics are not factors in routing decisions. (Refer to IETF RFC 2702, "Requirements for Traffic Engineering over MPLS.")

In practice, there has been zero impact from CSPF CPU utilization on even the largest networks. After the path is calculated, you need to signal it across the network.

To reserve any bandwidth so that other LSPs cannot overload the path and to establish an LSP for loop-free forwarding along an arbitrary path, a path setup is done via PATH messages from head to tail and is similar to "call setup." A PATH MESSAGE carries a LABEL_REQUEST, whereas RESV messages are done from tail to head and are analogous to "call ACK." RESV messages transport the LABEL.

Other RSVP message types exist for LSP teardown and error signaling. The principles behind path setup are that you can use MPLS-TE to forward traffic down a path other than that determined by your IGP cost and that you can determine these arbitrary paths per tunnel head-end.

Figure 3-19 describes the path setup operation.

Path Setup

- PATH message: "Can I have 40Mb along this path?"
- RESV message: "Yes, and here's the label to use."
- LFIB is set up along each hop.

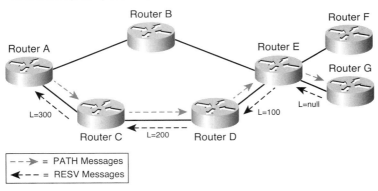

Figure 3-19 *Path Setup*

After having established the TE tunnel, the next step in deploying MPLS-TE is to direct traffic down the TE tunnel. Directing traffic down a TE tunnel can be done by one of the following four methods:

- **Autoroute**—The TE tunnel is treated as a directly connected link to the tail IGP adjacency and is *not* run over the tunnel. Unlike an ATM/FR VC, autoroute is limited to single area/level only.

- **Forwarding adjacency**—With autoroute, the LSP is not advertised into the IGP, and this is the correct behavior if you are adding TE to an IP network. However, it might not be appropriate if you are migrating from ATM/FR to TE. Sometimes advertising the LSP into the IGP as a link is necessary to preserve the routing outside the ATM/FR cloud.
- **Static routes**
- **Policy routing**

With autoroute and static route, MPLS-TE provides for unequal cost load balancing. Static routes inherit unequal cost load sharing when recursing through a tunnel. IP routing has equal-cost load balancing but not unequal cost. Unequal cost load balancing is difficult to implement while guaranteeing a loop-free topology. Therefore, because MPLS does not forward based on IP header, permanent routing loops do not occur. Further, 16 hash buckets are available for the next hop, and these are shared in rough proportion to the configured tunnel bandwidth or load-share value. Autoroute, forward adjacency, and static and policy routing are further explained in Chapter 8. To summarize, MPLS-TE operational components include the following:

- Resource/policy information distribution
- Constraint-based path computation
- RSVP for tunnel signaling
- Link admission control
- LSP establishment
- TE tunnel control and maintenance
- Assignment of traffic to tunnels

MPLS-TE can be used to direct traffic down a path other than that determined by your IGP cost. Fast Reroute (FRR) builds a path to be used in case of a failure in the network and minimizes packet loss by avoiding transient routing loops. To deploy FRR, you must pre-establish backup paths such that when a failure occurs, the protected traffic is switched onto backup paths after local repair and the tunnel head-ends are signaled to recover. Several FRR modes, such as link node and path protection, exist. In link protection, the backup tunnel tail-head is one hop away from the point of local repair (PLR). In node protection, the backup tunnel tail-end is two hops away from the PLR. Figures 3-20 and 3-21 depict link, node, and path protection mechanisms.

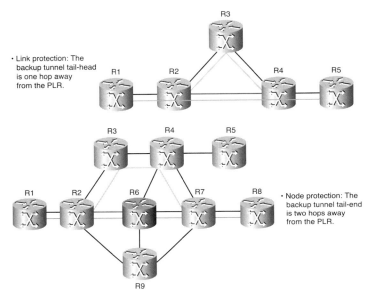

Figure 3-20 *FRR Link and Node Protection*

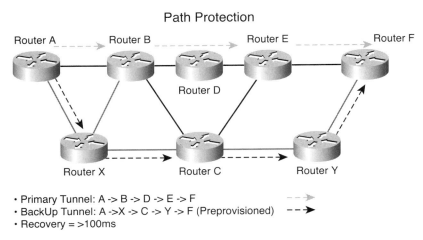

Figure 3-21 *Path Protection*

One application for MPLS-TE is to implement a virtual lease line (VLL) with bandwidth guarantees. This can be done via MPLS-TE or differentiated service-traffic engineering (DiffServ-TE) with QoS. Diff-Serv is covered in the next section of this chapter. Figure 3-22 shows an example of VLL deployment via MPLS-TE.

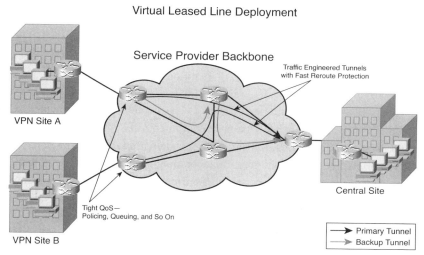

Figure 3-22   *Virtual Leased Line Deployment*

The next section discusses class of service implementation based of the differentiated service architecture or DiffServ. Details of DiffServ are described in Chapter 9. The next section highlights the architecture and provides linkage to service development.

DiffServ

DiffServ architecture relies on a broad differentiation between a small number of service classes. Packets are identified as belonging to one class or another through the content of the DiffServ field in the IP header. Packets are classified and marked at the network edge depending on the kind of traffic contract or SLA between the customer and the service provider. The different classes of packets then receive different per-hop behaviors (PHBs) in the nodes of the network core. Service differentiation also implies different tariffs depending on the QoS offering to flows and packets belonging to different classes. The DiffServ architecture consists of a set of functional elements embodied in the network nodes.

- Allocation of buffering and bandwidth aggregates corresponding to each PHB
- Packet classification (FEC)
- Traffic conditioning, metering, marking, and shaping

The sophisticated operations of packet classification are implemented at the edge of the network or in the customer equipment. The architecture avoids the requirement to maintain per-flow or per-user state within the network core.

The implementation, configuration, operation, and administration of the PHB groups supported of a DiffServ domain are dependent on sufficient resources being available. You must ensure that the amount of resources available is adequate, given the traffic conditioning parameters for contracted SLAs.

The DiffServ field (IETF RFC 2474) replaces the existing definitions of the TOS byte in IPv4 and the traffic class byte in IPv6. Six bits of the DiffServ field are used in the form if the differentiated services code point (DSCP) identifies the PHB to be received by a packet at each node.

In addition to traditional best effort, considered to be the default PHB, two other PHBs have been defined by the IETF. These are expedited forwarding (EF) (IETF RFC 2598) and assured forwarding (AF) (IETF RFC 2597). The EF PHB is designed to provide an end-to-end service with low packet loss, delay, and jitter and a guaranteed bit rate. It can be used to create a virtual leased line as described previously under MPLS-TE. The AF PHB group permits a service provider to offer differentiated levels of performance to different traffic aggregates received from customers. For example, AF packets can be divided into four subclasses with a separate resource allocation for each class.

Using DiffServ in MPLS (IETF RFC 3270) the following two types of LSPs exist:

- **EXP-Inferred–PSC LSP (E-LSP)**—Can transport different service classes and the differentiated handling of packets being carried out at the level of the LSR on the basis of the EXP field where up to eight PHBs per LSPs can be deployed.

- **Label-Only-Inferred-PSC LSP (L-LSP)**—Handles only one type of DiffServ aggregate, the label defining the LSP corresponding to a DiffServ class. The information on the DiffServ class is provided when the LSP is set up using LDP or RSVP protocol. An LSR can merge L-LSPs only if they belong to the same DiffServ class. The EXP field can be used for the discard priorities of DiffServ classes.

The advantages of E-LSP are that multiple PHBs (8) per LSP are supported, thus reducing the number of labels required; implementation is a bit easier in that you just need to configure LSRs to map EXP values to PHBs. The disadvantage is that, although 8 PHBs can be supported, DiffServ actually supports up to 64 PHBs and cannot be implemented when the shim header is not used—for example, in ATM or FR.

The advantages of L-LSP are that it can support an arbitrarily large number of PHBs in excess of 64 and can use multiple paths for different PHBs via traffic engineering. The disadvantages of L-LSP are that it consumes more labels and is more difficult to configure. For example, you need to configure LDP to signal PHBs during label establishment.

The majority of current deployments consist of less than 8 PHBs in the core. Actual deployment models on Router-LSRs consist of a single E-LSP for all CoS or 1 E-LSP per CoS (for example, 1 E-LSP for voice + 1 E-LSP for data). A strict priority queue exists for EF and a high weight exists for premium/AF (for example, 90%) with WRED for in and out-of contract. Additionally, a low weight exists for best effort (for example, 10%) with RED. The L-LSPs used today on ATM-LSRs might be required in the future on Router-LSRs, if and when more than 8 PHBs are needed.

MPLS DiffServ and MPLS TE can coexist because MPLS TE is designed as a tool to improve backbone efficiency independently of QoS. MPLS TE computes routes for aggregates across all classes and performs admission control over the "global" bandwidth pool for all classes (that is, MPLS TE does not consider the bandwidth allocated to each queue). MPLS TE and MPLS DiffServ can run simultaneously and provide their own benefits. For example, TE distributes aggregate load and DiffServ provides differentiation. This construct is referred to as differentiated services-traffic engineering (DS-TE). DS-TE makes MPLS TE aware of DiffServ in that DS-TE establishes separate tunnels for different classes and takes into account the "bandwidth" available to each class (for example, to queue).

DS-TE also considers separate engineering constraints for each class. Here are two examples: I want to limit voice traffic to 70% of link max., but I do not mind having up to 100% of best effort traffic, or I want an overbook ratio of 1 for voice but 3 for best effort.

DS-TE can take into account different metrics (for example, delay) and ensures that a specific QoS level of each DiffServ class is achieved. DS-TE provides a mechanism where different tunnels can satisfy various engineering constraints as summarized in Figure 3-23.

DS-TE Implementation Example

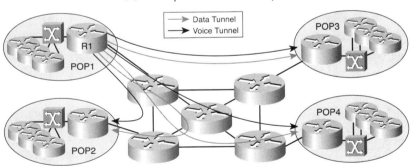

• So, with DS-TE:
  – R1 can build a voice tunnel and a data tunnel to every POP.
  – If R1 sends a data packet in a data tunnel (with EXP = Data), it will get the right QoS for data.
  – If R1 sends a voice packet in a voice tunnel (with EXP = Voice), it will get the right QoS for voice.

Figure 3-23 *DS-TE Implementation Example*

MPLS DiffServ and DS-TE are discussed further in Chapter 9.

Layer 2 VPNs

There is a broad taxonomy for Layer 2 transport consisting of the following components:

- **L2 Transport**—Provides point-to-point Layer 2 connectivity.

- **L2VPNs**—Use Layer 2 transport as a building block to build a Layer 2 VPN service that includes autoconfiguration, management, QoS, and so on. A concept of pseudowires to emulate a Layer 2 service is a key attribute for a Layer 2 VPN over MPLS.

- **Virtual private wire service (VPWS)**—Has a characteristic of a fixed relationship between an attachment-virtual circuit and an emulated virtual circuit. VPWS-based services are point-to-point (for example, Frame-Relay/ATM/Ethernet services over IP/MPLS).

- **Virtual private LAN switching service (VPLS)**—It's fundamentally an end-to-end service. It is "virtual" because multiple instances of this service share the same physical infrastructure; it is "private" because each instance of the service is independent and isolated from the others. It is "LAN service" because it tries to provide a multipoint connectivity among the participant endpoints that looks like a LAN. A dynamic relationship (learned) exists between an attachment-virtual circuit and emulated virtual circuits that is determined by customer MAC address. An example of a VPLS-based service is an Ethernet multipoint service.

- **IP LAN services (IPLS)**—A service similar to VPLS, in that all LAN interfaces are implemented in promiscuous mode and frames are forwarded based on their MAC destination addresses. However, the maintenance of the MAC forwarding tables is done via signaling rather than via the MAC address learning procedures of IEEE 802.1D. Further, the Address Resolution Protocol (ARP) messages are proxied, rather than carried transparently. You could use routers and a single MAC address rather than the more complex bridging of customer LANs. IPLS is currently an IETF draft.

Figure 3-24 summarizes the Layer 2 taxonomy.

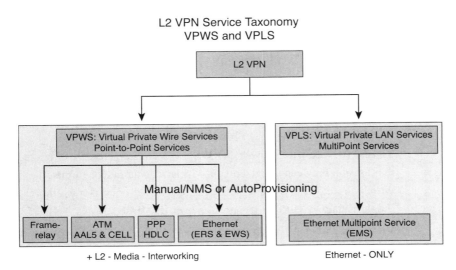

Figure 3-24   *L2 VPN Service Taxonomy: VPWS and VPLS*

A Layer 2 transport over MPLS is referred to as *Any Transport over MPLS (AToM)* by Cisco. Any transport over MPLS is required to support several services, such as Layer 2 transport over packet-based infrastructure. ATM and Frame Relay service is popular, and the provisioning of these services is easily understood. Currently, VPNs are built using either IPSec tunnels or PVCs with ATM or Frame Relay.

Layer 3 VPNs are available to offer branch office connectivity; however, this connectivity is limited to IP-based services and other protocols must be encapsulated in IP. First, encapsulating everything in IP might not always be possible. Second, service requirements, such as ATM cell transport, IGP trunking, and non-IP transport, are also needed. This trunking of Layer 2 frames can be done with Any Transport over MPLS in MPLS IP networks.

While deploying IP core, the trunking of Layer 2 can be considered because there might be existing revenue generating services for service providers or service providers might want to offer services similar to point-to-point virtual leased lines to their customers. Service providers are used to build Layer 2 services. These services are attractive in terms of revenue because the provider is not required to participate in any customer routing information. Because MPLS can transport both Layer 2 and Layer 3, it offers a viable alternative and convergence point for diverse infrastructures. Moreover, specific services, such as transparent LAN connectivity, extension of broadcast domain, virtual leased line, and voice trunking, can be easily built when AToM functionality is combined with MPLS QoS and traffic engineering.

An AToM overview is depicted in Figure 3-25.

Any Transport over MPLS (AToM)

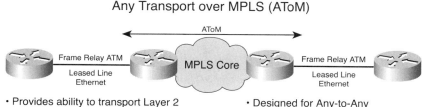

- Provides ability to transport Layer 2 traffic across MPLS packet-based core networks, extending the richness of MPLS capabilities to L2 VPNs.
- A scalable architecture that supports the multiplexing of subscriber connections.
- A standards track open architecture allows extensibility to many transport types.

- Designed for Any-to-Any connectivity.
- Service provider does not participate in customer routing.
- Allows service providers to combine with QoS and MPLS traffic engineering to provide virtual leased line like services.

Figure 3-25 *Any Transport over MPLS (AToM)*

Layer 2 transport options include Frame Relay, ATM AAL5 and ATM Cell Relay, Ethernet, 802.1q (VLAN), Packet Over Sonet (POS), TDM, and Cisco HDLC and PPP. The architectural elements of AToM consist of the following: a control connection performed by directed LDP, a transport component called a *tunnel header* or *tunnel label*, a tunnelling component that consists of a demultiplexer field or virtual circuit label, and a Layer 2 protocol data unit (PDU) that provides an emulated virtual circuit encapsulation via the control word attribute. Figure 3-26 summarizes the AToM architectural elements.

Layer-2 Transport across MPLS

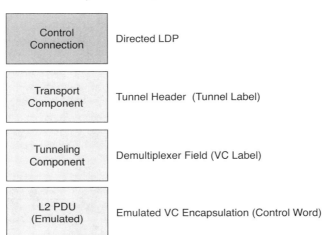

Control Connection	Directed LDP
Transport Component	Tunnel Header (Tunnel Label)
Tunneling Component	Demultiplexer Field (VC Label)
L2 PDU (Emulated)	Emulated VC Encapsulation (Control Word)

Figure 3-26   *Layer 2 Transport Across MPLS*

- AToM is used for the point-to-point transport of Layer 2 PDUs across an MPLS-enabled core via directed LDP sessions to negotiate virtual circuit labels between participating peers. AToM can use a control word to preserve relevant information in transported PDUs (for instance, Frame Relay BECN, FECN, or DE). AToM can also interwork with native service management protocols, such as ILMI/LMI, to indicate the local circuit status to remote peers. Layer 2 service interworking enables the interconnection of different encapsulations to offer hybrid Layer 2 services (for example, Ethernet to Frame Relay Interworking) over an IP/MPLS core and can facilitate the convergence of existing services. The Layer 2 service interworking construct is shown in Figure 3-27.

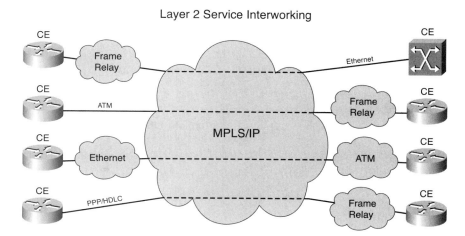

Layer 2 Service Interworking

Enables the interconnection of different encapsulations to offer
hybrid Layer 2 services (for example, Ethernet to Frame Relay Interworking).

Figure 3-27   *Layer 2 Service Interworking*

Layer 2 and Layer 3 VPNs are summarized as follows:

Layer 3 VPNs are concerned primarily with looking at the Layer 3 information and making forwarding decisions. MPLS VPNs require a CE-to-provider edge routing process plus PE-to-PE signaling via mutiprotocol BGP. With Layer 2 VPNs, the information used to make forwarding decisions is based on Layer 2 information—for instance, via a MAC address, via a VLAN ID, on DLCI information, or on an input interface for lease line connectivity. Figure 3-28 provides a comparison between Layer 3 and Layer 2 VPNs. Figure 3-29 depicts the L2VPN constructs as has been discussed.

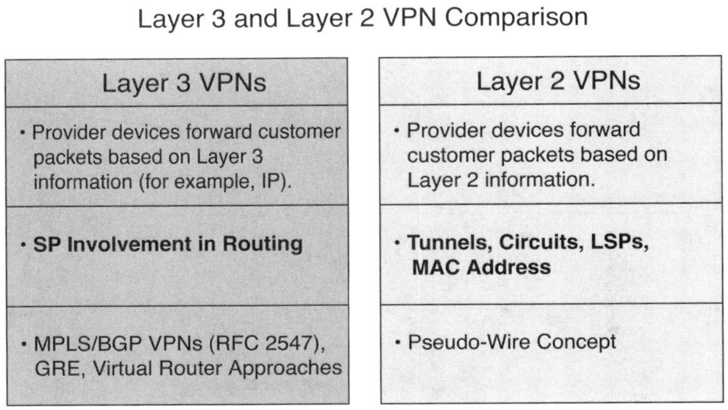

Layer 3 and Layer 2 VPN Comparison
Layer 3 VPNs
• Provider devices forward customer packets based on Layer 3 information (for example, IP).
• SP Involvement in Routing
• MPLS/BGP VPNs (RFC 2547), GRE, Virtual Router Approaches
Layer 2 VPNs
• Provider devices forward customer packets based on Layer 2 information.
• Tunnels, Circuits, LSPs, MAC Address
• Pseudo-Wire Concept

Figure 3-28 *Layer 3 and Layer 2 VPN Comparison*

L2VPN Constructs
• An L2VPN is comprised of switched connections between subscriber endpoints over a shared network. Non-subscribers do not have access to those same endpoints.
Provider Edge
SP Interconnection
Remote Subscriber Location
SP Network
Provider Edge
Pseudowire
ATM
PPP
Ethernet
HDLS
FR
Many subscriber encapsulations supportable.

Figure 3-29 *L2VPN Constructs*

Layer 2 VPNS are further discussed in Chapter 4.

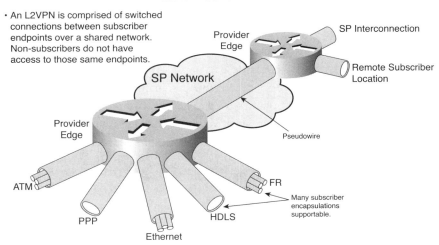

Summary

MPLS technology is fundamentally a service enabler for Layer 3 VPNs and provides for support of CoS and QoS guarantees along with traffic engineering, DiffServ-TE, and fast reroute that are required to manage tight SLAs for such services as voice, video, and data. Multicast VPNs can support enhanced services for push applications, such as streaming, IPTV, videoconferencing, and e-learning. As IP commences to dominate the majority of public network traffic and the requirement for bandwidth increases the need to reduce management, service providers definitely require configuration and provisioning in the network.

With GMPLS, the IP routing tables of an optical LSR enable you to activate a lambda of dense wave divisional multiplexing (DWDM) immediately, according to the needs of the network. It therefore becomes possible to establish connections in a dynamic fashion for rapid provisioning through the SDH/Sonet, optical, or packet network layers.

GMPLS could be used to support bandwidth-intensive applications, such as GRiD, which is emerging in the industry amongst auto, financial, and pharmaceutical vertical segments. Thus, MPLS technology is flexible and can be used to develop and implement services serving current and future market needs.

We have technically deconstructed Layer 3 VPNs as these apply to MPLS and have described the functionality of traffic engineering and differentiated services essential for the deployment of services that require tight SLAs, such as voice and videoconferencing.

We have further provided an overview of Layer 2 VPNs that can be implemented over an MPLS core. Layer 2 service interworking as part of an evolving convergence strategy can facilitate the migration of legacy Layer 2–based services over an MPLS infrastructure. Finally, we have provided a building block of the MPLS service architecture essential to highlighting its value-added proposition, particularly toward developing service provider NGNs for implementing LAN/WAN virtualization within enterprise organizations.

PART 3

MPL SERVICES AND COMPONENTS

CHAPTER 4

LAYER 2 VPNs

Layer 2 *virtual private network (VPN)* is perhaps the most overused term in the networking industry when it comes to MPLS networks. It has a different meaning for everyone. However, this term has been around since the days of both Frame Relay networks and Asynchronous Transfer Mode (ATM), which are commonly deployed L2 technologies.

Perhaps a simplistic way to describe Layer 2 VPNs is like this: They are a group of sites connected together at Layer 2 by point-to-point ATM VCs, Frame Relay data link connection identifiers (DLCI), or Point-to-Point Protocol (PPP) sessions. The most important concept is that IP routing is done at the edge of the Layer 2 network. As mentioned earlier, the service that is delivered to the end customer is a Layer 2 service; hence, the core network or the service provider network is not responsible for Layer 3 routing.

Each Layer 2 connection is an independent interface for routing. Routing must be configured at the end device to communicate across the Layer 2 circuits. Because these point-to-point circuits are provisioned, managed, and billed as one group, they are referred to as a *Layer 2 VPN*. For example, an enterprise might be buying Frame Relay circuits or ATM circuits from a provider and building its own enterprise IP wide area network (WAN) but connecting various sites with these L2 circuits. The service provider (SP) has no knowledge of IP connectivity and is delivering pure L2 circuits. The enterprise is responsible for all the IP connectivity that is using these circuits. In some cases, the enterprise might choose to implement Ethernet bridging across the wide area using these Layer 2 circuits, as shown in Figure 4-1.

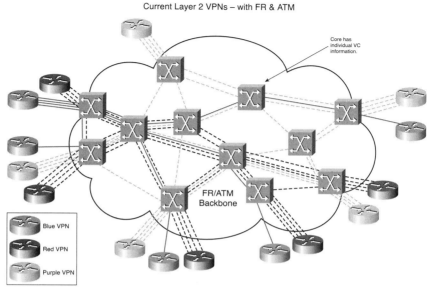

Figure 4-1   *Three Layer 2 VPNs*

Figure 4-1 shows three Layer 2 VPNs (Red, Blue, and Purple) for various customers. All sites within each VPN are connected to each other via Layer 2 circuits using either Frame Relay or ATM. The total number of Layer 2 circuits needed to connect *n* sites in a Layer 2 VPN is n(n-1). Each site within the VPN has direct connectivity with other sites, and the service provider cloud is transparent to the VPN. Using Layer 2 circuits, full-mesh or hub-and-spoke VPNs can be built. In Figure 4-1, Red and Purple VPNs are full-mesh, whereas the Blue VPN is hub-and-spoke.

The delivery mechanism of a Layer 2 VPN is either via a dedicated physical connection with a data link, such as PPP or via a virtual connection, such as an ATM VC or a Frame Relay DLCI.

Taxonomy

To get a better understanding of Layer 2 VPNs, it is important to clarify the taxonomy of Layer 2 VPNs.

Referring to Figure 4-2, you can see that the entire category of Layer 2 VPNs can be easily classified into two main types (through network-based technology used to deliver the services)—namely, packet-based Layer 2 VPNs and circuit, or switched, network-based Layer 2 VPNs as shown in Figure 4-2.

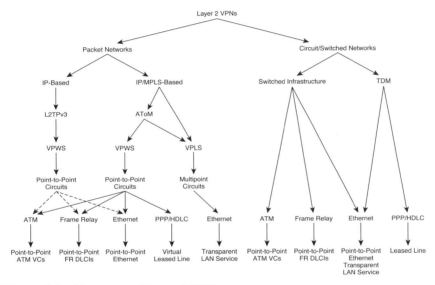

Figure 4-2   *Taxonomy of Layer 2 VPNs*

Packet-based Layer 2 VPNs are defined as Layer 2 VPNs that are delivered using a packet infrastructure, whereas circuit-based Layer 2 VPNs are Layer 2 VPNs that are delivered using the traditional Layer 2 infrastructure, such as ATM or Frame Relay switches or traditional Ethernet switches.

The circuit or switched network-based Layer 2 VPNs are the most common means of delivering Layer 2 VPNs today and are well known in the industry. Today, most providers, including incumbent local exchange carriers (ILEC), deliver Layer 2 VPN services using ATM/FR switched infrastructure. In this chapter, we do not address the topic of how to build Layer 2 VPNs using traditional Layer 2 switches. Instead, we focus on how to build Layer 2 VPNs using packet infrastructure with MPLS. We provide only a cost differential comparison in building complete networks for delivering various services. In that context, we compare Layer 2 VPNs built using Frame Relay (FR) or ATM switches with that of packet infrastructure.

Moving to the second layer of the taxonomy, packet-based Layer 2 VPNs can be delivered using IP/MPLS or native IP-based infrastructure using pseudowires. The Internet Engineering Task Force (IETF) defines a pseudowire as follows: "A pseudo-wire (PW) is a connection between two provider edge (PE) devices which connects two pseudo-wire end-services (PWES) of the same type."

Layer 2 frames are encapsulated in IP/MPLS packets and transported across the packet network. At the remote end, the encapsulation is removed, the packet is converted to native Layer 2 format, and the packet is transported to the customer site. The IETF defines a reference model, known as the "PWE3 reference model" within the PWE3 (Pseudowire Emulation Edge-to-Edge) working group in RFC 3985. Refer to *http://www.ietf.org/html.charters/pwe3-charter.html* for more details. The PWE reference model is applicable to both IP- and MPLS-based networks. To better understand the terminology, refer to Figure 4-3.

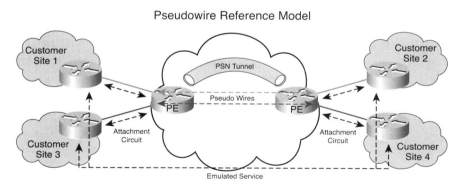

Figure 4-3   *Pseudowire Reference Model*

IETF has organized the area of packet-based L2 VPNs into two areas: the PWE Working Group and L2 VPN Working Group. The PWE3 Working Group deals with the signaling, transport, and encapsulation of a single point-to-point connection/pseudowire across the packet-based network, whereas the L2VPN Working Group discusses the auto-discovery and provisioning of L2 end points.

The connection between the customer edge (CE) and the provider edge (PE) is a native Layer 2 circuit called the attachment circuit (AC). An AC can be any of the following:

- Point-to-Point Ethernet
- Ethernet VLAN
- Frame Relay DLCI
- ATM VPI/VCI
- Point-to-Point Protocol (PPP) connection on a physical or logical
- High-Level Data Link (HDLC) link
- Packet over SONET (POS) link
- Time Division Multiplexed (TDM) channel, such as a DS0, T1/E1/DS1, or T3/E3 circuit

In short, it attaches a CE device to a PE device. Figure 4-2 diagrams all the types of attachment circuits.

The virtual connection between the PEs that connects the two attachment circuits on either side of the network is called a *pseudowire*, as shown in Figure 4-3. The pseudowire (PW) carries Layer 2 frames, with or without Layer 2 headers, across the packet infrastructure. The pseudowire is set up using signaling mechanisms, such as directed LDP in the case of an IP/MPLS network or L2TPv3 signaling for a native IP network. You can use other signaling protocols for signaling a pseudowire, but that usage is not covered in this chapter. Only the two most popular methods of building pseudowires are discussed in this chapter.

When Layer 2 frames arrive at the PE router, they can be appropriately encapsulated and forwarded onto the pseudowire. The pseudowire is mapped to a packet switched network (PSN) tunnel setup using some encapsulation mechanism. The PSN tunnel is a mechanism of forwarding frames from PE1 to PE2. In the case of MPLS, the PSN tunnel could be a traffic-engineered tunnel or a PE1-PE2 labeled switched path (LSP).

Now let us examine the MPLS-based Layer 2 VPNs in more detail. As mentioned earlier, the basic building block of MPLS-based Layer 2 VPNs is AToM.

Introducing AToM

AToM stands for Any Transport over MPLS. The name comes from the ability of AToM to transport any frames over an MPLS network using MPLS as an encap and LDP as a signaling mechanism. AToM is a basic building block of Layer 2 VPNs over MPLS in Cisco. This is a Cisco term and not an industry term. The industry refers to this as *pseudowires*. We will also refer to this as *pseudowires* in the subsequent sections of this chapter and in the rest of the book. The development of AToM came about in an interesting manner.

Luca Martini, now at Cisco, was at Level 3 Communications, Inc., and had a requirement for the delivery of Frame Relay service to end customers. Level 3 had an IP/MPLS network in deployment. Martini brought that requirement to Cisco and, working with Cisco, built a prototype to deliver Frame Relay frames across the MPLS infrastructure. The prototype was tested and sometime during the project, the requirement was changed and the new requirement was to deliver ATM AAL5 frames across the MPLS network. In extending the same concepts of Frame Relay over MPLS, the ATM AAL5 over MPLS became possible—thus allowing ATM over MPLS capability. This prompted the idea of generalizing the concept of delivering Layer 2 frames to other Layer 2 transports, such as Ethernet VLAN, ATM cells, PPP frames, and High-Level Data Link Control (HDLC) frames. The marketing team, along with engineering department, coined this technology AToM. An IETF draft was also published, and it received wide industry acceptance and became a defacto standard. This is now known as draft-martini. The pseudowires for MPLS network setups using this mechanism are known as martini tunnels after Luca Martini.

Moving down the layers of the taxonomy diagram in Figure 4-2, you can see that pseudowires can be used to deliver two types of services to end users: virtual private wire service (VPWS) and virtual private LAN service (VPLS). VPWS includes the ability to deliver a point-to-point wire connecting the end customer devices (routers). The customer is responsible for managing the IP routing, and the provider delivers the equivalent of a leased line. The VPWS can have either the same transport type at each end (like-to-like) or any transport type at each end (any-to-any). In the case of disparate transport types, the interworking must be done at the PEs to translate the Layer 2 frames from one transport type to another.

Pseudowire Systems Architecture

Let us consider an example of Frame Relay over MPLS and see how it works in detail. Consider a Frame Relay VC being delivered to end customers. The series of configurations needed on the network elements to deliver the VC are shown in Figure 4-4.

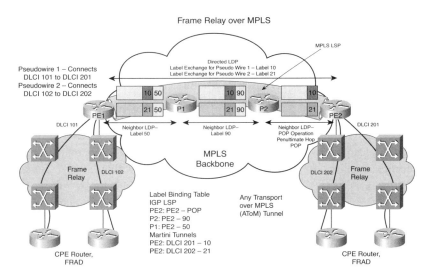

Figure 4-4 *Frame Relay over MPLS—Technical Overview*

Assuming an operational MPLS network, the IGP LSPs are established using MPLS LDP. P2 advertises Label 90 for destination PE2, P1 advertises label 50 for destination PE2, and PE2 advertises a POP operation to its neighbors for destination PE2. The LSP from PE1 to PE2 has the labels 50, 90, POP from PE1 to PE2 via P1 and P2. This label sequence represents a label switched path. At this point, a live MPLS network has been set up with LDP signaling.

Now consider two attachment circuits on the left side of Figure 4-4. The two DLCIs are DLCI 101 and DLCI 201. They need to be switched to the customer sites at the far end as DLCI 201 and DLCI 202, respectively. On PE1, the following configuration is required:

1   Cross-connect DLCI 101 to pseudowire 1, and the destination for the pseudowire 1 is PE2.

2   Cross-connect DLCI 102 to pseudowire 2, and the destination for the pseudowire 2 is PE2.

On PE2, the following configuration is required:

1   Cross-connect Pseudowire 1 to DLCI 201, and the source of pseudowire 1 is from PE1.

2   Cross-connect pseudowire 2 to DLCI 202, and the source of the pseudowire is from PE1.

Upon configuration of the two PEs, the PEs then initiate signaling to set up the pseudowire. PE1 signals using directed LDP to PE2 and exchanges the VC type, and other parameters as part of LDP forwarding equivalence class (FEC). PE2 assigns a label of 10 for pseudowire 1 and label 21 for pseudowire 2. Now both PEs populate their forwarding tables with the label information as shown in the Figure 4-4. Note that the knowledge of pseudowires is only between PE1 and PE2. P1 and P2 routers in the core do not have any knowledge of the pseudowire labels. They know only about the IGP LSP or how to reach PE1 and PE2 via MPLS LSPs. However, when P routers load-balance traffic, they look at the payload. In L2 service, the payload is a non-IP packet; hence, the P routers in this case load-balance traffic based on the pseudowire label.

Packet Forwarding

When the setup is complete, the frames can be forwarded. Frame Relay frames now are received on the PE1. After the frame received on DLCI 101 is received, the header is stripped and a control word is added. (Refer to the IETF RFC 3985, RFC 4385, RFC 4447, and RFC 4448.) The control word is 4 bytes. It is used to carry the length of the frame, L2 flags, and a sequence number of the frame for sequence-sensitive applications. In the case of Frame Relay, the control word carries the following bits: Frame Relay forward explicit congestion notification (FECN), backward explicit congestion notification (BECN), discard eligible (DE), and command/response (C/R). The label assigned to the pseudowire is imposed; in this case it is label 10.

Similarly, for the frame received on DLCI 102, the label 21 is imposed. The frames (now MPLS packets) need to be forwarded to PE2. The IGP LSP toward PE2 had the label 50 assigned by P1. The PE1 now imposes another label of 50 onto the MPLS packet and forwards it toward P1. The P1, core router, forwards the MPLS frame to P2 on its LSP by swapping label 50 with label 90. P2 does the same and forwards it to the destination. Because the advertised operation by PE2, which is the next hop from P2, was a POP operation, P2 strips the outer label and forwards the pseudowire packet to PE2 as the destination. PE2 looks up the pseudowire label, recognizes that label 10 matches DLCI 201, removes the label, attaches the frame relay header, and forwards the payload on Frame Relay DLCI 201 toward the destination. Similarly for DLCI 202, the PE2 recognizes the label 21 and forwards it appropriately. So, using labels as demultiplexers, Layer 2 frames can be forwarded to the destination across a packet network.

This concept can be easily extended to all other transport types, including Ethernet VLANs (in which the pseudowire labels designate VLAN information), PPP sessions, HDLC links, ATM VPI/VCI, and ATM AAL5 frames.

In some L2 transports, specialized frames or cells can be used for a management function called operations, administration, and maintenance (OAM). These OAM cells or packets can also be transported or mapped to pseudowire messages. More details of OAM are discussed in Chapter 12, "Network Management and Provisioning."

Layer 2 Transport Types (Like-to-Like)

This is the most commonly used L2 service. As mentioned earlier, like-to-like transport implies the same transport type exists at each end of the connection. The two attachment circuits that consist of the end-to-end connection (in this case AC1 and AC2—DLCI 101 and DLCI 201) have the same characteristics. They have the same frame types, encapsulation, and QoS characteristics (including, but not limited to, committed rates, burst sizes, delay, and characteristics). There must be no change in the L2 header information except the DLCI, VPI/VCI, VLAN ID, or PPP session value and TTL (if any).

This is similar to a classic Layer 2 service delivered using Layer 2 switches, except here it is delivered using an IP/MPLS infrastructure. The challenge in this type of service is delivering the same service characteristics that are similar to, if the not the same as, a traditional Layer 2 service. Let us discuss each of those services in some detail.

Ethernet Service

Ethernet service today is delivered using an optical long-haul infrastructure and Ethernet switches. The cost of this type of infrastructure can be very high depending on the availability of fiber, optical gear, optical switching, and termination equipment, although the Ethernet switches themselves are cheap.

In delivering Ethernet service using IP/MPLS infrastructure, the cost can be significantly reduced per Ethernet connection. Refer to the "Benefits of L2 VPNs" section for details. With Ethernet over MPLS, several services are possible, including a 10 Mbps Ethernet service, a subrate Ethernet service (for example, a 2 Mbps Ethernet service), and a VLAN service. The service is delivered on a dedicated 10 Mbps port, but it is rate limited or policed to a 2 Mbps Ethernet connection. Another example is a flexible rate service, also called a *bursting rate service*. In this type of service an Ethernet service is sold and billed according to usage. Alternatively, a user can sign up for an on-demand bandwidth service by scheduling via a web portal and requesting bandwidth during a certain anticipated period of usage.

Link Layer Service

Similarly, PPP or HDLC over MPLS can be used to deliver a virtual leased line service with PPP or HDLC encapsulation, respectively. A leased line service is characterized by a data rate (the rate at which the line is clocked by the TDM network, such as 56 Kbps, T1, E1, or T3 service) and is usually an unprotected circuit. There is no buffering and no protection against failures, and it is a bit-timed connection. This can be easily emulated on the packet network.

In addition to providing bandwidth guarantees, this service can be improvised by providing additional protection using MPLS fast reroute and MPLS traffic engineering. (MPLS traffic engineering is described in Chapter 8, "Traffic Engineering.") Packet buffering provides some buffering protection, especially for User Datagram Protocol (UDP) traffic. One can argue that there are situations in which buffering can hurt some types of services. However, for pure data services, buffering can also help you recover from unexpected packet loss.

Frame Relay Service

Unlike Point-to-Point Ethernet and PPP/HDLC services, the Frame Relay service is a little different when delivered over a packet infrastructure. Although you can carry Layer 2 parameters across the pseudowire such that the attachment circuits can be easily policed and updated, the QoS of the service delivered is a function of hardware and software features. Frame Relay requires delivery of in-order packets and notification of congestion information forward and backward using the FECN and BECN bits. Moreover, if the frame is out of contract based on the burst size or peak information rate, the network element might have to set the DE bit so that a switch/router can discard the Frame Relay frame. All these actions—DE bit marking, acting on FECN and BECN—can be done only by the PE devices in the network.

The P devices or core routers do not have any knowledge of the pseudowires and therefore do not see any FECN, BECN, or DE information. If the edge hardware is capable of enforcing traffic contract, it can act on any Layer 2 parameters it receives as part of the Frame Relay information. Alternatively, it can also translate core LDP signaling about label withdrawal and outages to Frame Relay Local Management Interface (LMI) and notify the status of the DLCI to the

CPE device. Frame Relay service can be delivered on a per-DLCI basis or per-port basis, where a group of DLCIs traverse the same ports that are cross-connected across the MPLS network. However, Frame Relay port mode service is actually achieved using HDLC over IP/MPLS.

Today, service providers deliver various flavors of L2 services with strict traffic contracts and loose traffic contracts. For example, some service providers in the United States deliver a zero-CIR Frame Relay service. Such a service is an easy candidate for migration to the IP/MPLS network. Other stringent-contract L2 services might or might not be suited for delivery on a packet-based IP/MPLS network depending on the available hardware and the strictness with which it can enforce the traffic contracts.

ATM Service

Similar to the Frame Relay services, ATM services can also be delivered to the customers. The types of ATM services that can be emulated are as follows:

- UBR data service using ATM AAL5 over MPLS
- ABR data service
- Transparent cell relay service for voice or other payloads (particularly useful for ATM AAL1/2)
- ATM VP service
- ATM VBR service
- ATM CBR service

Many ATM services depend on the availability of hardware that can appropriately police the data to enforce traffic contracts. Assuming capable hardware, ATM AAL5 over MPLS can be used to deliver UBR, ABR, or VBR data services. This mode is primarily used for data services. In ATM AAL5 over MPLS, the ATM VC is terminated at the PE device, cells are sent through the SAR, and the AAL5 frame is transported across the packet cloud. This is an efficient mode of service in which the overhead associated with each VC is minimal in the core. The AAL5 frames can be policed much in the same way as they are in any ATM edge device. The capability to deliver ABR depends on the PE hardware.

Although you might be able to fully emulate the ABR services delivered using a traditional ATM infrastructure, you can mimic it and deliver a limited ABR service.

Similarly, using the bandwidth management capabilities of MPLS, you also might be able to deliver ATM CBR services. Again, the ability to deliver true CBR service characterized by cell delay variation (CDV) and cell delay variation tolerance (CDTV) can be difficult and requires hardware that is capable of maintaining low CDVT within the specified limits. The current generation of packet hardware is certainly not capable of delivering a very low CDVT and low CDV according to strict requirements. Subsequent generations of line cards on the current hardware might be capable of helping deliver this service with ease. Often, CBR service is delivered only with a bit rate guarantee and no CDV or CDVT guarantee. This is equivalent to a VBR service in which the PCR = SCR. Such a service delivery is possible using IP/MPLS infrastructure.

Another mode of ATM service is the delivery of virtual trunks. Applications, such as voice trunking from central offices (CO) or PBX connectivity, require dynamic setup of switched virtual circuits (SVC). This can be achieved by delivering a virtual path (VP) mode service. With cell relay, all cells belonging to the same VP are tagged with the same pseudowire label and are delivered to the same destination. Cell relay can be done in VC mode, VP mode, and port mode.

Additional efficiency can be achieved using cell packing techniques based on cell loss priority (CLP) values or wait times, or both. For example, consider the VP mode cell relay. Visualize this as a VP between two ATM switches, but the VP in this case happens to traverse a packet IP/MPLS infrastructure. The two switches on either side of the network see themselves as peers because all traffic (including signaling) is trunked across the packet backbone. Various bandwidth guarantees are possible.

The limitations of packet network-based ATM services pertain to more OAM aspects and the visibility of ATM VCs in the packet network core. Chapter 12 discusses OAM.

Configuration of Pseudowires

For all of the previously mentioned transport types—namely, ATM, FR, Ethernet, PPP, and HDLC—the configuration steps of PEs and CEs are listed in this section. In the like-to-like (same transport type at each end as opposed to different transport types) L2VPN service, only the AC information is required at the CPE and no additional configuration is required. An enterprise might request a choice of L2 service based on its requirements and needs. For example, until IP QoS was offered, the only way to guarantee traffic contracts with dedicated bandwidth was by using ATM. Thus, enterprise requirements to carry voice or video across the network meant that enterprises preferred a technology that could guarantee the bandwidth, delay, and jitter characteristics. QoS is discussed at length in Chapter 9, "Quality of Service."

Assuming an operational MPLS network (LDP or MPLS TE is enabled appropriately in the network), the configuration requirements in this type of like-to-like connectivity are as follows:

1 Configure the CPEs (both sides) with the attachment circuit information, including VLAN IDs, DLCI values, and ATM VPI/VCI or PPP session information.

2 Configure PEs (PE1 and PE2) with the same AC information (AC1 on PE1 and AC2 on PE2).

3 Configure the PE1 with the cross-connect information with the AC1 and pseudowire.

4 Configure QoS parameters on the AC and pseudowire.

5 Map the pseudowire to the TE tunnel, if bandwidth guarantees are necessary or if you're using MPLS TE in the network.

6 Configure PE2 with the cross-connect information with AC2 and the pseudowire.

7 Configure the QoS information on PE2 for the AC2 and pseudowire.

The AC type is the same at each end, so no additional configuration is needed. The operational complexity of this configuration is similar to that of an existing ATM/FR Layer 2 network.

Layer 2 Interworking

In the previous section, we discussed at length the like-to-like model with the same transport type at each end. This like-to-like AToM model can easily be extended with the interworking of disparate transport types—that is, different transport type at each end. For example, one attachment circuit could be Ethernet and another could be Frame Relay VC. This type of interworking is not unknown to the industry. RFC 2684 and RFC 2427 are standard documents that specify how to encapsulate and deliver Ethernet and IP frames over ATM and Frame Relay VCs, respectively. With these models, customer devices can be interconnected using a Frame Relay VC or ATM VC, and Ethernet frames or IP frames can be transported across these devices. The interworking function is performed at the device where the VC is terminated, and the frames are either bridged nor routed to the destination.

Let us consider a case study to determine why this type of Layer 2 interworking can be an important service. Consider an enterprise with as many as 1000 branch sites that need to be connected to a head office site and a disaster recovery site. A traditional hub-and-spoke design for a Layer 2 VPN requires that at least one Layer 2 connection be terminated from each of the branch sites to the head office site and sometimes another one to the backup site. Because the enterprise is managing the IP routing, it might want to buy redundancy in the wide area network (WAN) and sign up for a strict SLA. The offer it gets from the service provider for this Layer 2 VPN might not be attractive if the enterprise is asked to terminate 1000 DLCIs or ATM VCs at the head office and backup site from the remote sites. Managing a large number of DLCIs or ATM VCs at the head office and branch sites might be an issue. Moreover, it might be costly because the charge of the circuit is usually per virtual connection.

Instead, the enterprise customer might ask for Ethernet connectivity at the head office and Frame Relay or ATM VCs at the remote sites. This is a Layer 2 service, so it implies that the Frame Relay or ATM frames from the branch sites needs to be translated to Ethernet frames at the head office. This requires the service provider to translate protocols from one side of the network to another.

The challenge of translating protocols from one to another is not trivial. The characteristics of the protocols, such as point-to-point versus broadcast, make it a challenging task. Routing protocols behave differently over broadcast medium such as an Ethernet as opposed to over a point-to-point link, such as FR DLCI or an HDLC link. Hence, translating between broadcast protocols, such as Ethernet, and point-to-point protocols, such as Frame Relay or ATM, require additional configurations, not just on the PE devices, but also on the CE devices. For example, route bridge encapsulation (RBE) configuration can be required if bridged interworking is configured.

Interworking Modes

The two main Interworking modes are bridged interworking and routed interworking. Sometimes these two modes are also referred to as Ethernet interworking and IP interworking.

Ethernet interworking or bridged interworking allows delivery of Ethernet frames across the two transport types. This requires the capability to use the pseudowire as a bridge for Ethernet frames between the different transport types at each end. The CPE configuration required in this case is no different from like-to-like service.

Routed interworking or IP interworking allows the delivery of IP frames across the various transport types. This is a common service where IP routers or hosts are connected across the interworking pseudowire. For example, a router is connected to a point-to-point HDLC link on one side of the network and another router is connected with an Ethernet connection to the same network. Now these two routers need to establish a Layer 2 adjacency so that routing information can be exchanged. Using IP interworking, these two routers can peer with each other across the packet network despite the fact that each uses a different transport type for physical connectivity. Address resolution is done from IP to MAC using a proxy ARP function.

Interworking Models and Applications

With five transport types, several combinations of Layer 2 interworking are possible, including the following:

- Ethernet-to-Frame Relay interworking
- Ethernet-to-ATM interworking

- ATM-to-Frame Relay interworking
- Ethernet-to-PPP/HDLC interworking
- Frame Relay-to-PPP/HDLC interworking
- ATM-to-PPP/HDLC interworking

All these models have two modes, such as Ethernet interworking or IP interworking. Depending on the service model, any of these modes can be used. These combinations provide flexibility in the connectivity of different sites in a Layer 2 VPN. For example, the problem described at the beginning of this section can easily be addressed by interworking remote DLCIs with Ethernet VLANs, avoiding termination of 1000 DLCIs at the head office or disaster recovery site.

Assuming an operational MPLS network (LDP or MPLS TE is enabled appropriately in the network), the configuration requirements in this type of Layer 2 Interworking are as follows:

1   Configure the CPEs (both sides) with the attachment circuit information, including VLAN IDs, DLCI values, and ATM VPI/VCI or PPP session information.

2   Configure PEs (PE1 and PE2) with the same AC information (AC1 on PE1 and AC2 on PE2).

3   Configure the PE1 with the cross-connect information with the AC1 and pseudowire and specify whether the PE should do the interworking.

4   Configure QoS parameters on the AC and the pseudowire.

5   Map the pseudowire to the TE tunnel if bandwidth guarantees are necessary or you're using MPLS TE in the network.

6   Configure PE2 with the cross-connect information with AC2 and the pseudowire. Similar to PEI, you must specify whether interworking is required.

7   Configure QoS information on PE2 for the AC2 and pseudowire.

8   Configure the CPE with RBE/IRB capability depending on the interworking mode.

The operational complexity of this configuration is higher than that of an existing ATM/FR Layer 2 network, but the flexibility this mode provides can offset some operations costs associated with it. Refer to the section titled "Benefits of L2VPNs" for more details.

Virtual Private LAN Service

Using AToM/pseudowires as a building block and adding MAC-based forwarding capability to Ethernet over MPLS, a VPLS can be offered. VPLS offers LAN and broadcast domain extensions with multipoint connectivity between sites. Ethernet over MPLS that provides point-to-point Ethernet connectivity is used as a building block. The same signaling procedures can be used to set up the pseudowires between PE devices as in Ethernet over MPLS.

A BGP-based signaling mechanism has also been proposed in the IETF to set up the pseudowires between PEs for VPLs. However, in VPLS on the PE, a virtual switch instance (VSI) is needed. A *VSI* is a MAC table of the attached devices on the LAN segment or on the remote sites connecting to the VPLS domain. To provide multipoint connectivity, a mesh of pseudowires is set up connecting all PEs that carry the same VSI. The PE forwards the Ethernet frames onto the attached LAN segments that are in the same VPLS domain, or within the same VSI. The PE also forwards frames based on MAC addresses to the pseudowires. This implies that the PE must be capable of learning MAC addresses not just on the local LAN/VLAN segments, but also on the pseudowires. Each PE behaves like a "half bridge" and a PE-pseudowire-PE constitutes a bridge/switch.

All bridging rules apply in the VPLS design and configuration. The PE behaves like an Ethernet switch; in fact, the entire MPLS network behaves like an Ethernet switch, connecting LAN segments at customer sites. This network provides simple forms of connectivity and works well in a metro region with a small number of sites that need to be connected. This might not be the desirable mode of connectivity for a large number of sites in a VPLS domain, though. Scalability of VPLS is discussed in the subsequent section.

Considerations for VPLS

Because the PE devices are forwarding traffic based on the MAC address, as the number of devices grows in the VPLS domain, the MAC table size also grows. The PE must be capable of MAC aging and caching. If the MAC is not found in the MAC table, the frame is broadcast on all ports just as it is done on an Ethernet switch.

With a large number of sites in a VPLS domain and with many devices (PCs, workstations, servers, printers, and so on) in a single VPLS domain, broadcast becomes an issue. Broadcast storms can occur, and these storms can result in network outages. The classic issues of bridged networks are also applicable. Care must be taken to consider the number of sites in the VPLS domain and the number of MAC addresses per VPLS domain as part of the network design.

Loop-free topology can be built using spanning tree or rapid spanning tree in the VPLS domain. However, it is not advisable to run spanning tree over the MPLS network. A full mesh of pseudowires connects PEs with the same VPLS instance, so a split-horizon configuration mode is available. Split-horizon allows PEs not to forward the frames back onto the pseudowire if they learn the MAC address on another pseudowire.

Due to its bridging nature, VPLS has poor scalability. Nevertheless, it is a useful service in small or metro environments. In dynamic provisioning, some level of diverse path routing can be achieved using constraint-based routing mechanisms, although this is not as accurate or comprehensive as the manual provisioning. However, the advantage is that, while provisioning an SPVC, there is no need to touch all the network elements along the path because the diverse routing path is computed by the network elements and set up dynamically via the signaling protocol. This LAN service to IP end points is called IP LAN service (IPLS). Optimizations to VPLS can be done for IPLS for some efficient setup of circuits. However, setup was not the main issue with VPLS; MAC address scale was more of a concern.

Provisioning and Signaling

The provisioning of traditional Layer 2 VPNs involves setting up PVCs or soft PVCs (SPVC) between customer sites or CEs. If the network supports only PVCs, the PVC must be configured on every switch/network element along the path of the PVC connecting the two CE sites. If the network supports dynamic signaling, SPVCs can be set up using point-and-click provisioning.

In the ATM SPVC setup, the network operator clicks the two end points to which the PVC must be built. The network elements dynamically signal a path using the PNNI signaling protocol and set up the SPVC between the end points. This eases the provisioning of ATM networks at the expense of network control.

Manual provisioning has the advantage of explicit control of the network w.r.t placement of PVCs. PVCs can be routed along explicit paths, and resiliency can be built using diverse path routing. In dynamic provisioning, some level of diverse path routing can be achieved using constraint-based routing mechanisms, although this is not as accurate or comprehensive as manual provisioning is. However, the advantage is that while provisioning an SPVC, there is no need to touch all the network elements along the path because the TBDs are computed by the network elements and set up dynamically via the signaling protocol.

MPLS-based Layer 2 VPN provisioning is similar to that of ATM SPVC provisioning. Using network management applications, pseudowire and attachment circuit provisioning can be done. Similar to the traditional Layer 2 VPNs, the PVC is configured between the CPE and the PE. As stated earlier, the configuration of the PE triggers signaling in the network core for the establishment of the pseudowire. If the standard pseudowire wire emulation edge to edge (PWE3) signaling method is used, LDP signaling is initiated, labels are exchanged, and the pseudowire is set up without any additional configuration on the network core routers. This is equivalent to the concept of the dynamic signaling of SPVC in the ATM PNNI network.

In the MPLS case, there is no explicit placement of pseudowires in the network core. In fact, the network core devices do not have any knowledge of the pseudowires. As explained earlier, this is achieved by label stacking, where the network core routers know only about the IGP label and have no visibility inside the payload unless it is destined for them.

Comparing the MPLS-based provisioning to traditional provisioning models for other Layer 2 transport types, such as Ethernet, Frame Relay, PPP, and HDLC, we see that provisioning these circuits in an IP/MPLS network is easier than a traditional network. The SPVC model of dynamic signaled pseudowire applies to all Layer 2 transport types, including Ethernet, PPP, and HDLC. For example, in a traditional PPP or HDLC setup, the TDM channel is manually set up along the entire path (from one CE through the network and to another CE) on ADMs, DACs, and NTUs. Then a PPP or HDLC encap is enabled on the two end points of the PPP or HDLC link. In IP/MPLS-based Layer 2 VPNs, the circuit is provisioned only in the access layer, between the PE and CE. The edge network provisioning follows the same procedure as described in the ATM or Frame Relay case. Although the gain realized might not be significant, delivering a PPP or HDLC service is simpler on the IP/MPLS network.

At the time of writing this book, a hot debate is raging in the industry about which signaling protocol is better suited for pseudowire signaling. There are two proposals in the IETF. One uses LDP, supported by Cisco and a host of other vendors, and another uses Border Gateway Protocol (BGP), supported by Juniper Networks. The pros and cons of each are discussed in the following sections.

LDP Signaling

LDP is a simple protocol for label exchange to set up pseudowires. As described in the operation of pseudowire reference model, directed LDP is used for signaling and exchanging labels between the pseudowire end points. LDP exchanges Layer 2 FEC type and sets up the label binding of the pseudowire. The Layer 2 FEC type determines the type of pseudowire, such as Frame Relay, ATM, Ethernet, PPP, or HDLC. The labels are used to identify the pseudowires and determine the Layer 2 circuits where the frames must be forwarded.

LDP is by nature a point-to-point protocol. The information exchanged between the LDP end points is relevant to the two peers that exchange the information. With LDP signaling, the PE routers that form the end of the pseudowire have a peering relationship with each other. This one-to-one relationship between PE routers has several pros and cons:

- **Scalability**—LDP signaling uses a directed LDP session between a pair of routers, between which a pseudowire must be established. This can imply the following: If the number of routers is large, say n, in a random environment, potentially n-1 LDP sessions are required from any router to all other routers. If n is large, a large number of LDP sessions can become a bottleneck depending on the platform. However, this might not be a concern because the network sizes seen today are about 700 PE devices, which requires a PE to support approximately 700 LDP sessions. This is easily achievable.

- **QoS**—Provisioning QoS is easy due to simple point-to-point configuration. Pseudowires are easily identifiable and are explicitly provisioned. The network operator has explicit control of the pseudowires and their QoS characteristics.

- **Failure notifications**—LDP signaling can be easily tied into the LMI/ILMI signaling or OAM capability on the attachment circuit. This ensures prompt notification of the signaling status to the end points. For example, a circuit might be down on the remote end. In such as case, the PE can immediately withdraw the label with LDP and the local PE can take one of three actions: send an OAM cell in case of ATM VC/VP, use LMI/ILMI in case of Frame Relay/ATM, or use carrier shutoff for Ethernet to signal to the local CE device that the remote end of the Layer 2 circuit is down. This signaling is immediate with LDP—unlike BGP, which relies on a damper, scanner, and timer.

- **Simple paradigm with low overhead**—LDP signaling follows a simple and well-understood paradigm of traditional Layer 2 VPNs. Only the two end devices that need to communicate on a particular pseudowire exchange messages, without any third device hearing or snooping it. The fact that no unnecessary information is sent or received makes LDP signaling efficient with a low CPU or memory overhead for an operational network. Each device must maintain an LDP session (directed LDP) with which it needs to build one or more pseudowires. Thus, the number of directed LDP sessions required on any given network element is equal to the number of devices this network element must talk to in order to build the pseudowire. Thousands of directed LDP sessions can be created on the Cisco routers today, allowing for a large-scale setup of pseudowire service.

- **No broadcast of information**—In this case, no information is replicated across all the directed LDP sessions. There are no broadcast messages.

- **Label management**—Labels are dynamically allocated and withdrawn by LDP. No preconfiguration of label information is required. The network element dynamically manages labels in the most efficient manner, reusing unused labels. The results are better scalability and easier management.

- **Contiguous labels or attachment circuit values**—Neither the label values nor the attachment circuit values need be contiguous. Any random AC number can be bound to any label/pseudowire and can be made part of any Layer 2 VPN, making it extremely efficient and flexible. There is no wasting of label, DLCI, or VPI/VCI space.

- **Hub-and-spoke topology**—Most Layer 2 VPNs are hub and spoke. By using a point-to-point setup procedure, building a hub and spoke or an arbitrary mesh topology is much easier because the operator has explicit control over the pseudowire setup.

BGP Signaling

An alternative way of signaling Layer 2 information to the PEs is using BGP. However, because BGP is great at taking a piece of information and communicating that to everyone, optimizing Layer 2 signaling or the pseudowire setup is possible. For example, you can use BGP signaling with VPLS. In this method of signaling, all attachment circuit information and label information is preallocated and sent to the PEs in the BGP update. An ordered list of ACs is created in each PE, and a label block is allocated. Each PE then uses its site ID as the index, retrieves the label information from the label block, and programs the hardware or forwarding tables. No exchange of information between PEs on a per-pseudowire basis occurs. However, using BGP signaling of pseudowires for VPLS only does not require sending an AC list because only one VSI services all the ACs within a VPLS domain.

Here are some pros and cons of this method of signaling:

- **Scalability**—Although there are no PE-PE LDP sessions in this case, the pseudowire information (label bindings and AC list) is carried in the extended community attribute in the BGP signaling. This can be made to work with PE-PE iBGP sessions or via route reflectors. The number of PEs supported in this configuration scale with the number of BGP sessions (in case of iBGP full mesh) or RR capability, when route reflectors are used. However, the scalability is not just about BGP sessions. It is also about the memory needed to store information and the CPU needed to process BGP updates in addition to the number of BGP sessions. The information about any pseudowire (AC list and its label binding) is sent to everyone, so each PE must filter the BGP update to look only at the pertinent information. If an L2VPN contains a large number of sites, the entire AC list and the label information are sent to all the PEs in the network, regardless of whether the AC list applies to PEs. In a random environment with a large number of Layer 2 VPNs and a large number of sites per VPN, this causes a huge processing overhead, resulting in less overall scalability of the equipment.

- **QoS**—As we explained earlier, in Layer 2 VPN QoS guarantees are almost taken for granted. This means the requirements of QoS and bandwidth guarantees on the pseudowire must be met. Moreover, there might be a requirement for different QoS characteristics on each pseudowire. With BGP signaling, the QoS information must also be sent into the BGP extended community. This can unnecessarily increase the information sent, thereby reducing the overall scalability. Moreover, there is no way of dynamically updating the QoS on a pseudowire. The BGP signaling model assumes that there is no requirement for different QoS characteristics on the pseudowires. It works with difficulty on the assumption that the same QoS characteristics are applicable to all pseudowires. Ways to make it work with different QoS characteristics are available, but it can become extremely complicated with a large number of sites and a large number of VPNs. So, the savings it brings in terms of provisioning are offset by the management requirements.

- **Failure notifications**—Failure notifications must be sent across with the BGP update. If the updates are triggered each time a failure occurs, a significant churn in the network can occur. This occurs because failure information is propagated to everyone because they are all peering with each other or with a common route reflector. Given any large operational network, link or VC failures occur often, especially when networks span large geographical regions. This means that the overhead the failure notification provides is significant and becomes worse as the failure rate increases. Moreover, it is not clear why the failure information must be sent to everyone. For example, if the AC or pseduowire fails between router A and B, the only affected components are routers A and B in a Layer 2 service; other routers in the network, such as routers C, D, or E, therefore, do not need to know about the failure notification or the changes in Layer 2 service affecting A and B. However, with BGP signaling, all routers are sent the failure updates, resulting in high processing overhead and poor scalability.

- **Complicated paradigm**—One of the arguments made in favor of BGP signaling is that it is used for Layer 3 VPNs, and with some small set of changes, Layer 2 VPNs can be easily added to the network. However, as networks grow larger, the number of policies and filtering that must be met to accommodate both Layer 2 and Layer 3 VPNs becomes complex. Managing all the changes—especially when new sites are added and removed—becomes an issue as the number of sites and the number of VPNs grows. QoS policies, therefore, cannot be applied easily and uniformly.

- **Label Management**—To avoid a flooding of individual labels of all the pseudowires to every PE in the network, a handy "hack" was developed. It involves sending a block of labels, with each site using the site ID as an index and setting up the pseudowire. This requires operators to statically allocate a block of labels for a given number of sites. If the number of sites changes and no more labels are left in the label block, either a new label block must be allocated and stitched to the previous block or the label block must be renumbered. This can also mean an interruption of service to the entire VPN when a new site is added. This can result in a fragmentation of label space, resulting in management overhead to maintain and manage the label space. This overhead can easily offset any gains achieved through the ease of provisioning full-mesh pseudowires.

- **Contiguous VC values**—Contiguous VC values must be allocated to attachment circuits to keep track of which AC connects to which site. Sifting through the list of VC/DLCI values each time a problem must be traced becomes difficult. With a large number of sites, separate external applications must be used to track the DLCIs, sites, and VPNs. It is not impossible, but it is certainly cumbersome. Much like label block assignment, when contiguous labels run out, VC blocks must be stitched or reallocated. Thus, over a period of time with many VPNs added and deleted and sites added and deleted, provisioning the DLCI/VC values without collisions becomes difficult. Automated tools must be used that keep track of the changes for provisioning such values.

- **Hub-and-spoke topology**—BGP-based signaling makes the setup of full mesh of pseudowires easier. To set up hub-and-spoke VPNs, more policies must be applied to filter advertisements of BGP updates, so that pseudowires are not built between spoke sites. This gets more complicated as the number of sites grows larger.

- **Management**—Irrespective of the signaling protocol used, after the pseudowires are set up, the management of them is similar in both cases. PWE MIB provides indices and tables so that packet/byte counts can be obtained in addition to pseudowire types and pseudowire parameters. However, debugging pseudowires signaled using LDP might be easier than debugging pseudowires set up using BGP. As explained earlier, the tracking of BGP-signaled pseudowires is done using the labels in the preallocated block, whereas the tracking of pseudowires signaled using LDP is done by looking up the LDP table.

Additionally, OAM message mapping and status signaling have not been defined in the standards bodies yet. Some of the previously mentioned drawbacks disappear if BGP signaling is used solely for the purpose of VPLS setup. For VPLS, there are no requirements for point-to-point pseudowires; therefore, the complexity of contiguous VC assignment and label block allocation is unnecessary. With VPLS, one or more Ethernets that are attached to the PE are usually part of the same bridging domain. Hence, the VC allocation is typically one or more VLANs that are part of the same bridging domain. The label assignment is also done per VSI. So, no label blocks are needed because a single label can now be broadcast to all PEs belonging to the same bridging domain. This results in a considerable reduction in complexity. However, other issues, such as failure notification and OAM message mapping, still remain with this method of signaling.

Benefits of L2VPNs

Delivering Layer 2 VPNs over an IP/MPLS infrastructure has several benefits, including the following:

- **Common infrastructure**—No new infrastructure is required to offer Layer 2 VPNs. The same IP/MPLS network can be used to deliver Layer 3 VPN services and Layer 2 VPN services. This is extremely cost effective when compared to building out completely new networks with one for Layer 2 and another for Layer 3. With this, equipment as well as operations costs can be duplicated. However, many providers have existing separate networks that provide both Layer 2 and Layer 3 services, respectively. Both those networks can be migrated to a converged network, based on packet infrastructure, for cost-effective delivery of Layer 2 and Layer 3 services. This is the reason many service providers are evaluating or migrating to the converged networks. Convergence is a hot topic. Many issues must be considered when planning a converged network, though. Most of them relate to three categories—namely, technical, business, and operational issues. Installed networks are also one of the inhibitors to a single IP/MPLS network for Layer 2. Many providers have investments that must remain in use to complete the amortization of the existing Layer 2 equipment, and until the value of this equipment is fully depreciated, providers are reluctant to take on the added cost of new equipment and to lose the write-offs of installed equipment. However, most providers should see the majority of installed-base hardware fully depreciated within the next 12–24 months because minimal new investment has been made in Layer 2 switches in the past 1–2 years.

- **Service flexibility**—Because Frame Relay and ATM networks allow service providers to offer FR and ATM service only, if the same service provider wants to offer Ethernet services, the service provider must undertake a completely new build-out of Ethernet network. As the service portfolio expands, the network must also expand in the same way, resulting in the significant expansion of management products and operations costs. Using an MPLS network allows the SP to offer Ethernet, Frame Relay, ATM, PPP, or HDLC service on the same network without building a completely new network. As the service portfolio expands, more line cards might need to be added to the existing IP/MPLS-capable network devices for connecting the correct transport type.

- **Value-add services**—Using MPLS-based Layer 2 VPNs, many new service types can be offered. For example, with PPP over MPLS or HDLC over MPLS, a new service can be created equivalent to a leased line—a virtual leased line. This service emulates a PPP or HDLC link across the IP/MPLS network. By combining this functionality with MPLS traffic engineering and QoS, a tight SLA can easily be offered for this service. A physical leased line does not offer any protection against the failure of network core components. In contrast, the virtual leased line service can be protected against link, node, and path failures using MPLS TE and MPLS Fast Reroute. A service provider can show value by offering a PPP- or HDLC-protected link capability with the bandwidth guarantees to mimic leased lines.

- **Back-haul services**—PPP/HDLC over MPLS can be used for back-hauling PPP connections from remote pops to central termination points in the network. For example, a national provider in the Asian Pacific is back-hauling DSL PPP connections from remote POPs to a central POP that houses all the user authentication capability. This means the national provider need not provide all the authentication and termination equipment at remote pops, thereby reducing the operations costs by using the available technology to back-haul to a few central locations and administer them through the central points.

- **Remote peering**—Using interworking and virtual leased line capability, remote peering can be offered as a service to local regional providers. For example, one national provider in Europe uses PPP-to-Frame Relay interworking to offer peering capability on a PPP connection to small regional service provider with global service providers on Frame Relay or ATM connections. This is done without requiring the regional providers to physically buy a connection to the global gateway point. This results in cost savings for the regional providers, as well as a new service for the national provider.

- **Wholesale trunks**—Using AToM, point-to-point trunks can be sold for ATM and or Frame Relay networks. This is a useful application for selling central office-to-central office (Co-to-CO) voice trunks. In the enterprise environment, PBX tie lines, previously carried through ATM service, can now be carried across the converged network, which provides both Layer 3 and Layer 2 capability.

- **Transparent LAN services**—Ethernet connectivity is popular for metro region transport. VPLS allows a service provider to offer Layer 2 Ethernet service in a metro region connecting the enterprise. Alternatively, the enterprise can either deploy or buy Ethernet connectivity to branch sites and maintain control over its own routing and addressing plans.

- **Leverage the high-speed packet core**—Any Layer 2 network cannot be expanded natively to a core bandwidth of OC-48 or greater due to limitations of available hardware and the technology. For example, no Frame Relay networks exist with OC-48 core bandwidth. In addition, until recently no ATM OC-192 interface was available from any vendor. The maximum speed for Ethernet is 10 Gbps. When Layer 2 connections are aggregated, the core trunks must be high bandwidth to carry aggregated traffic between PEs. Using an IP/MPLS network, higher bandwidth core networks can be built up to OC-768 and large amounts of Layer 2 and Layer 3 traffic can be aggregated easily.

The real benefit of Layer 2 VPNs over MPLS comes from the overall cost savings due to the possibility of building a converged backbone. Otherwise, for multiple services, multiple networks must be built—which impacts the bottom line. With the planning of various service providers to build a next-generation network (NGN) that converges Layer 2 and Layer 3 services, L2VPN becomes a critical service as part of the NGN portfolio. In addition, IP/MPLS provides the cost savings needed to build one infrastructure.

Inter-AS L2VPNs

When building pseudowires across an AS boundary within a provider or across service providers, the PEs must have a directed LDP session to exchange labels for that pseudowire across the AS boundary. This means PE reachability is needed inside the AS; this could be considered a security issue. To prevent malicious access, service providers do not allow the building of sessions with a PE router in their domains from anyone outside their own domains. You must have PE reachability to build a contiguous pseudowire from one PE to another, so LDP signaling solution is not desirable from a security standpoint.

To overcome this problem, segmented pseudowires can be built between ASs. For example, one pseudowire can be built from the PE1 to ASBR1, another pseudowire can be built between ASBRs 1 and 2, and a third pseudowire can be built between the ASBR2 and the remote PE2, as shown in Figure 4-5.

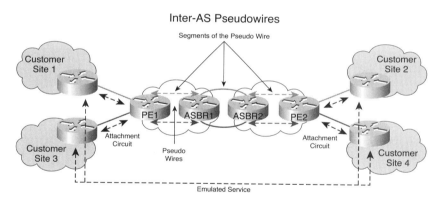

Figure 4-5   *Inter-AS Pseudowires*

The segments are then stitched together at the ASBR routers to complete the end-to-end Layer 2 connection. This allows SPs to maintain their security while building pseudowires independently. The handshake at the ASBR boundary and stitching of pseudowires enables independent control of the respective autonomous systems domains while maintaining a pseudowire-specific SLA between providers.

Supported IETF Standards

Cisco's implementations of AToM and VPLS are based on IETF drafts and standards. The standardization of AToM and VPLS is being tackled in the IETF PWE3 Working Group, while the signaling and autodiscovery aspects are being looked at in the L2VPN Working Group of the IETF. Cisco either fully or partially supports the following IETF drafts and RFCs at press time:

- RFC 3916, "Requirements for Pseudowire Emulation Edge-to-Edge (PWE3)"

- RFC 4448, "Encapsulation Methods for Transport of Ethernet over IP/ MPLS Networks"

- RFC 4447, "Pseudowire Setup and Maintenance Using LDP"

- RFC 3985, "PWE3 Architecture"

- RFC 4197, "Requirements for Edge-to-Edge Emulation of TDM Circuits over Packet Switching Networks (PSN)"

- RFC 4446, "IANA Allocations for Pseudowire Edge-to-Edge Emulation (PWE3)"

- "Requirements for Virtual Private LAN Services (VPLS)"

- "L2VPN Framework"

- "Virtual Private LAN Service"

- "Virtual Private LAN Services over MPLS"

- "Pseudowire (PW) Management Information Base"

- "Pseudowire (PW) over MPLS PSN Management Information Base"

- "Definitions for Textual Conventions and Object Identities for Pseudowire Management"

- "SONET/SDH Circuit Emulation over Packet (CEP)"

- "Ethernet Pseudowire (PW) Management Information Base"

- "PWE3 Fragmentation and Reassembly"

- "Encapsulation Methods for Transport of Frame Relay over MPLS Networks"

- "Encapsulation Methods for Transport of ATM over MPLS Networks"
- "Encapsulation Methods for Transport of PPP/HDLC over MPLS Networks"
- "Pseudowire Virtual Circuit Connectivity Verification (VCCV)"
- "PWE3 Frame Check Sequence Retention"
- "Structure-aware TDM Circuit Emulation Service over Packet Switched Network (CESoPSN)"
- "PWE3 ATM Transparent Cell Transport Service"
- "Pseudowire (PW) OAM Message Mapping"
- "Requirements for Interdomain Pseudowires"
- "Segmented Pseudowire"
- "Control Protocol Extensions for Setup of TDM Pseudowires"
- "Dynamic Placement of Multi-Segment Pseudowires"
- "An Architecture for Multi-Segment Pseudowire Emulation Edge-to-Edge"
- "Target Choice of Pseudowire Type"
- "Pseudowire Attachment Identifiers for Aggregation and VPN Autodiscovery"
- "Encapsulation Methods for Transport of Fibre Channel Frames over MPLS Networks"

Summary

In this chapter, you have seen and understood Layer 2 VPNs and how they work in IP/MPLS networks. You have also seen several examples of how AToM can be used to offer various types of Layer 2 services. Several value-added services can easily be built by combining AToM with MPLS traffic engineering to offer services, such as virtual leased lines and bandwidth-guaranteed Layer 2 connections. This chapter also compared and contrasted the signaling techniques of LDP and BGP for pseudowire signaling and examined the benefits of Layer 2 VPNS built over an IP/MPLS network.

Standards and References

L2VPNs: http://www.cisco.com/en/US/products/sw/iosswrel/ps1829/products_feature_guide09186a0080223a1b.html

CHAPTER 5

LAYER 3
VPNs

In this chapter, we discuss another important application of MPLS, which was mentioned in Chapter 4, "Layer 2 VPNs"—namely, Layer 3 VPNs. This is also known as Border Gateway Protocol (BGP) MPLS VPNs. Layer 3 VPNs (commonly referred as RFC 2547 VPNs; the new RFC is RFC 4364) was one of the first applications of MPLS. This is the most common MPLS application and the most widely deployed network-based IP VPN technology. This chapter starts with a technology overview and then discusses how Layer 3 VPNs can be offered as a service. We further discuss value-added services and how these services can be bundled with Layer 3 VPNs for additional revenue for service providers.

IT managers struggle with the question of whether to outsource the corporate wide area network (WAN) to a service provider or to manage the WAN themselves. However, the migration of corporate applications, such as customer relationship management (CRM) and enterprise resource planning (ERP), to IP further prompts these IT managers to consider adopting a managed Layer 3 service offering from a service provider (SP). Many have outsourced the managed Layer 3 service, whereas others have taken the plunge to build it in-house. Many who have outsourced their virtual private networks (VPN) have bought a Layer 3 service from the SP. These services can consist of a tunneling technology, such as generic routing encapsulation (GRE) or IPSec, layered across a Layer 2 data link. Or the services might include the latest network-based IP VPN technology based on MPLS technology as a service foundation.

The GRE or IPSec tunnel-based alternatives provide IP-based connectivity in small networks. They are, however, limited in scalability for large networks because they do not scale well with their requirement of n^2 tunnels to connect sites in full mesh. This means that each customer router maintains a tunnel adjacency with other customer routers despite the routing relationship with provider routers. In the IPSec case, secure/encrypted tunnels are set up over public/private infrastructure. As the number of sites increases in any VPN of size n, to maintain an any-to-any connectivity, $n-1$ number of tunnels must be established from each site. With MPLS-based L3VPNs, the scale is much better and there is no requirement of setting up $n(n-1)$ tunnels – $O(n^2)$ (read as order of n^2) tunnels between sites. The subsequent sections discuss how MPLS VPNs work.

Technology Overview

In network-based VPNs, the VPN is built in to the provider network. The service provider defines the rules and policies for connectivity. The customer routers (CE devices) that are connected to the provider network forward IP packets toward the network core. The provider network is responsible for maintaining and distributing customer routes. No tunnel adjacencies are required between customers' routers, and the provider network is responsible for maintaining the route separation from one customer's VPN to another.

The three main components to MPLS-based VPNs are as follows:

- Separation of routing information between VPNs

- Constrained distribution of routing information to sites within a VPN

- Forwarding of packets through the network core

Let us now examine each of those components in some detail.

Separation of Routing Information Between VPNs

Separation of routing information between VPNs is a fundamental requirement for a network-based VPN service. If the routing information were to intermingle, packets from one VPN would be forwarded to another VPN, and this goes against the fundamental definition of the VPN network itself.

Within each VPN, the VPN customer advertises routes and addresses that are carried by a routing protocol. The routes advertised in one VPN by the routing protocol need to be separate from another VPN's.

The provider edge (PE) routers are responsible for keeping VPN A routes separate from VPN B routes. The PE devices hold each VPN's routes in a table called the virtual routing and forwarding (VRF) table. Each VRF within the PE holds customers' routes. All the PEs that connect to the same VPN must have a VRF for that VPN, and all routes within the VRF must be unique. However, because a separate routing and forwarding table is maintained per VPN in the PE device, the IP addressing can be reused between VPNs. For example, VPN A can have a 10.20/16, VPN B can also have a 10.20/16 prefix in its routing tables, and both VPNs can be on the same PE box. The PE always maintains the routing context of the VPN and forwards packets appropriately, without mixing the traffic from one VPN to another.

Routes are imported into a VRF or exported from a VRF. Routes can also be imported into multiple VRFs, creating overlapping VPNs or extranets. More details on extranets are provided later in this chapter. The PE always routes packets within a VPN unless by configuration, in which case it can send packets to a global table or other VPNs (extranets). The VRF table grows with the number of routes within a VPN. The VRF table is maintained only on the PE router, and no provider core router has any knowledge of the VRF table. (Subsequent sections examine how the core router forwards VPN packets.)

When CEs connect to PE routers, as shown in Figure 5-1, the CEs distribute routing information. The local PE then learns the information from the attached CEs and populates the VRF table. After all the PEs in the network learn the attached CE routes, they need to communicate with each other to exchange routes so that packets can be forwarded within the VPN.

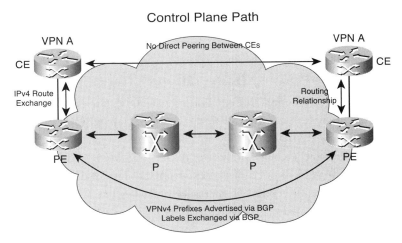

Figure 5-1   *Control Plane Path*

Constrained Distribution of Routing Information

As stated earlier, after the PEs learn local information from the CE either through dynamic routing protocols or through static configuration, they need to distribute the routing information to other PEs in the network. For this routing distribution to happen, the following two things are required:

- A core addressing plan to separate routing information from VPNs is required. Remember that IP addresses can be reused within VPNs or even private addresses can be used within VPNs.

- A protocol for distribution of routing information between PEs is required. It must provide a peering relationship between PEs so that routing information about VPNs can easily be exchanged between the PEs without having to propagate/redistribute all this into the provider core.

The first problem can be solved by creating an addressing scheme that makes VPN addresses unique by prepending the VPN IP address by a route distinguisher (RD)—for the lack of a better name, we can call this a VPN identifier. The details and formats of RD are the Cisco Press book *MPLS and VPN Architectures*, Vol 1, by I. Pepelnak and J. Guichard. By prepending the RD to the VPN IP addresses, by virtue of assignment, these VPN IP addresses become globally unique.

- VPNv4 prefix = RD + VPN IPv4 prefix

- RD = * byte field uniquely assigned by the provider—significant to the provider network only

These globally unique VPN addresses are also referred to as *VPNv4 addresses*. The PE routers exchange these VPNv4 addresses between themselves and learn about the remote routes and sites that require connectivity within the VPN. For more details on the allocation of RDs and an explanation of VPN addresses, you can also refer to the IETF RFC 4364.

The protocol used for distributing routing information is Multi-Protocol BGP (MP-BGP). BGP has been extended to carry VPNv4 addresses as part of the extended community attributes in the BGP network layer reacheability information (NLRI). An *extended community attribute* is an attribute carried in the NLRI. The PE receives the BGP updates, processes them, and populates the VRFs with the remote routes. To receive the updates, the PEs must peer with each other or peer with a route reflector.

A *route reflector* is a dedicated device that helps in BGP scalability by distributing routing information to the PE routers. MPLS labels are also distributed along with the VPNv4 addresses. The PE routers identify a VPN prefix by looking up the associated label and forward packets. We provide more information on packet forwarding behavior later in this chapter.

It might have been theoretically possible to use another protocol, such as LDP, for VPN routing distribution. However, the use of another protocol requires scaling properties for route updates to support a large number of sessions and requires a mechanism, such as a route reflector, to scale the number of sessions and information/routing distribution. The protocol must also be capable of providing mechanisms for filtering and creating flexible routing maps and policies. BGP is the only protocol that has proven to scale for IP routing with the Internet and to be capable of providing flexible routing policy configuration. BGP is naturally suited for the distribution of VPN routing information because it is currently used for Internet routing distribution.

For details of the routing relation ships between PEs, refer to Figure 5-1.

Forwarding Packets Through the Network Core

As stated earlier, labels are distributed with the VPN prefixes. However, for packets to reach the destination PE—and ultimately the destination CE—the reachability information for the BGP next-hop must be available through an Interior Gateway Protocol (IGP). Examples of IGPs include OSPF, IS-IS, EIGRP, and the Routing Information Protocol (RIP). A label distribution protocol, such as LDP or RSVP-TE (when using traffic engineering), is needed to distribute labels for reachability of the PEs. The label-switched paths (LSP) established between PEs provide a path for forwarding VPN packets between them. This LSP is formed by the first label (outermost label) in the label stack. Remember that VPN packets themselves have a VPN label; this is usually the second label in label stack. The VPN-labeled packets are forwarded onto the LSP that has been set up between PE routers. The resulting MPLS packet carries multiple labels. The outermost label is called the IGP label, and the innermost label is called the VPN label.

Packet Flow Through the Network

To explain the forwarding of packets clearly, refer to the Figure 5-2.

Data Plane Path

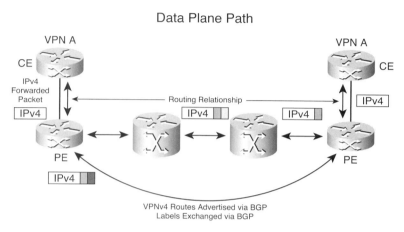

Figure 5-2 *Data Plane Path*

The CEs in VPN A have a single routing relationship with only the attached PEs. The dual-attached CEs (CEs attached to two PEs) maintain two routing relationships with the attached PEs. The routing information is distributed to the CE by the PE via this routing relationship. The CEs wanting to send packets to other CEs in the VPN forward plain IP packets toward the PE. When the PE receives the packet, the PE knows from which VPN the packet is received, and it imposes the VPN label, which was distributed to other PEs. The PE now must forward the VPN labeled packet to the destination, and the ingress PE then imposes the IGP label and forwards the VPN packets on the LSP toward the network core. Thus, the PE imposes two labels (a VPN label and an IGP label) on the VPN IP packet. The core routers (P routers in the diagram) forward the packets toward the destination PE based on the outermost label. The penultimate hop along the LSP can remove the IGP label and forward the VPN-labeled packet to the destination PE. This is called the *penultimate hop pop (PHP)* operation. In some devices, the penultimate hop pop might be disabled, in which case the egress PE first pops the IGP label and then looks up the VPN label. The destination PE looks up the VPN label, removes the label, and forwards the IP frame to the attached CE.

When routes are withdrawn—depending on the type of routes that change—reconvergence must occur in the IGP or BGP. The LDP must also reconverge for any IGP changes. However, the LDP will not reconverge if only the BGP routes change, and BGP will not converge if the IGP routes change (unless the BGP next-hop changes). This provides some level of isolation of VPN routes from the provider core network. We investigate the convergence and how this can affect the offered SLA in Chapter 13, "Design Considerations: Putting it All Together."

Corporate Intranet

MPLS VPNs are an ideal way of building scalable corporate intranets. Corporate intranets can span local area networks (LAN) and wide area networks (WAN). They can be built over public or private backbones. In addition, they can have full or partial sites within a VPN and can have remote users over a DSL connection or a dedicated connection. No matter what the connectivity in terms of transport protocol, the intranet must work. These requirements provide several challenges to the network designer. If the corporate intranet is built using MPLS VPNs in the WAN, the MPLS network must support several features. Some of these requirements are as follows:

- The MPLS network must be capable of supporting all transport types, such as a data link—Ethernet, Frame Relay, Point-to-Point (PPP), High-Level Data Link Control (HDLC), Packet over SONET (POS), and ATM.

- It must be possible to map VLANs in a LAN to MPLS VPNs at the PE or the CE.

- It must be possible to map remote users and dial-in users to the MPLS VPNs.

- It must be possible to connect full sites to MPLS VPNs.

- It must be possible to use either dynamic routing protocol or static routing between the PE and CE.

- It must be possible to build a corporate intranet across geographic boundaries and across multiple provider networks using MPLS VPNs.

- This is a generic requirement for the technology and not for an individual corporation.

- It must be possible to scale the corporate intranet to a large number of sites—maybe even thousands of sites—in the intranet using MPLS VPNs.

- Quality of service (QoS) must be supported with MPLS VPNs.

- It must be possible to physically connect sites in an arbitrary manner, but any-to-any connectivity is required logically.

- It must be possible to define routing policies to allow partial connectivity.

- It must be possible to also build hub-and-spoke VPNs.

MPLS VPNs can easily satisfy all the previously listed requirements because of the following reasons:

- MPLS supports all the data links for L3 VPNs.

- VLANs can be mapped to VRFs in MPLS VPNs at either the CE or PE.

- Remote access users can be mapped to MPLS VPNs by terminating the IPSec tunnels either on a dedicated IPSec concentrator or directly on the PE itself.

- Sites can be connected to multiple VPNs, or all the sites can be connected to a single VPN. The attached customer port (CE) belongs to a VPN site. Any static or dynamic routing protocol (OSPF, IS-IS, RIPv2, eBGP, or EIGRP) can be used between PE and CE.

- Techniques, such as Inter-AS VPNs or Carrier Supporting Carrier (CSC), can be used to scale VPNs to large networks that span multiple geographies and provider networks. For details on Inter-AS and CSC, please refer to IETF RFC 4364.

- Because the PE needs only to know information about the attached VPNs, you can scale MPLS VPNs to connect thousands of sites within a VPN and thousands, or even tens of thousands, of VPNs per network. Each device within the network needs to hold information only of the attached VPNs/sites, and more PEs can be added to support more VPNs. Hence, the scalability is not hampered by the scale limitations of a single device.

- By managing the VPNv4 route advertisements via BGP and appropriate filtering, you can easily build full-mesh or hub-and-spoke VPNs.

- Corporate intranets can be extended to dedicated sites and remote sites including DSL/cable users and dial-in users by mapping the remote users appropriately to VRFs using a mix of technologies, such as VLAN-to-VRF mapping and VRF-aware AAA.

Corporate Extranet

Another important requirement is the capability to build extranets without compromising the security of the intranet. For example, an automobile manufacturer might want a corporate intranet for communicating between sites and factories but also require an extranet to communicate to dealers. The auto dealers are selling the cars, so it is crucial for the automobile manufacturer to be able to communicate quickly and effectively with the dealers regarding ordering, shipping, and maintenance and recalls. All this must be done without compromising the intranet's security.

With MPLS VPNs, communication is fairly easy. Let us suppose that an intranet contains the following routes:

10.20/16

10.30/16

10.100/16

All the transaction hosts for order entry and tracking that are accessed by dealers are in the 10.100/16 domain. The dealer extranet contains all the dealer routes. Those can be any public or private routes. For the dealers to access the transaction servers for order placement, only the 10.100/16 routes need to be imported into the extranet VRF, in addition to the dealer routes. This provides connectivity between the dealers and the automobile manufacturer without compromising the security of the automobile manufacturer's intranet. If the attackers in the dealer networks send packet to hosts in different subnets, such as 10.20/16 or 10.30/16, the PEs won't know where to send those packets because there are no routes for 10.20/16 in the extranet VRF; thus, packets to all routes outside the extranet are dropped.

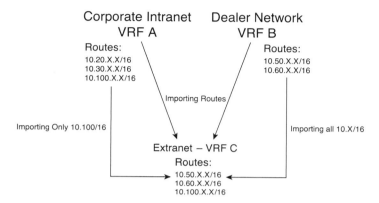

Figure 5-3 *Importing Routes into VRFs*

Refer to Figure 5-3 for details on how routes are imported into VRFs. From the previous example, it can be easily observed that in the MPLS VPNs environment, you can create extranets just by performing a few simple configuration steps on a PE.

Internet Access

Another important service that is required with MPLS VPNs is Internet access to VPN customers. There are several ways of providing Internet access, one of the simplest ways of which is to provide access to the gateway holding Internet routes to the VPN customers. This can be done by configuring a default route for all nonVPN prefixes and forcing the traffic to be routed via a firewall between the Internet and VPN. Each time a new VPN needs access to the Internet, a new dedicated gateway or a virtual gateway is required. There are several other ways of offering Internet service to MPLS VPN customers. Some of them include a shared centralized gateway; others move the ownership of Internet connectivity to the VPN customers themselves.

Let us briefly discuss the following four ways of offering Internet services (refer to Figures 5-4 and 5-5).

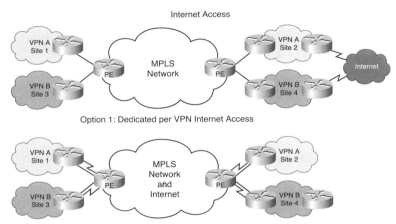

Figure 5-4   *Fnternet Access (Options 1 and 2)*

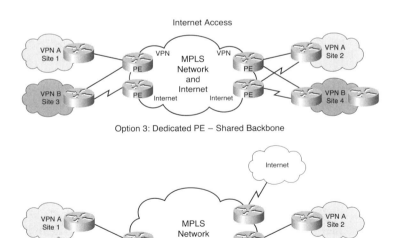

Figure 5-5   *Internet Access (Options 3 and 4)*

- Option 1: Dedicated per-VPN Internet access

- Option 2: Shared PE—Internet and VPNs

- Option 3: Dedicated PE—Shared backbone

- Option 4: Managed central service—Shared Internet access

Let us discuss each one in detail.

Dedicated Per-VPN Internet Access

As shown in Figure 5-4, the Internet access is via the VPN. No direct connection to the Internet exists from the VPN provider network. The Internet connectivity is through one or more VPN sites. Traffic to the Internet from the VPN goes through a firewall or gateway. The Internet connectivity is independent of the VPN connectivity, so the VPN subscriber has the opportunity to buy Internet service from any provider. The VPN subscriber must pay for another dedicated connection. Although, this model of connectivity is simple, the VPN provider has no play in the Internet connection. This can be advantageous because the VPN provider can claim this is a pure private IP network.

Shared PE—Internet and VPN

This model of connectivity is simple: The PE is shared between Internet and VPN. In addition to carrying VPN routes in a VRF, the PE usually carries Internet routes in the global table. To connect to the Internet from a VPN, the VPN subscriber must buy another circuit, such as a data-link connection identifier (DLCI) or a DS1/DS3 channel from the VPN site(s) to the nearest PE. The CE then routes traffic on two interfaces based on whether the traffic is destined to the Internet or to another VPN site. As the number of Internet connections increases, an operator can reflect these additions from the CE within a VPN by provisioning a DLCI, VC, or dedicated DS1/DS3 channel to the PE. The result of such an implementation is an efficient traffic flow that forces the Internet traffic to the nearest PE rather than always being routed via a single VPN site (HQ or Internet gateway site). If all CEs have connectivity to both an Internet and a corporate

VPN, the Internet traffic is offloaded at the first hop and will not traverse the VPN path to reach a gateway.

This method of connectivity is relatively simple, and all isolation and firewall techniques can be applied to the Internet connectivity. However, this implementation might not be the most secure due to the perceived threat from the Internet to the PE routers. Additionally, PE routers carry the burden of Internet routes and instabilities with the VPN routes, and these affect scalability and convergence. It is not our intention to deal with security and convergence issues in this chapter. They will be dealt with in Chapter 13.

Dedicated PE—Shared Backbone

To separate the VPN routes from the Internet routes, dedicated PEs can be deployed that carry Internet routes and VPN routes only. The PE carrying VPN routes does not peer or have connectivity with the PE carrying Internet routes. However, they share the same backbone or core network. This can be viewed as two planes of connectivity riding on the same network core where paths (LSP) from one plane do not intersect with LSPs from the other plane. Plane 1 carries VPN information, and LSPs for VPN traffic are established by the VPN PEs. LSPs for the Internet traffic are established by Internet PEs. The core network can be BGP free with neither Internet nor VPN routes but simply IGP connectivity. The CEs responsible for routing Internet traffic connect to both PEs.

This method of connectivity provides a good separation of VPN and Internet traffic. Security issues are minimized when compared to the shared PE model. However, the cost of this method of connectivity is high because of the requirement of a dedicated PE for each function. From a VPN subscriber point of view, the cost is the same as the shared PE model due to the requirement to buy multiple connections—one for the Internet and another for VPN.

Managed Central Service—Shared Internet Access

The fourth model leverages VRF-aware IP services to provide Internet access. It makes use of IP services such as Dynamic Host Configuration Protocol (DHCP), network address translation (NAT), firewalls, and on-demand address pools (ODAP) being VRF-aware. This means that these IP services (NAT, ODAP, and firewall) understand VRF context and maintain separation between the traffic of one VRF and another.

Let us assume that several VPNs are using private address space. This means that when performing NAT from any VPN to the public address space (Internet), the gateway/PE must be able to maintain the VPN contexts. By using VRF-aware NAT, a PE can distinguish between 10.1/16 of VPN A and 10.1/16 of VPN B. Therefore, a single PE can now become the gateway to the Internet for all the VPNs, as shown in the diagram. The Internet gateway PE contains the VRFs (VPN information) and routes traffic for multiple VPNs to the Internet. This gateway PE can be located at a central location, providing easy Internet connectivity to all the sites.

As the name suggests, this model of connectivity is used for centrally building the Internet access and sharing it across all VPNs. It can be used to build bundled services providing value add for the VPN provider. The important advantages include both cost reduction through the use of fewer gateways and reduced management requirements caused by the capability to enforce a single security policy centrally in the network.

Several variations can be created with these four basic models of Internet access for VPN customers. These are discussed in detail in several books and whitepapers from Cisco including the following:

- Pepelnak, J. Guichard, et al. *MPLS and VPN Architectures*, Volumes 1 and 2. Indianapolis, IN: Cisco Press.

  —*Definitive MPLS Network Designs*. Indaianpolis, IN: Cisco Press.

- B. Davie et al. *MPLS: Technology and Applications*. San Francisco, CA: Morgan Kaufmann.

- Behringer, Michael D. and Monique Morrow. *MPLS VPN Security*. Indianapolis, IN: Cisco Press.

Scaling MPLS VPNs to Multi-AS, Multi-Provider, and Hierarchical Networks

Any VPN technology must scale to a large number of sites per VPN and a large number of VPNs per network. Using a tunneling technology, such as GRE or IPSec, limits the number of sites per VPN or the number of VPNs to a small number due to the number of tunnels a network element supports. Hence, the size of the VPN is dependent on the network elements and their scale numbers. While we will not discuss the details of how MPLS VPNs scale here, it is important to understand that a technology being evaluated for VPN deployment must be able to scale to large (>10000) sites per VPN and a large number (>10000) of VPNs per network. The VPN technology must be capable of accommodating such large routing information easily without a meltdown occurring in the network.

When building an IP network using MPLS, the VPN technology must provide a means to build a VPN across IGP areas, across BGP autonomous systems, and across multiple domains and routing boundaries. These are termed Inter-AS or Carrier Supporting Carrier (also known as Carrier's Carrier) VPNs. Before we discuss the details of each of these VPNs, we have deliberately decided to ignore whether the autonomous system (AS) or a stub network is controlled and managed by the same provider or different providers.

Inter-AS VPNs

RFC 4364 discusses the ability to build MPLS VPNs across the autonomous system boundaries. The three basic models discussed in RFC2547bis for Inter-AS connectivity are as follows:

- Back-to-back VPN connectivity between ASBRs
- VPNv4 exchange of routes and peering between ASBRs
- IPv4 exchange of routes and peering between ASBRs

All three models focus on propagating VPN routes from one AS to the other AS. The first model is a simple one in which the ASBRs connect back to back via logical circuits or VLANs one per VRF. The back-to-back connections enable VPN connectivity and the exchange of routes between ASBRs on a per-VPN basis. For example, if ASBR1 and 2 need to exchange routes for 10 VPNs, 10 logical circuits exist between ASBR1 and ASBR2—one for each VPN.

In the second model of connectivity, ASBRs exchange VPNv4 routes among each other. As stated earlier, a VPN can span multiple ASes, the peering points between ASes. ASBRs advertise the VPV4 routes learned from the other AS and use themselves as the next hop for those routes. The PEs then forward the traffic toward the ASBR, which in turn forwards it to the destination. For multiprovider networks—each managing its own set of ASes—the same model of connectivity applies. If the providers are peering just for VPN routes, this mode of connectivity might be sufficient. However, if they are peering for VPN routes and IP routes, the ASBRs here have the additional burden of carrying IPv4 and VPNv4 routes. The third model of IPv4 route exchange solves this problem. In the third model, only the IPv4 routes are exchanged between provider ASBRs and VPNv4 routes are exchanged between the VPN route reflectors in each AS. This frees up the ASBRs to carry only IPv4 routes.

Each method of connectivity has advantages and drawbacks. What we are trying to illustrate is that, irrespective of AS boundaries, MPLS VPNs can be built across them. Some providers choose to partition their networks to make them more manageable from a routing standpoint, such as BGP confederations and so on. MPLS VPNs can work over all such routing paradigms and have the capability to seamlessly connect customer sites no matter in which AS or confederation they reside.

Carrier Supporting Carrier

Another method of scaling MPLS VPNs is to create hierarchical VPNs. Consider a national or international carrier that is selling a VPN service to smaller stub carriers. The smaller stub carriers might in turn be selling another MPLS VPN service to end users (enterprises). By nesting stub carrier VPNs within the core or national carrier VPN, a hierarchical VPN can be built. With the CSC mode described in RFC 2547bis, the stub carrier VPNs and their routes do not show up in the core carrier—only the stub carrier IGP routes are part of the core carrier VPN. So, the core carrier does not need to learn or understand end user routes because the end user of the core carrier is the stub carrier. The core carrier needs only to provide VPN connectivity so that the core carrier's CEs (ironically, they are stub carrier PEs) are reachable. These CEs are called *CSCCEs*, whereas the PE that connects to the stub carrier and has MPLS enabled on the PE-CE link is called the *CSCPE*.

Carrier's Carrier can also be used by a single provider. For example, let us assume that the core network of a carrier is managed by a different department from that of the edge network. The edge network might sell services to enterprise customers. The core network might also sell services to other departments (one might provide Internet service, another might provide content-based services, and so on) or even directly to VPN customers. Using the CSC model, the core network need not be aware of the VPN routes of the CE network. The core network in this manner is isolated from the routing changes of customer VPNs. Similarly, this can be extended to the enterprise customers. For example, say an enterprise customer buys a VPN service from a service provider. The enterprise customer wants to build his own VPNs or virtual networks (LANs and so on) within the VPN. By using CSC connectivity, the enterprise can build multiple VPNs within the provider VPN.

The exact details of label forwarding, route exchange, and configurations are beyond the scope of this chapter and can be easily learned from Cisco Press's *MPLS and VPN Architectures*, Volumes 1 and 2 by I. Pepelnak, J. Guichard, et al. Our point is to show you how this technology scales and can be used to build large IP VPNs.

Heterogeneous Networks

So far, we have assumed that a network on which MPLS VPNs are being built is a homogenous MPLS network. This implies that the edge of the network is MPLS enabled and that the core of the network is also MPLS-enabled. Hence, we assumed that the paths set up in the core of the network were label-switched paths (LSP). However, you might be building an MPLS VPN that is required to transit over nonMPLS networks or network elements. In such cases, the MPLS traffic must be tunneled across the nonMPLS network. This can be done in several ways:

- MPLS in IP tunnel
- GRE tunnel
- MPLS in L2TPv3 tunnel
- MPLS in IPSec tunnel

All the previously listed methods enable tunneling of MPLS VPN packets from ingress PE to egress PE. This implies that the VPNv4 route exchange and that label distribution of VPNv4 routes do not change at all. Using the procedures described in the preceding sections, the VPN routes are imported and traffic labeled. However, in forwarding the traffic to the destination PE instead of imposing an IGP label as described in Figure 5-2, the tunnel header is imposed and the traffic is tunneled across the nonMPLS network to the egress PE.

The method of establishing the tunnel to go across the nonMPLS network can be either static or dynamic. In static establishment, the tunnels are manually preestablished between PE devices where it must cross the nonMPLS boundary. In the dynamic establishment, the tunnels are established by some signaling mechanism that uses its own signaling protocol, such as IPSec end point discovery, or by using BGP extensions, such as the L2TPv3 tunnel. The details of how these tunnels are established can be found in various IETF drafts and also RFC4364.

For example, MPLS packets can be carried across an IPSec tunnel setup across the public network. This provides the security that is needed by the VPN and leverages the public infrastructure that is low cost. Now extend this principle to a network in which only the edge network is MPLS-enabled and the entire core network is a nonMPLS or a pure IP backbone. This becomes the ultimate case of tunneling across the nonMPLS network. In this case, the entire forwarding of frames from one PE to another is done over the IP network. The VPN labels are exchanged in BGP, just as before, and packets are forwarded by the PE devices with a VPN label. The IGP label is replaced by the generic IP tunnel.

The biggest advantage to having this capability to transport MPLS VPN packets across the nonMPLS network is the flexibility it provides in connecting all types of networks and making them appear to be a single network from the VPN's point of view.

Managed Central Services

We stated that VRFs are used for storing VPN routes. Packets coming from a VPN are looked up in a VRF and forwarded to the destination PE. We also briefly discussed how Internet access can be provided to the VPN customers. We also learned that a protocol, such as NAT, can be made VRF-aware to understand the

VRF context. This enables the automatic performance of address translation from private to public addresses without compromising security or connectivity. The concept was to make a protocol or service (address translation) so that it could be used to offer the same service to any VPN.

This is called *managed central or shared service*. A number of SPs who have deployed MPLS VPNs and are growing their networks each day are also interested in what is next with MPLS VPNs. Managed central services includes any service that is deployed centrally and offered as a value add to all the VPNs.

Now let us consider a few services that service providers might be interested in offering to enterprise customers or that large enterprises might be interested in offering to the VPN clients:

- Managed hosting

- Content distribution

- IP address management

- Redundancy solutions—hot standby solutions

- Managed security

- Managed Internet access

- Subscriber self-management

- On-demand QoS for VPNs

Each of the previously listed service types is designed to create a centralized service that can be configured and hosted at a central location and can easily be shared across the VRFs and VPNs. In this case, by simply making them VRF-aware, a single service can be shared across the different VPNs.

Making Applications and Services VRF-Aware

Protocols and services running on a network element must be VRF-aware and must be able to distinguish between requests from VPN A and VPN B. Otherwise, packets will be forwarded on the wrong paths and to the wrong destinations. For example, suppose a network element, in this case a router, has voice ports and supports voice over IP (VoIP). The router also supports a VoIP signaling protocol, such as H.323 or SIP. When this router is used in a VPN context to offer VPNs services to multiple customers and voice services are being targeted towards these customers; the router must be able to distinguish between a VoIP signaling request from VPN A and one from VPN B; perform a correct routing table lookup; and then forward the signaling requests. Note the distinction in function between voice signal differentiation and VPN instantiation. If the VoIP signaling protocol is not VRF-aware, the voice call requests from the VPNs would be looked up in the global routing table and either sent to the wrong voice gateways or dropped. Dropping the requests does less damage than forwarding the requests to incorrect destinations.

To make protocols or features VRF-aware, the protocols or features must be implemented to look beyond the global routing table for information into VRFs. Internally a VRF can be implemented as an additional routing table that is handled by the routing protocol. In the case of Layer 3 VPNs, we have seen how the VRF is handled by BGP. The following are some examples of protocols that are or can be made VRF-aware:

- VRF-aware address management (NAT, DHCP, ODAP, and DHCP Relay)
- VRF-aware NAT
- VRF-aware firewall
- VRF-aware HSRP/VRRP (Virtual Router Redundancy Protocol)
- VRF-aware SIP/H.323/MGCP (Media Gateway Control Protocol)
- VRF-aware management tools (Ping and SNMP)
- VRF-aware policy routing

To illustrate the point further, let us now discuss one of these in detail.

VRF-Aware Address Management

Let us assume that address management is offered as a service to the end customers. This is frequently the case when the ISP offers DHCP service to broadband users. In this context, let us also assume that an L3VPN provider is planning to offer address management service to small enterprises that have a few sites per VPN and a small number of IP devices per site. Now an SP can develop an attractive service for this small enterprise and offer IP address management by offering DHCP and NAT service as part of the bundled package of VPN connectivity.

A corresponding cost is associated with IP address management that comes with offering DHCP and NAT services to enterprise customers. For each enterprise customer to which the SP sells this service, a dedicated gateway and server must be deployed to avoid the confusion of a 10.1/16 address from VPN A versus a 10.1/16 from VPN B. This can be cumbersome to implement and manage. Let us now see how this would change if we had VRF-aware NAT and VRF-aware DHCP/DCHP Relay.

The SP can deploy VRF-aware NAT and DHCP Relay at the PE router itself without a dedicated gateway or external server. So, the PE is now enabled with VRF-aware DHCP and NAT function. When a client in the VPN sends a DHCP request, the PE now understands the DHCP request, appends the VPN name in the options field, and sends the DHCP request to a centrally located DHCP server. The DHCP server recognizes the VPN name, allocates a new address in the VPN A address pool, and sends a DHCP reply. The DHCP reply reaches the PE, and the PE then forwards the DHCP reply to the VPN client on the correct interface to the VPN client.

In this manner, instead of replicating DHCP servers and NAT gateways, by making DHCP and NAT VRF-aware, a cost-effective, alternative deploying address management system is found. The same principle can be extended to other protocols and services. Refer to Figures 5-6 and 5-7 for before and after scenarios.

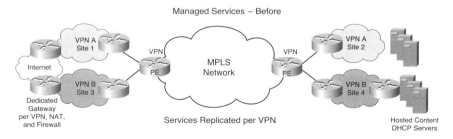

Figure 5-6   *Managed Services—Before*

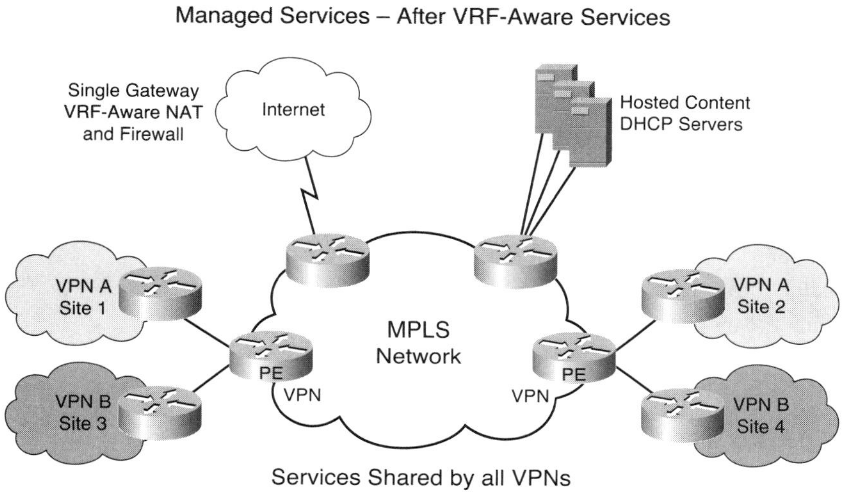

Managed Services – After VRF-Aware Services

Figure 5-7   *Managed Services—After VRF-Aware Services*

Managed shared/central services is an excellent way for a service provider to add value and move beyond plain IP VPN connectivity for a better bottom line. In this section, you have seen how MPLS makes that possible.

Supported IETF Drafts

MPLS-based L3VPNs were first defined in the Informational IETF RFC 2547. It came about as a result of a tag switching invention from Cisco. The RFC 2547 was later revised to draft-ietf-2547bis. This is now a final approved RFC 4364. RFC 4364 adds the capability to support Inter-AS, Inter-Provider VPNs, and Carrier Supporting Carrier VPNs. The RFC 4364 also describes how MPLS VPNs can be built over an IP core using point-to-point GRE tunnels or IPSec tunnels.

Summary

This chapter started with an L3VPN classification and focused attention on network-based VPNs using MPLS. You have seen what MPLS L3VPN is and how it works using MP-BGP. You have also seen how Internet services can be bundled with VPN services and the options available for Internet connectivity. The chapter explained how MPLS L3VPNs VPNs can be easily extended to multiautonomous systems and multiprovider networks and how they scale to large networks due to the fact that not all PEs need to hold all the VPN information. Lastly, you have seen how value-added services can be cost effectively built with MPLS L3VPNs using the managed central services model.

Standards and References

Guichard, Jim, Jeff Apcar, and Ivan Papelnejak. *MPLS VPN Architectures*. Indianapolis, IN: Cisco Press.

CHAPTER 6

REMOTE ACCESS AND IPSEC INTEGRATION WITH MPLS VPNs

Corporate virtual private networks (VPN) must not only provide secure site-to-site connectivity, but must also integrate remote access technologies for dial, DSL, and cable users of the VPN networks. Enterprise customers cannot just outsource wide-area network (WAN) connectivity to manage only remote access connections for corporate remote users. A decision to outsource for enterprise managers can also mean considering the outsourcing of remote access connectivity, including managing virtual home gateways and subscriber management.

From a service provider (SP) point of view, it is only a natural progression to offer remote access connectivity to users of corporate VPNs. For example, cable providers can extend the last mile reach of corporate VPNs by offering remote access connectivity to corporate VPNs in partnership with the MPLS VPN provider.

Remote users can access corporate VPNs using dial connections or dedicated connections. In either case, the traffic might need to be encrypted because it might traverse public networks.

This chapter discusses how remote access and IPSec can be integrated with MPLS VPNs. Remote access is one of the most important services with Layer 3 VPNs.

Technology Overview

To understand this better, let us quickly create a reference model. In this reference model, we limit the discussion to the connection between the provider edge (PE) and the customer edge (CE) indicated by the remote access arrow in Figure 6-1.

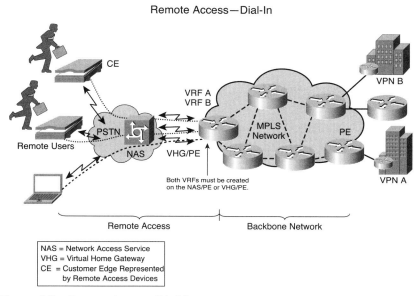

Figure 6-1 *Remote Access: Dial-In*

The remote users can connect via cable, dial, or DSL and are terminated either directly on the PE or on another device, commonly referred to as a *virtual home gateway (VHG)* within the point of presence (POP). The method of access can vary depending on the service provider's facilities, service offerings, and protocols.

Remote access integration involves the mapping of users and their traffic to the appropriate MPLS VPNs. This requires the authentication and termination of sessions and the distribution of customer routes. L2TP or point-to-point tunnels might be required between customers' routers or user PCs and the provider's termination gateways. To understand these better, let us categorize them into three main components for a complete remote access integration solution with MPLS VPNs. They are as follows:

- Dial access

- DSL access

- Cable access

Let us now examine each of those components in some detail.

Dial Access

Dial access is used when a user is connected to the corporate VPN via a dial link. Dial access consists of both dial-in and dial-out to and from the PE device. A user can dial in to a network access server (NAS) device that terminates the user connection and maps the associated traffic to a VHG. Because each VRF within the PE holds customer routes, these VRFs must be populated with the dial user/ route information. (Refer to Figure 6-1.)

Several components are common to various types of dial access. They are as follows:

- **Virtual access interface**—The virtual access interface is an instance of a virtual profile or template used in the dialer configuration, and it must be VRF-aware.

- **Authentication, authorization, and accounting (AAA)**—By using AAA, users are authenticated and per-user accounting stats can be maintained. Making the AAA servers aware of VRFs enables the sharing of AAA servers for use across AAA functions for multiple VPNs. Otherwise, a separate AAA server must be configured per VRF. The AAA server usually authenticates based on the user's domain and password to identify the VPN and then sends the configuration to the PE for the mapping of the user traffic to a particular VPN. Another authentication mechanism commonly used for dial users is Remote Access Dial-In User Service (RADIUS). RADIUS's usage principles are the same as those of AAA and can easily be adopted to authenticate remote users and map them to MPLS VPNs.

- **Address management**—AAA servers can also perform address management using on-demand address pools (ODAP) and can provide addresses to clients. Address reusability is also possible using overlapping address pools. The Dynamic Host Configuration Protocol (DHCP) can be used to provide addresses to the VPN clients, and VRF-aware DHCP allows the sharing of the same DHCP server among multiple VPNs. Address pools can grow using ODAP for automated address management, and network address translation (NAT) can also be used for address translation from private to public address space.

One or more of these components is needed to enable dial access to MPLS VPN. Dial access can be further subdivided into the following categories:

- Individual users dialing in using an ISDN or PSTN network

- A CE dialing in to a PE creating a backup connection when the primary has failed

- A PE dialing out to remote CEs triggered by incoming traffic from the network

Let us now discuss each in detail.

Individual Access

One of the most common dial-in methods is dialing using public switched telephone network (PSTN) to a local or an 800 number. Figure 6-1 shows individual users dialing in to access a corporate VPN. The networks access server (NAS) then terminates the call and initiates a VPDN tunnel using L2TP to the appropriate customer VPN. This can include PPP, multilink PPP, or multichassis multilink protocols that are used for a better bandwidth connection. The sequence of events is fairly standard: The remote user initiates a PPP connection to the NAS via PSTN dial or ISDN dial. The NAS accepts the connection, authenticates the user, checks to see whether a tunnel exists with the VHG, and extends the user's PPP session to terminate on the VHG or PE in the appropriate VRF. The authentication process determines the specific VRF that this user needs mapped. If the L2TP tunnel does not exist between the NAS and VHG, the NAS establishes a new L2TP session.

The PE must then map remote users' sessions to the correct VRF and forward traffic. The PE can impose another level of authentication for PPP sessions to ensure that the correct users are being mapped to the correct VRFs. Additionally, the SP provides address management in such scenarios via DHCP using the VRF services discussed in the previous chapter. The rest of the route management and advertisement is standard to MPLS VPN operation and has been discussed in detail in the previous chapter.

Another option is to have the user directly dial in to the PE that is also a NAS device. In such a situation, the NAS/PE might authenticate the user and map the traffic to VPNs. This conforms to a collapsed NAS/VHG environment.

CE Dial Backup Access

Should the primary connection fail for any reason, dial backup is a common technique used as a cheap redundancy option for providing PE-to-CE connectivity. (See Figure 6-2 for details.)

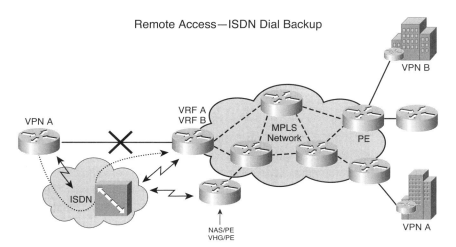

Figure 6-2 *Remote Access—ISDN Dial Backup*

The choice of using a redundant link for connectivity or dial backup is usually based on cost. In many places, using a redundant link is expensive; hence, dial backup is an affordable option especially for lower-speed connectivity between PE-CE devices.

The most common dial backup technique is to use ISDN dial backup to VHG or PE devices from the CE. The dial backup process can be to the same PE (if it also acts as a VHG for remote connections) or another PE that is a dedicated VHG. Either static routing or dynamic routing can be enabled on that dial connection.

The route learning and advertisement process is the same as in regular MPLS VPNs. However, dial backup usually works well with static routes. With dynamic routing protocols, though, the work involved with provisioning static routes can be less than that in a dynamic routing configuration.

If the service involves multiple CoS for the VPN, dial backup needs to take care of multiple classes. Special attention must be paid to address CoS requirements. For example, on the dial backup interface (due to lower available bandwidth) traffic is restricted to either high priority only or just high and medium priority and best effort is discarded or throttled down to accommodate high-priority traffic. This requires that different quality of service (QoS) templates be applied to regular interfaces and dial backup interfaces. In short, you must be sure to address dial backup for multiple classes of service.

Dial-Out Access

Instead of a remote CE initiating a connection to the VHG or PE, in this case, the PE dials out to the remote CE for connectivity. The PE-CE dial-out can be triggered based on incoming traffic from the network destined to the CE or scheduled at a particular time of the day. (See Figure 6-3.)

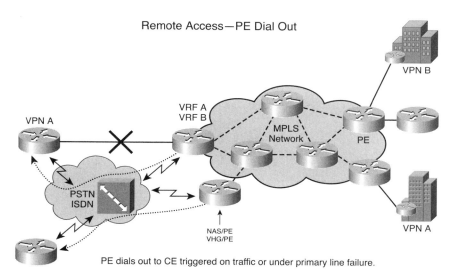

Remote Access—PE Dial Out

PE dials out to CE triggered on traffic or under primary line failure.

Figure 6-3 *Remote Access—PE Dial-Out*

For example, a PE might dial out to remote point of sale sites to collect data or remote vending machines to collect inventories and sales data. This is useful for the retail market, where this function is automated. An example is discussed in a later section.

Dial-out uses the following sequence:

- Upon receiving the traffic, the PE brings up an L2TP tunnel and initiates a PPP session with the NAS. The NAS then dials out to the CE based on the information provided as part of the L2TP negotiation.

- In the direct dial-out case, the NAS directly dials out to the CE.

Much more complicated configurations can be easily created for load-balancing of NAS devices with a VHG/PE for large-scale dial-in/dial-out.

DSL Access

To understand DSL access to MPLS VPNs, let us examine the simple reference model shown in Figure 6-4.

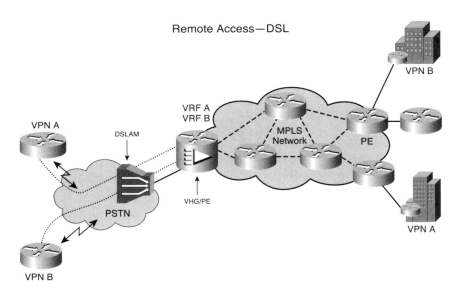

Figure 6-4 *Remote Access: DSL*

In this reference model, the subscriber is connected to customer premises equipment (CPE)—a DSL modem—and is homed to a DSL access multiplexer (DSLAM). Multiple subscribers are aggregated to a DSLAM. Multiple DSLAMs can connect to a DSL aggregation router where the DSL connections (Point-to-Point Protocol [PPP] sessions) are terminated and routed into the network.

DSL access methods and configuration have several variations depending on the CPE configurations and the aggregation used in the access network. They are briefly described in the section that follows.

Routed Encapsulation

When the CPE equipment is a DSL modem with an integrated router, this encapsulation is used in the configuration. At the aggregation site, the interfaces are statically mapped to VRFs. For example, the PVC from DSLAM is terminated into a VRF on the PE. A normal interface configuration is required at the PE or the aggregation point, but no user authentication is required by the VHG or VHG/PE. The DSL router address assignment is done dynamically using DHCP and by using VRF-aware DHCP. A service provider can assign DHCP addresses to the CPE devices based on the VPN assigned. The PVC originating from the DSL router passes through the DSLAM and terminates at the VHG/PE. Static or dynamic routing can be enabled; however, in most cases static routing is used.

Bridged Encapsulation

CPE can also use bridged encapsulation. With the bridged encapsulation mode, the DSL modem provides transparent transport to user traffic. The ATM permanent virtual circuit (PVC) originates at the CPE and terminates at the aggregation point or the VHG/PE. The VHG/PE must be configured with IRB for packets to arrive as bridge encapsulation and then be routed to the VPN network. In this mode of operation, all user PCs/accounts sitting behind the DSL modem are assigned addresses by the provider and are authenticated by the provider. This can be an attractive option if the SP wants to bill based on the number of devices/connections using remote access connections. However, the provider might have to manage more than one user authentication per site. Address assignment is similar to that of the routed encapsulation except that it is now done for all devices behind the DSL modem.

The authentication mechanism here can be PPP over Ethernet (PPoE), and this can be done at the VHG/PE. The users are then mapped to VRFs after they are authenticated.

Cable Access

One of the most popular access method for remote access connectivity is cable. Cable is available in many more households than DSL. In fact, the *Wall Street Journal* reported in its September 13, 2004 *Journal Report* that a Harris Interactive study shows that cable modems have a slight advantage over DSL with 22 percent adoption versus DSL's 19 percent adoption across U.S. households. In-Stat/MDR (a market research firm) states in a 2003 report that more than 15 million households in the United States alone have access to cable broadband. The number reported for worldwide cable broadband access is 27 million subscribers. More and more corporations allow users to work from home or have remote offices. Getting cheap cable Internet access is easy and is almost the norm in metropolitan areas. To enable these sites and users to connect to corporate VPNs, these sites can nail a user-based IPSec tunnel to a VHG; then, the traffic is mapped to a VPN from the VHG.

The UMTS can also act as a PE device. For example, the Cisco uBR 10K can be the broadband router that performs the PE function in addition to terminating the broadband connections. Users are mapped to a VPN based on authentication. A simple identification procedure involves checking a user's domain name and authenticating the user with a password. The domain part identifies to which VPN the user needs to be mapped, and the password authenticates whether the user is allowed to access that VPN. VPN client software can be bundled to include such information as the nearest home gateway for authentication and authorization. Figure 6-5 depicts a remote access example for cable deployments.

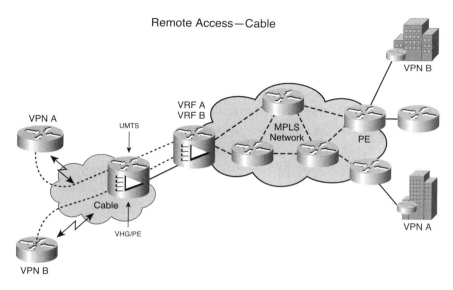

Figure 6-5 *Remote Access: Cable*

PE-CE Routing Protocols

Most of the deployments today use static routing for PE-CE connection for remote access with a default route pointing from the CE/remote access site toward the VHG/PE. If you need to run a dynamic routing protocol between PE and CE over the ISDN dial connection, this can also be supported. Although most providers we know do not run a dynamic routing protocol, such as OSPF or EIGRP on the PE-CE connection, doing so is possible.

For example, in the case of dial backup, a CE can use a dynamic routing protocol between itself and the PE over the directly connected link. Because the directly connected link is the primary link, the provisioning and the addressing are the same as any other VPN connection. However, as a redundancy option, the CE might use dial backup to the PE/VHG. In such cases, you might want to continue using the dynamic routing protocol even on the dial backup connection. This can mean slightly higher convergence, but it is better than not having dial backup at all. Through the use of a dynamic routing protocol, you can mitigate against the complexity of address summarization and static routing configuration for dial backup connection.

For the PE dial-out case, a dynamic routing protocol is rarely used. As stated earlier, the PE dial-out is usually triggered by traffic or a time schedule. Because the purpose of this connection is temporary—for example, a triggered data collection event—you do not need to add the complexity of dynamic routing and add the negotiation and route advertisement process, only to withdraw the routes in a short time. The PE dial-out case might not have any routing configuration at all because there might be cases where you can deal with this in a manner similar to how you would handle directly connected routes.

Scalability and Network Convergence for Remote Access

Remote access capability is not without challenges when it comes to scalability and network convergence time. First, in sizing the PE/VHG, you must note how many L2TP or IPSec connections the VHG/PE can terminate. This number helps you determine the number of remote access users that can use the PE. Second, you also must note that VHG might need to have all the VRFs configured because any given user from any VPN can dial in to any local POP. This implies that VPN information must be present at those POPs and PEs and VHGs must have the relevant VPN information for the user to be authenticated and mapped. One technique to improve scale is to partition the user space to dial/connect to specific PEs for their VPN access. This distributes the load between different PEs. For example, VPNs A through F could be mapped to VHG/PE1, and VPNs G through K could be mapped to VHG/PE2.

Another important aspect to consider is the convergence of the remote access network. If dynamic routing protocols are used, a setup latency exists on the remote access connections due to the establishment of the tunnel's (PPP, IPSec, or L2TP) routing adjacency setup and exchange of routing information. Hence, static routing is commonly used for faster convergence. If the convergence takes a long time, the remote access user might terminate the remote access connection, thinking it has not connected, and try again. If the entries do not age out quickly on the VHG/PE, this can cause a buildup of aged entries and reduce the number of total accepted connections for a certain period of time. This causes unnecessary network churn and user dissatisfaction.

Summary

This chapter started with an explanation of the various methods of remote access. We described why remote access is useful to providers offering L3VPN service. Different types of remote access address different needs of providers. Dial access can be used as a simple backup solution when the primary connected link fails. The dial-in access is useful for both business and individual users.

Dial-out is also a useful technique for triggered events such as stats gathering or inventory management for banks and retail chains and their ATMs.

DSL cable access can easily be substituted for a dedicated connection between PE-CE because it is really a semipermanent connection. This is the most common mode of access for broadband users and small businesses. Flexible mapping of such users on a broadband network can provide users multiple solutions for their VPN access.

CHAPTER 7

MPLS SECURITY

This chapter commences with an overview of security and its role within a next-generation network (NGN) framework. The discussion progresses to an overview of MPLS security in terms of the following three security attributes: the relevant architecture, the technology implementation, and operating the technology. Breaking any of these security attributes exposes the customer to a corresponding security attack.

The chapter concludes with MPLS security best practice guidelines that identify attack vectors and recommended responses to these attack vectors. Security must be integral in an overall operations, management, and administration (OAM) policy, which is further discussed in Chapter 12, "Network Management and Provisioning."

Security and NGN

As networks and services converge under the framework of NGN constructs, security is a key attribute because convergence suggests a level of complexity that the industry overall must balance between discreet capabilities and robust services. Transforming to an NGN framework does solve critical business issues in the service provider community and for large enterprises evolving to virtualized architectures—most notably in capital expenditure efficiency and in operating expense reduction as goals. In this time of ever-increasing threat sophistication, an evolution of the miscreant adversary, and an ever-increasing complexity of effective solutions, the information technology industry must short-circuit the solution.

The sophistication in attack techniques is one of the more frightening trends occurring in the security industry. Attacks were once primarily the work of hackers who wanted to temporarily take well-known sites offline to get media attention or brag to their friends. Now attacks are increasingly being used as the foundation of elaborate extortion schemes. In addition, some attacks are motivated by political or economic objectives, costing businesses and service providers millions of dollars each year.

The effect of this trend, and its financial implications, will result in a more defined value proposition of protecting assets from attack for the entire industry. This security trend will enhance the general perception in the marketplace of the value of security-enabled services. This phenomenon also presents service providers and enterprise organizations with opportunities to charge more for their services.

Security has therefore become more pivotal for both service providers and enterprise organizations to protect core assets; security is indeed a component for NGN architecture.

The Cisco IP NGN is a vision and architecture designed to deliver a broad, sweeping transformation of the service provider network and business. It provides a sustainable competitive advantage and increases profits by helping service providers develop and plan for the future of their organizations, network architectures, and business models.

In the IP NGN architecture, security is fundamental to a service provider's ability to protect its infrastructure, deliver the intended services in a manner that complies with specific service levels, and control the business. Security is resident in all four layers of the IP NGN architecture. Cisco IP NGN security solutions help create an environment in which service providers can extend services to generate increased revenue and differentiate themselves more clearly from competitors. In addition, Cisco IP NGN security solutions help service providers achieve greater efficiencies with highly available service and minimum downtime and to apply better control for network and business success.

Let's look at how security operates in various layers of the NGN service architecture. In the operational layer, security spans the entire IP NGN architecture, protecting a service throughout the network to maintain service availability and enabling service survivability when attacks occur. In the network layer, security is built in to the foundation of the infrastructure and its hardware and operating systems to secure the transport of services. In the service layer, part of the Service Exchange Framework, security plays a role in creating services and service features to generate revenue and service differentiation. For example, security functions, such as detecting and responding to denial-of-service attacks, ensure that the service can continue without interruption. This noninterruption of service enables the operation of billing functions that are key to revenue settlements between service providers and their customers. In the application layer, security is resident in the applications themselves and in the links to the service layer to secure the integrity of the applications as they interface with the network.

The intelligent operational layer operates through and helps connect the three IP NGN convergence layers—network, service, and application—and makes intranetwork and internetwork communications as efficient and productive as possible. Intelligent networking simplifies the complexity of operating an IP NGN by making it more resilient, integrated, and adaptive. Together, the three convergence layers, the cohesive operational layer, and intelligent networking enable you to build integrated features that are consistent across product lines and that enable these products to function as a global system—an IP NGN. Security is fundamental to the IP NGN and is implemented through a combination of processes, technologies, and solutions.

Within the framework of NGNs for service providers and enterprise customers, there is an opportunity to deconstruct security roles commencing at the access role. Specifically, this involves the customer premise edge router from one end of the service architecture and includes the data and control planes at the other end in a service provider or enterprise peering implementation. Security roles can include a firewall, an intrusion detection system (IDS), and anomaly detection via reporting applications, such as Netflow or Arbor.

For CIOs today, security has taken on even greater importance with the passage of regulatory requirements in Sarbanes-Oxley and other regulations. Although Sarbanes-Oxley does not explicitly define security requirements, it does state that CEOs and CFOs must personally attest to their companies having proper "internal controls." It would be difficult for companies to certify the validity of data if the systems maintaining and transmitting the data were not secure. A company's accounting system is part of the corporate IT system. So, if the IT systems are not secure, the internal controls will not be viewed favorably by the government if a security incident occurs or a Sarbanes-Oxley review is performed. Therefore, understanding MPLS security aspects provides inputs to the enterprise IT security framework.

Security Overview and MPLS

When talking about security concepts, the first question you must answer is, "What is meant by the term *secure*?" In a normal family house, for example, a good door lock is considered adequate security. In a jeweler's shop, though, a door has to be considerably more robust to be secure, and a bank might have guards in addition to several strong doors. In every scenario, the first step is to define *secure*; only after this is done can the next step of actually securing a network be performed.

Early discussions on MPLS VPN security had exactly this problem: To some users, *secure* was equivalent to encryption of data. Of course, with this definition, MPLS VPNs as such would be insecure. Many enterprises, however, do not necessarily require encryption—for them, *secure* means a separation of their network traffic from other networks. These two viewpoints clash because they are based on different definitions of the term *secure*.

Both enterprises and service providers define corporate security in a *security policy*. The starting point is a *threat model*, which defines security exposure on different levels—for example, physical security (somebody carrying out a computer) or network security (hackers gaining illegitimate access to network resources). The threat model serves as a basis for the definition of security requirements. Note that a threat model is not just limited to MPLS, but rather is generic to security overall.

In the MPLS VPN environment, security can be viewed from two angles: from the VPN customer's perspective and from the service provider's perspective. Both possess different threat models. For a customer, it is important to safeguard against network intrusions from outside his VPN. Therefore, one of the main threats to a VPN customer is intrusions into his domain. For a service provider, one of the key issues is the availability of the core network. Thus, one of the main threats to a service provider is denial-of-service attacks. Both aspects are important in MPLS VPN scenarios, but each part of the network has a different emphasis in its threat model.

The security reference model allows the clear distinction of the network zones in an MPLS VPN environment and defines the so-called *zones of trust*. Each of these zones of trust has its own security policy and threat model. So, the formally correct way to define *secure* in a certain context is to start by defining the zones of trust in a given environment and then develop a threat model for each zone and for the overall environment. *Secure* can then be defined through the requirements coming from the threat model. There is no absolute, 100 percent system security despite the fact that single components of a given system can be 100 percent secure. Entire systems can never be 100 percent secure—mainly because of the human factor involved.

For example, the One-Time-Pad in cryptography is a 100 percent secure encryption algorithm. Every bit in the clear text is encrypted using a bit from a key string. If the key string is as long as the plain text and is never reused, and if the bits in the key string are entirely random, the encryption as such is 100 percent secure. However, this key string has to be carried from the encrypting to the decrypting side, so it can be intercepted. Or the device used for writing the message might have a backdoor that allows sniffing the plain text. Thus, the overall system will never be 100 percent secure.

The first problem that occurs when engineers are asked to work on new projects is that they are often given rather sloppy guidelines, such as "it must be secure," without any further explanation. One of the issues here is, as explained previously, that the term *secure* needs to be defined in painfully precise terms before it can be implemented. As with many things, the devil is in the details! Furthermore, security requirements can be a moving target as organizations evolve.

The second problem is that, even if you have a clear understanding of what is meant by the term *secure* in a certain context, security is not an absolute value and can never be achieved 100 percent. A more reasonable approach is to define a system as "sufficiently secure against a list of perceived threats." This is also one of the reasons a security policy must contain a threat model. Security must always be measured against perceived threats. Many discussions about MPLS VPN security have commenced by analyzing the architecture. One example is asserting that nobody can intrude from the outside of a customer network into a customer VPN because the service provider core would not accept labeled packets from outside the service provider network. Then the customer discovers that if an operator misconfigures a provider edge (PE), VPN separation will not be guaranteed any longer. The conclusion is, therefore, that MPLS is insecure. This is an incorrect conclusion, though, because the problem of the misconfiguration is an operational problem, which can occur in any technology. These discussions confuse architecture and the operations of that architecture.

Even more confusing, when looking at traditional VPN technologies, such as ATM, people had to admit that they had essentially the same problems, yet the technologies were assumed to be secure. So what went wrong in these discussions? The previous example with the One-Time-Pad gives an idea that even if an algorithm is proven to be 100 percent secure, the overall system might still have weaknesses in other areas.

Therefore, when classifying the overall security of a system, such as an MPLS VPN network, you have to analyze the three fundamental parts that comprise the system:

- **Architecture or algorithm used**—This is the formal specification. In cryptography, it's the algorithm itself; in the case of MPLS VPNs, it's the formal specification as defined in RFC2547bis.

- **Implementation of that architecture or algorithm**—Implementation refers to how the architecture or algorithm is actually implemented in reality. Programming issues play a role here.

- **Operation thereof**—For cryptography, key handling is involved; in the case of networks, an example is weak router passwords.

Of course, security is a broad field, and it is impossible to capture all the details in a short introduction. However, some additional security concepts are worth mentioning briefly:

- **Confidentiality, integrity, availability**—The three basic properties of security (some text books add authenticity as a fourth). When defining *security*, you can be more precise by defining which of the security properties is required to which extent. For example, in a military environment the most important security property is probably confidentiality. In a bank, confidentiality is important, too, but even more important is the integrity of the data. For an online shopping site, however, availability of the web page is an important factor. Overall security can usually be defined with these three properties.

  In the MPLS context, every VPN customer has slightly different requirements in these parameters. Customers expect that their data will be private (confidential) for their VPN.

- **Defense in depth**—Because one weak link is sufficient to endanger the security of an overall system, it is common practice to construct several layers of security around a solution, such that if one single component breaks, others still defend the assets. The best example in enterprise networks is the demilitarized zone: Servers of a company are usually highly protected. However, even if this protection fails and a hacker gains access to a server, a firewall is still there that the hacker must overcome to get into the network.

It is good practice to add several layers of defense around everything that needs to be protected. This design principle is also important in MPLS networks.

- **Secure failure**—The primary mode of operation of any technology is usually well considered and well secured. However, when the primary method fails, the backup method also needs to be appropriately secured. It is common practice today to use secure shell (SSH) for router configuration; however, you need a backup method of getting to a router in case the SSH server fails. This is usually done through out-of-band access, mostly over the telephone network. It is important that this backup mode be as secured as the principal access mode.

MPLS-based VPN services have increased significantly over the last years. One of the reasons is that they can be provided more easily than traditional layer 2 VPNs, such as ATM and Frame Relay. This ease of provisioning often leads to attractive pricing models for the customer.

MPLS VPN and Security

One of the reasons MPLS VPNs, or specifically BGP-VPNs, are easy to provision is that MPLS VPNs are not connection oriented. Whereas most traditional VPN types consist of a number of provisioned point-to-point connections, MPLS is connectionless.

The connectionless nature of MPLS VPNs has many implications for the scalability of the overall MPLS network, but also for security: On an ATM network, for example, a VPN customer is typically presented with a number of virtual connections from a given router to all other routers that need to be connected. However, the customer needs to configure her router to use these virtual connections. The disadvantage here is that many virtual connections have to be configured on both the customer side and the service provider side. The advantage is that the customer has full visibility of her VPN and controls the connections. On an MPLS network, the same customer router is in most cases presented with a single connection into the MPLS network, and it is the MPLS network itself that decides where to forward packets. The customer loses the view of the connections through the core. The advantage of this approach is scalability: The provisioning complexity is reduced to a single connection for each customer router. However, the customer does not have visibility of the core network anymore. A service provider could maliciously or inadvertently introduce a router that does not belong there into the VPN of a customer. The customer might not detect this and might lose the integrity of her network.

VPN users have certain expectations and requirements for their VPN service. In a nutshell, they want their service to be private and secure. Neither concept is black or white, and the concepts need to be defined for a real-world implementation. In discussions about MPLS security, a number of questions typically arise that are outside the scope of the MPLS architecture. This means that these issues have nothing to do with the standards and can therefore not be controlled by the architecture. The following list describes these issues and explains why they are outside the scope of the architecture:

- **Protection against misconfiguration or operational mistakes**—The standards describe the architecture, define the protocols, and recommend best practices for both the architecture and protocols. This chapter examines MPLS VPNs based on this architecture. This architecture can also be misapplied, leading to security issues. For example, as long as the PE is configured correctly according to the standard, the solution is secure. However, any operator could misconfigure a PE, thus breaking the security. This is not an architectural issue, but an operational issue.

- **VPN data confidentiality, integrity, and origin authentication**—VPN users have no guarantee that packets are not read or corrupted when in transit over the MPLS core. MPLS as such does not provide any of the previously listed services. It is important to understand that a service provider has the technical possibility to sniff VPN data, and the VPN user can either choose to trust the service provider(s) not to use her data inappropriately or encrypt the traffic over the MPLS core (for example with IPSec, as discussed later in this chapter).

- **Attacks from the Internet through an MPLS backbone**—If the MPLS backbone provides any Internet access to a VPN, attacks from the Internet into this VPN are outside the scope of MPLS. The task of the MPLS core is to forward packets from the Internet to the VPN, and vice versa. This includes potential attacks. It is, however, within the scope of MPLS security to ensure that an attack against a given VPN does not affect other VPNs or the core itself.

Also outside the scope of the MPLS architecture is any kind of firewalling required for such cases.

• **Customer network security**—Every attack that originates in a customer VPN and terminates in that same VPN is outside the scope of MPLS security. The MPLS VPN architecture forwards packets between VPN sites; it is not concerned with the nature of these packets, which could also be attack packets. This also includes IP spoofing within a VPN.

| NOTE | When discussing the security of MPLS VPN networks, care should be taken to maintain a balanced view on the overall risks to a customer. It is irrelevant to argue about the chances of an attacker sniffing a core line if the customer network has unsecured wireless access points. It is also not important to worry about a service provider misconfiguring a PE when attackers have uncontrolled physical access to hosts in an enterprise.

Security is a question of balance: There is no point in putting extra locks on the door of your house if the windows are left open. |

Many enterprises have been using VPN services based on Frame Relay or ATM in the past and are considering a move to MPLS VPNs. Unfortunately, the discussion of this topic has often been emotional and unbalanced. Table 7-1 compares all the aspects of VPN security for the various VPN technologies.

Table 7-1 *Security Comparison Between MPLS and ATM/Frame Relay*

	MPLS	ATM/Frame Relay
VPN separation	Yes	Yes
Robustness against attacks	Yes	Yes
Hiding of the core infrastructure	Yes	Yes
Impossibility of VPN spoofing	Yes	Yes
CE-CE visibility	Not in MLPS IP VPNs; yes for MPLS pseudowire emulation	Yes

1 Reference: http://www.miercom.com/?url=reports/&v=16&tf=-3&st=v

New MPLS users are often concerned about the fact that an MPLS VPN service has a control plane on Layer 3. The typical VPN security requirements are

- VPN separation (addressing and traffic)
- Robustness against attacks
- Hiding the core infrastructure spoofing protection against VPN spoofing

BGP-VPN (for Layer 3 MPLS VPN) permits a separation between address and data plane constructs, whereas hiding the core infrastructure (that is, the service provider or a large enterprise implementing MPLS) is paramount to overall MPLS security (as depicted in Figures 7-1 and 7-2). Note that in both examples, the vulnerable security point is between the service provider PE and customer edge connection. The amount of topological information—for example, from the Interior Gateway Protocol (IGP)—announced outside a trust domain or leaked outside a trust domain is what is important.

We discuss attack scenarios in the next section, followed by the best practices for defending against attacks.

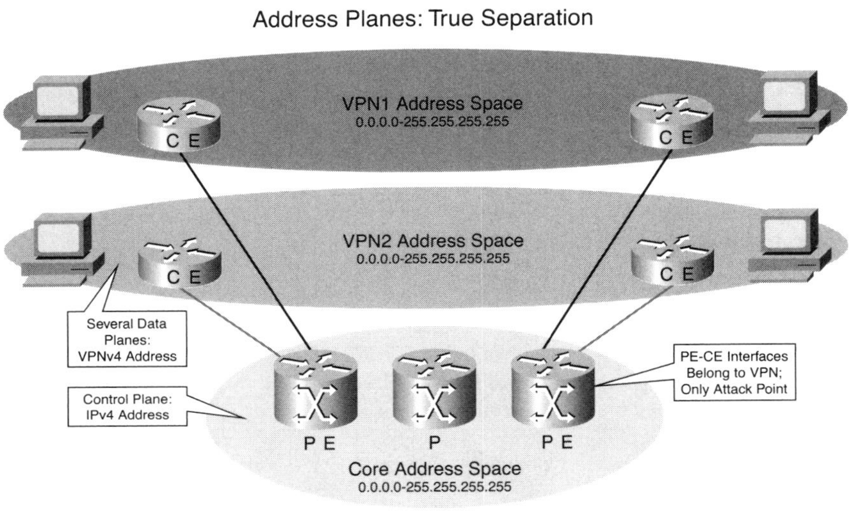

Address Planes: True Separation

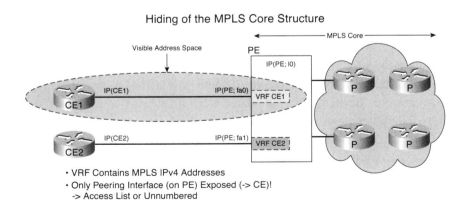

Figure 7-1   *Address Planes: True Separation*

Hiding of the MPLS Core Structure

Figure 7-2   *Hiding of the MPLS Core*

Attack Scenarios

To be able to evaluate security of MPLS, you must define a threat model for the various zones of trust. This section uses the zones of trust defined in the chapter introduction and outlines the threats against those zones.

A complete threat model (such as a security policy) must contain threats from outside as well as from inside a trusted zone because in practice many threats come from the inside. For example, a thief might come from outside an office building, but thefts actually are perpetrated in many enterprises much more frequently by internal trusted staff. Therefore, a complete threat model must take both internal and external threats into consideration. Physical threats, such as nonauthorized access to buildings, network operating centers, transmission links, and network infrastructure, also comprise the overall threat model. A network operations center (NOC) is the nerve center of a service provider and a large enterprise that deploys and manages services and networks because it applies OAM and security policies.

For the analysis of MPLS VPNs, only threats from outside a trusted zone are relevant because you must assume that internal threats are independent on the VPN architecture. In the example of the office building, this means the following: When analyzing the security of the building itself, internal thefts can be ignored. Translated back to the networking world, someone executing attacks on a local area network (LAN) with tools, such as ARP spoofing, can do so regardless of whether the site he is in is connected via MPLS to the other VPN sites or via Frame Relay. However, in the case of an operational error, such as a label mismerging that results in traffic being directed from one VPN to another, the trusted zone administrator must be able to detect and respond to such a condition. Note that this example is analogous to a Frame Relay Data Link Connection Identifier (DLCI) virtual circuit being swapped from one VPN to another. This is an operational error that is not inherent on the technology architecture overall.

This section discusses all the threats from the point of view of a VPN customer or user. Any VPN user, such as a bank that is using an MPLS VPN service, needs to analyze security based on the threats against its VPN. Threats that are potentially related to the MPLS VPN architecture include the following:

- **Intrusions from the outside**—For example, other VPNs, the core, or the Internet

- **Denial-of-service (DoS) from the outside**—For example, other VPNs, the core, or the Internet

- **Insider attacks**—For example, errors or deliberate misconfigurations made by internal service provider staff

Figure 7-3 depicts locations from which threats might come into a specific VPN. Threats come primarily from other VPNs (1), the core itself (2), or the Internet (3). Intrusions give an outsider control over parts of the VPN, including network elements, servers, PCs, or other networking equipment. To execute an intrusion, you need to insert control traffic into the VPN—in the simplest case a single IP packet to a destination in the VPN.

NOTE   Although most of today's intrusions use IPv4 packets, other data traffic can also be used to intrude into a network. This could be Layer 2 packets, IPv6 packets, or even the telephone system when dialing into a modem.

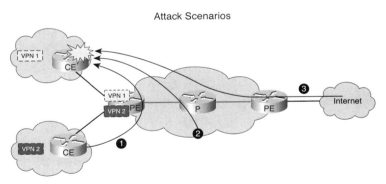

Figure 7-3   *Attack Scenarios*

Figure 7-4 shows the potential intrusion vectors into a VPN. Intrusions could potentially come from another VPN (1), the core itself (2), or the Internet (3). What they have in common is that they must directly target a piece of the infrastructure of the VPN. Therefore, to control intrusions into a trusted zone, it is sufficient to block all illegitimate data traffic into the zone. In traditional networks, this is being done using a firewall that controls traffic into a site and by separating the network from other outside networks, such as the telephone system.

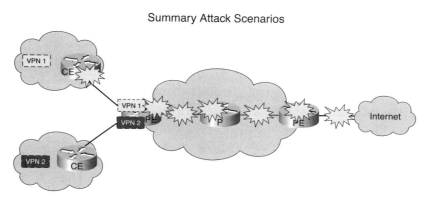

Figure 7-4 *Summary of Attack Scenarios*

In the MPLS VPN environment, the same principles prevail: It is best to provide separation against outside networks and control of inbound traffic into a VPN. Where traffic is filtered by a firewall, this filtering is usually independent of the MPLS architecture.

However, this assumes correct operation of the MPLS core network. If the engineer of the MPLS service provider misconfigures a PE router, an external site might become a member of the VPN, which enables intrusions from this external site.

Another threat against a VPN is DoS attacks from the outside. This threat could come from the Internet, another VPN, or the core itself. However, a key difference exists between intrusions and DoS attacks.

To execute an intrusion, a hacker needs to be able to send packets into the trusted zone of the VPN. Therefore, a VPN user can effectively protect herself by securing her own network edge. This assumes that the intrusion points are controllable—that is, that it has no hidden intrusion points. The threat model for a DoS attack against a VPN is different, though: A given VPN site might receive a DoS attack against its own networking infrastructure—that is, targeting parts of the VPN that are under the control of the VPN user. However, as opposed to an intrusion, a DoS attack can also affect a VPN user indirectly. For example, if a PE router is under a DoS attack, this might affect a given VPN connected to that PE, even though the attack is not directly against the VPN.

The *monolithic core* refers to the standard MPLS VPN architecture as defined in RFC 4364, "BGP/MPLS VPNs." One single autonomous system (AS) defines the core network, and all VPN sites connect to this single AS. The threats against a monolithic core are the same as those listed previously as threats against MPLS VPN architecture:

- **Intrusions from the outside**—For example, attached VPNs or the Internet.

- **Denial-of-service attacks from the outside**—For example, attached VPNs or the Internet.

- **Internal threats**—Operator errors or deliberate misconfigurations. These can cause security problems on the core or on connected VPN, so they must be taken into consideration.

Intrusions can first be targeted at core equipment, such as routers. The technical scope and the protection against this threat are comparable to those used for normal Internet core networks. However, the potential business risk is higher in the MPLS VPN case because the security of connected VPNs depends on the correct operation of the core, whereas sites connected to the Internet do not usually rely on the security of the service provider network.

Intrusions can also target the NOC and NOC equipment, such as AAA servers, Trivial File Transfer Protocol (TFTP), or File Transfer Protocol (FTP) servers, or management stations. The associated risk is high for both the core itself as well as for the connected VPNs: For instance, a maliciously modified PE configuration can allow external sites to access a targeted VPN.

An example of such a risk is extranet deployments in which external subsidiaries or corporate organizations present another threat to the service provider core.

Therefore, the threat of intrusions into the core or NOC carries a high business risk—typically higher than in normal IP service provider networks, but comparable to other VPN core networks, such as ATM or Frame Relay.

Intrusions can be prevented with standard security measures, such as securing access to devices and secure user management through AAA, firewalling, and so on.

The threat of a DoS attack against the core is often technically equivalent to the same threat in normal IP core networks. However, the business risk is potentially higher in MPLS VPN core networks, depending on the contracts with the VPN customers. Any part of the MPLS core is potentially vulnerable to a DoS attack from a VPN or the Internet, unless this part of the core has been appropriately secured and designed. In a correctly configured MPLS core, sending traffic directly to a piece of core equipment is impossible from the outside, VPNs, or the Internet. Although this completely prevents intrusions, overloading routers with transit traffic is still theoretically possible. This overloading results in resource starvation for other functions that the router or provide edge might be performing. However, mechanisms such as rate shaping at the edge mitigate against resource starvation.

The solution to this threat is the appropriate design of the core network. The routers and lines have to be correctly dimensioned—that is, even if an attack from a VPN loads an access line of that VPN completely, with minimum size packets, the connected PE router must be able to handle all the received traffic. The same principle applies to core lines. Where the aggregate traffic might exceed the provisioned capacities, appropriate quality-of-service (QoS) measures need to be taken to ensure that transit traffic meets the required service level agreements (SLA).

The last threat against MPLS core networks is insider attacks. This category contains all the errors or deliberate misconfigurations made by internal service provider staff. The threat is relevant to the core as well as to VPNs because such misconfigurations can also affect the security of connected VPNs.

A relatively simple misconfiguration of a route target could have potentially serious security consequences. For instance, if all the sites of a bank's VPN use a certain route target for importing and exporting routes, and if this route target is accidentally added to another VPN routing and forwarding (VRF) instance, the connected sites of this VRF are effectively part of the other VPN.

Example 7-1 shows a correct configuration on a PE router. The example uses Cisco commands and command line interface (CLI). Two VRFs are configured, each with its own route target. Customer edge equipment (CE) is connected to the

VRFS on the PE through the serial interfaces, and the route targets in the VRFs define how the routes from a given VRF should be treated. Here there are different route targets, and the routes are kept in their respective VRFs.

Example 7-1 *Correct Configuration of Two VRFs with Correct Route Targets on a Singe PE-Router*

```
ip vrf bank_A
  rd 1234:10
  route-target both 1234:33

ip vrf bank_B
  rd 1234:11
  route-target both 1234:34

interface serial 0/1
  ip vrf forwarding bank_A
interface serial 0/3
  ip vrf forwarding bank_B
```

Assume now that an operator accidentally typed the wrong route target. Example 7-2 shows the new configuration using Cisco commands and CLI. Here the routes from bank B are exported with a route target that belongs to bank A, and vice versa.

Example 7-2 *Incorrect Configuration: Wrong Route Target in the Second VRF*

```
ip vrf bank_A
  rd 1234:10
  route-target both 1234:33

ip vrf bank_B
  rd 1234:11
  route-target both 1234:33  <--- ERROR: 33 instead of 34

interface serial 0/1
  ip vrf forwarding bank_A
interface serial 0/3
  ip vrf forwarding bank_B
```

The effect of this simple error is that all the sites of bank B connected to this PE router belong logically to bank A and have full access to the entire VPN of bank A. For routing to work in this scenario, the address spaces of the two now "merged" banks would have to be unique, which is not necessarily the case in an accidental misconfiguration. Once again, MPLS VPN (BGP-VPN) permits address and data plane separation. With address separation, a service provider or large enterprise deploying BGP-VPN constructs can use private addressing for different VPNs that can overlap. In Example 7-2, we are referencing misconfiguration of route targets (RT).

The danger in this type of situation is that bank A, which just suffered a potential intrusion from an outside site, might not even detect this. After all, the existing network of bank A is not affected by this move, unless there is now some address space overlap with potential connectivity problems. Bank B, on the other hand, would probably quickly discover that its site is not connected correctly because many operations (such as connecting to intranet sites, like www.bank_B.com) would fail while its site is logically connected to bank A.

Therefore, if this misconfiguration was made accidentally, the security exposure of bank A would probably be limited because staff in this particular site of bank B would probably not notice where they are connected. Viruses and worms, or peer-to-peer applications, would now spread freely between bank A and the wrongly connected site of bank B.

Although this example reflects an extreme case where RT manipulation permits a VPN leakage situation (albeit rare), it should be stated that when traffic from two VPNs is received on the ingress PE router/routers, two labels are imposed on each packet and forwarded toward the service provider (SP) core. The intermediate routers in the SP core do not process the Layer 3 contents (the IP destination address and so on) of the VPN packet, but base their forwarding decision only on the top MPLS label. When the traffic reaches the egress PE router, packets are forwarded toward the CE router after examining the bottom label that is unique for each VPN/VPN destination. No two prefixes belonging to two different VPN customers can have the same bottom label; thus, sending VPN-A traffic to VPN-B traffic is impossible unless explicitly allowed to do so. In addition, SPs can mitigate this further by using automated tools to assign unique VPN ID labels for each customer VPN. That further reduces any chance of unintentional assignment of the wrong site to a customer VPN. This virtually eliminates the possibility of an incorrect site receiving traffic not intended for it.

However, if this type of misconfiguration is made deliberately by an operator of the service provider, the potential exposure is relatively high. In this case, the operator probably has enough knowledge to avoid overlapping address space, and bank A might not discover the intrusion.

There are a number of such potential misconfigurations, all of which might have severe security implications for the connected VPNs, and some of which are hard to detect. It is important to understand that although in the previous threats the solution was based on design, here this does not work. Instead, the threat is coming from the inside, for example, from the people designing the solution. An analogy might be an operator configuring a firewall. He is controlling the security device, so he automatically has the power to also subvert security by opening additional ports.

So, it is of paramount importance that service providers secure the architecture and the implementation as well as their operations, such that misconfigurations are at least detected and are prevented where possible.

In practice, many service providers use automated provisioning tools where such misconfigurations are unlikely to occur. So, the more realistic threat comes from deliberate misconfigurations of an operator. In practice, operational tools control running configurations and compare them against a correct configuration, such that even malicious changes are usually detected. Generally, a NOC is logically separated from the core network. There might be more than a single NOC, in which case each NOC site can be treated as a standalone entity.

A NOC needs connectivity to the network, and it needs to operate. In most cases, there are also links to outside networks: the corporate intranet, the Internet, and possibly others.

Threats from the Internet and other external networks include intrusions into the network management system and the various other systems, such as FTP/TFTP servers, AAA servers, and so on. These threats are extremely serious because they might endanger the secure operations of the entire network. But they are the same as in any other NOC environment and not discussed here in detail.

From the MPLS side, the same threats prevail in principle: intrusions into management systems with the potential to alter any type of the network operations, introduce fake sites into VPNs, or join VPNs. Additionally, DoS attacks against any part of the network or its operations center are possible. Overall, the NOC is the most important part from a security point of view because the entire network can be controlled from it.

Internet/Extranet and MPLS Security

The Internet is usually positioned as the insecure part in any network deployment, so threats normally come from the Internet. Although this view is completely correct, it is not complete. In other parts of the Internet, other users require security, and from their point of view, the threat also comes from "the Internet," which now includes your own network. For any given service provider network—MPLS or not—this means that a threat is originating in this network toward the Internet. One could assert that threats may be 50 percent from the Internet and 50 percent from internal sites or hybrids of sites outside the trust zone.

Some service providers take the view that security is unidirectional and that they have to secure their part of the Internet, including their customers, against the rest of the Internet—but not the other way round. There are at least two reasons this attitude is inappropriate in the global Internet. First, the Internet is a global system and requires all participants to do their share in securing access to it. Second, and more practically, an attack from a customer of a service provider often affects the service provider network as well, or other customers of that service provider. This can be observed where worms are spreading, with e-mail spam relays, and many other security incidents.

For all these reasons, operators of networks that connect to the Internet must also secure the Internet *from* their customers, such as by applying source address spoofing prevention as described in RFC 2827 (BCP 38).

In the specific context of MPLS VPNs, the threat originates from every VPN customer who has Internet connectivity through this MPLS VPN service. Customers who do not receive Internet connectivity from the MPLS provider can still be the source of security incidents through other paths, such as through other Internet service providers.

The CIA has published a report that shows that the majority of security incidents occur on the inside of an enterprise. More generically speaking, this refers to a zone of trust. In many networks, the insider is more of a threat to the networks than the outsider.

This principle applies in the same way to MPLS VPN deployments, for each zone of trust separately:

- **The zone of a given VPN**—This is essentially the enterprise intranet, and the previously mentioned report refers directly to this zone of trust.

- **The core network**—Also in the core, an insider can easily modify configurations, endangering the security of the core or connected VPNs. Where this affects VPNs, it is strictly speaking not a threat from within the zone. This is discussed earlier in this chapter.

- **For extranets and other external networks**—Threats, such as information being changed, can be originated in these zones.

A number of potential security issues that originate in the same zone of trust exist and are thus not related to the fact that the underlying infrastructure is an MPLS network. Examples for such issues are as follows:

- An unsecured wireless access point in an enterprise, which has an MPLS VPN service.

- A DoS attack from the Internet to a web server in a VPN network, where the VPN with Internet service is provided on the same MPLS core. If an MPLS core provides Internet connectivity to a given VPN, this connectivity can also be used to attack the VPN from the outside. The same would be true in other VPN deployments, such as Frame Relay or ATM.

- An intrusion from one MPLS VPN into another VPN that results in a compromise of a customer's data. Such deployments should normally be secured by a firewall, and the security depends on the correct configuration of that firewall.

- Worm infections from a VPN site to an extranet site, where such connectivity was deployed consciously. In this case, firewalls are typically deployed and security depends on correct operation of the firewall, plus standard security measures within the end systems.

In summary, within a single zone of trust, or wherever connectivity between zones of trust has been specifically designed, security issues relating to such connectivity are outside the scope of this chapter. In these cases, traditional security solutions, such as firewalls, need to be used to separate the zones as required.

To analyze security in any environment, a threat model is required and security requirements are then evaluated against it. This chapter has defined the threats against the various zones of trust in the MPLS VPN environment.

Threats against VPNs include intrusions and DoS attacks from other VPNs, the Internet, or the MPLS core. Each other zone has similar threats. Threats that are not related to the MPLS architecture, such as internal threats within a zone of trust, are not considered in this chapter because they also exist in other VPN environments, such as ATM or Frame Relay.

In network environments where both private network and Internet access are provided by one infrastructure, the security considerations applicable to the MPLS VPN assume the added significance of the Internet component's impact or potential impact on the service provider backbone and the customer edge connections. Not only are two corporate entities involved in the network services provisioning, but the Internet and its millions of connections and users are now closely coupled with the corporate data networks.

This necessitates stringent adherence to service provider security best practices to ensure the security and reliability of the backbone. In addition, you must address network design issues to guarantee that corporate (once private network) data is not adversely impacted by the vagaries of the Internet data flows. Of course, high volumes of corporate data (for instance, large image transfers or data backups) could also impact the infrastructure to an extent that Internet traffic suffers. However, Internet traffic is typically viewed as best effort traffic with little or no expected service levels, and as such, as long as user performance is not unduly hindered, this should not be a major issue. As the usage profiles of the Internet change to support traffic that has more stringent latency or jitter restrictions, more attention might be required with respect to general traffic performance.

Of greater import are intrusion-oriented security concerns and DoS attacks that are more likely to be sourced from the Internet than the corporate space and must be addressed to mitigate impact to the VPN traffic flows. At an overview level, there are three basic approaches to providing Internet and MPLS VPN services to a given set of customers.

These are as follows:

- Totally distinct networks
- A shared core network with separate PE and CE components and connections
- Shared resources end-to-end

Clearly, the provisioning of totally separate networks ensures that the only Internet-driven security vulnerabilities will be through the customer's own interconnect points within his network. This is a very costly approach for the service provider, though, and it will be reflected in the costs passed on to the consumer of such services.

Clearly, there is an incentive for some sharing of resources with due consideration given to the degree of conjoined infrastructure that is prudent.

In general, it is recommended that the VPN service network interconnects and the Internet access be run over separate links and to separate routers (not the VPN-supporting routers), rather than attempting to homogenize them over a single facility.

That is, the service provider should provision separate PEs for VPN versus Internet access even if the backbone P routers are convergent. As well, the interconnections between the VPN and Internet PEs should be unique and preferably be terminated on separate CE routers. This allows for the greatest degree of configuration flexibility (thereby policy control) and reduces the concern that Internet-launched DoS attacks will have an immediate impact on the VPN performance. Internet traffic can be directed through DMZ facilities at centralized customer sites where firewall-based control and intrusion detection systems can be readily deployed. Internet access can then be provided to other sites through default routing propagated through the corporate VPN.

The use of default routing to direct traffic through the DMZ ensures that corporate security policies are applied to traffic that traverses the Internet and provides a single connection point where problems can be identified and controlled. This approach also minimizes the memory usage on the PE and CE routers, which can be considerable if the entire Internet table is propagated.

The third alternative—sharing end-to-end resources—ensures that the network deployment costs are minimized, at least from a hardware and facilities perspective.

However, this approach is fraught with considerable security risks. Both services (MPLS/VPN and Internet access) must be tightly controlled to avoid any adverse interactions. In this scenario, the SP backbone, the PE router, the interconnection facility between the CE and PE, and the CE router itself are shared resources with respect to both the VPN and Internet traffic flows. The CE router needs to implement some mechanism to groom VPN and Internet traffic into different channels. The Internet traffic must be directed through a firewall device before re-merging with the corporate traffic. Policy-based routing or multilite-VRF can be used to perform the traffic direction. Indeed, some security perspectives suggest the use of doubled firewalls to provide an additional level of protection.

In addition, the use of IDSs is highly recommended to provide early warning and information leading to quicker resolution of Internet-driven attacks.

Due to the inherently greater degree of control and security mechanisms available, static or eBGP routing should be used between PE and CE in this scenario. The recommended CE-PE routing mechanisms are discussed later in this chapter.

Clearly, firewalling should be viewed as a necessary component of any Internet access, whether accomplished by any of the following means:

- A firewall at the central site with centralized Internet access

- A firewall at each CE site

- A firewalling through an SP service offering either through stacked or shared approaches

In addition, many current implementations of customer networks have been based on the use of private address space. Interconnecting to the Internet requires the use of global addresses that generally necessitate some form of network address translation (NAT). In addition to firewalls, this NAT functionality can be implemented either through shared services provided at a central customer site or by the SP.

IPSec

IPSec and MPLS are not competing technologies. In fact, as you learned in Chapter 6, "Remote Access and IPSec Integration with MPLS VPNs," IPSec can be deployed with MPLS. Regulatory policies, such as those in the banking sector or government agencies, might dictate the use of IPSec and end-to-end encryption for implementation. Guidelines for the use of IPSec and MPLS are as follows:

- Encryption of traffic

- Direct authentication of CEs

- Integrity of traffic
- Replay detection
- Enhanced traffic separation from the standard level offered by the service provider

Various deployment options are available for IPSec, such as CE-to-CE via cryptomap, hub and spoke via dynamic cryptomap, and full mesh with tunnel endpoint discovery (TED). In fact, MPLS VPN and TED are a recommended combination due to the scalability and the requirement for direct CE authentication. A service provider could also provide an additional site-to-site or spoke encryption service to its customers, as shown in Figure 7-5.

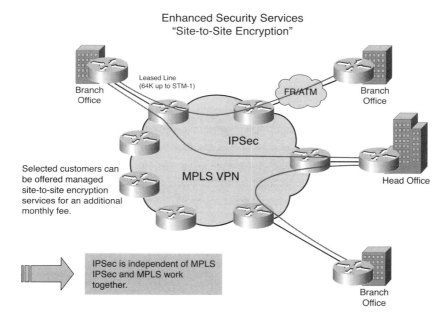

Figure 7-5   *Enhanced Security Services Site-to-Site Encryption*

The IPSec standards specify a requirement to "copy down" the original IP DSCP values into the encapsulating IPSec header. This copy function is performed automatically by the crypto engines.

In the case of Generic Routing Encapsulation (GRE) +IPSec, the encapsulation is done by the GRE process to perform a copy down of the differentiated services code point (DSCP) from the original IP header. Subsequently, IPSec performs encryption (usually in transport mode such that another IP encapsulation is not done) and retains the IP DSCP provided by the GRE/IP packet.

Regarding QoS implementations using classic IPSec tunneling, the transit routers (that is, the PE devices) have visibility only to the DSCP and the IPSec tunnel end points. These transit routers have no visibility to other protocols. For this reason, the QoS mappings must be accurate before reaching the encryption engines.

Regarding QoS on the CE, the CE and PE are generally able to work on aggregate queues only (that is, all the point-to-point IPSec flows in a common set of queues). The CE performing the encryption can have visibility to other protocols prior to encryption (that is, IP protocol, source port, and destination port). However, most customers simply use the DSCP for queuing to achieve general QoS consistency.

MPLS VPN (BGP VPN) Security Issues and Options

Typically, the most important security requirement for VPN users is that their traffic is kept separate from other VPNs' traffic. This refers to both the VPN's own traffic not being seen in other VPNs and the other VPNs' traffic not intruding into the user's VPN. Referring to the threat model from the previous chapter, this section analyzes a threat against a VPN, specifically intrusions into and from other VPNs.

Another requirement is that each VPN can use the complete IP address space without affecting or being affected by other VPNs or the core.

The service provider has the requirement that the core remains separate from the VPNs in the sense that the address space in use does not conflict with any VPN and that VPN traffic remains separate on the core from the control plane traffic on the core.

In other words, a given VPN must be completely separate from other VPNs or the core in terms of traffic separation as well as address space separation. To analyze how the standard addresses these requirements, let's first examine how addressing, data, and control traffic are kept architecturally separate.

The purpose of the route distinguisher (RD) is to allow the entire IPv4 space to be used in different contexts, such as in our example for VPNs. On a given router, a single RD can define a VRF in which the entire IPv4 address space can be used independently.

NOTE   IETF RFC 4364 defines a semantic for RDs, but this serves only administrative purposes to make selecting unique RDs easier. For security considerations, it is important only to understand that the RD makes the IPv4 routes of a VPN unique on the MPLS VPN core.

Due to the architecture of MPLS VPNs (BGP VPNs), only the PE routers have to know the VPN routes. Because PE routers use exclusively VPN-IPv4 addresses for VPNs, the address space is separated between VPNs. They use IPv4 internally in the core, which is a different address family from the VPN-IPv4 address family, so the core also has address space independent from the VPNs. VPNs use the VPN-IPv4 address family, whereas the RDs are used to distinguish between VPNs. The core uses the IPv4 address family, which is architecturally separated from other address families. This provides a clear separation between VPNs and between VPNs and the core.

There is only one special case in this model: The attachment circuit on a PE, which connects a VPN CE, is part of the VRF of that VPN and thus belongs to this VPN. However, the address of this PE interface is part of the VPN-IPv4 address space of the VPN, and therefore, inaccessible from other interfaces on the same PE, from other core routers, and from other VPNs.

For practical purposes, this means address space separation between VPNs and between a VPN and the core is still perfect because this PE interface to the CE belongs to the VPN and is treated as a VPN address. However, this also means that addresses exist in the VPN that belong to a PE. Consequently, a PE can by default be reached from a VPN, which might be used to attack that PE from the VPN.

VPN traffic consists of VPN data plane and control plane traffic. This section examines both. The VPN user's requirement is that his traffic (both types) not mix with other VPNs' traffic or with core traffic. Specifically, his packets must not be sent to another VPN and other VPNs cannot send traffic into his VPN.

On the service provider network, this definition needs to be refined because VPN traffic must be transported on the MPLS core. Here we distinguish between control plane and data plane traffic, where the control plane is traffic originating and terminating within the core and the data plane contains the traffic from the various VPNs. VPN traffic consists of traffic from and to end stations in a VPN and traffic between CEs (for example, if IPSec is implemented between the CEs).

Each interface can belong only to one VRF, depending on its configuration. So for VPN customer "red," who is connected to the PE on a fast Ethernet interface, the interface command **ip vrf forwarding <VPN>** determines the VRF.

Traffic separation on a PE router is implemented differently, depending on which type of interface the packets enter the router through.

- **NonVRF interface**—If the packet enters on an interface that is associated with the global routing table (the **no ip vrf forwarding** command), the forwarding decision is made based on the global routing table and the packet is treated like a normal IP packet. Only core traffic uses nonVRF interfaces, thus no further separation is required. (Inter-AS and Carrier's Carrier scenarios are exceptions to this rule and are discussed later in this chapter.)

- **VRF interface**—If the packet enters on an interface that is linked to a VRF using the **ip vrf forwarding <VPN>** command, a forwarding decision is made based on the forwarding table (or forwarding information base [FIB]) of that VRF. The next hop from a PE perspective always points to another PE router, and the FIB entry also contains the encapsulation method for the packet on the core. Traffic separation between various VPNs is then achieved by encapsulating the received packet with a VPN-specific tag. You have various options for encapsulating and forwarding VPN packets on the core: Through a label switch path (LSP), an IPSec tunnel, an L2TPv3 tunnel, or a simple IPinIP or GRE tunnel. All the methods keep various VPNs separate, either by using different tunnels for different VPNs or by tagging each packet with a VPN-specific label.

P routers have no active role in keeping traffic from VPNs separate—they just connect the PE routers together through LSPs or the other methods, which were previously described. One of the key advantages of the MPLS VPN architecture is that P routers do not keep VPN-specific information. This aids the scalability of the core, but it also helps security: By not having any visibility of VPNs, they also have no way to interfere with VPN separation. Therefore, P routers have no impact on the security of an MPLS core. (As always in this chapter, we assume here correct operation and implementation.)

In summary, VPN users can expect their VPNs to be separate from other VPNs and the core because

- An interface on a PE (the user's attachment circuit) can belong only to a single VRF or the core.

- The attachment circuit to this interface belongs logically to the VPN of the user. No other VPN has access to it.

- On the PE, the address information of the VPN is held as VPN-IPv4 addresses, making each VPN unique through a unique route distinguisher.

- VPN traffic is forwarded through the core through VPN-specific paths or tunnels, typically tagging each packet with a VPN-specific label.

- P routers have no knowledge of VPNs and thus cannot interfere with VPN separation.

The service provider can expect her core to be separate from the VPNs because PE and P addresses are IPv4 addresses. VPNs use exclusively VPN-IPv4 addresses and cannot access PE and P routers.

We can therefore summarize the MPLS security requirements as follows:

- Address space and routing separation

- Hiding of the MPLS core structure

- Resistance to attacks

- Impossibility of VPN spoofing

In any network, security considerations devolve into essentially two sets of two types of issues. Compromises are either accidental (through misconfigurations, growth, or anticipated changes in the network) or deliberate (attacks by some entity bent on causing havoc). The risk vectors are either external (issues driven by events external to the network in question) or internal (problems that are sourced from within the network itself). Additionally, most security-related problems fall into the categories of DoS or intrusion. DoS events can be intentional or accidental, whereas intrusion issues are by definition intentional. It is essential to harden the network components and the system as a whole to minimize the likelihood of any of these scenarios. However, as with all resource-consuming features, a balance must be struck between maximizing security and offering the performance and usability the service is intended to provide. Clearly, a wholly disconnected host or router has total security, but its ability to forward data or provide services is substantially compromised.

The state of the network from an availability and security viewpoint can also differ with respect to the perspective of the interested party. That is, the concerns of the service provider and the customer are an intersecting, but not completely overlapping, set of needs. Indeed, the perspective of the current status of the network might not be identical for the two parties.

The service provider's concerns can be generalized into the following set of issues:

- Protecting the backbone infrastructure in terms of availability, accessibility, load, manageability, and so on

- Ensuring that committed service level agreements (SLA) are maintained

- Ensuring that billing support functions are uncompromised

- Maintaining segregation between different customer domains

- Verifying that customers are receiving the services to which they are entitled—no more and no less

The customer has a somewhat differing perspective on the network from the service provider.

The customer's concerns include the following:

- Ensuring that data/routes are transferred reliably and unhindered to all appropriate end points.

- Ensuring that data/routes are not leaked to other service provider customers.

- Ensuring that the service provider is attaining committed SLAs in terms of availability and throughput.

- Expeditious troubleshooting of a network problem by the SP.

- Expeditious problem analysis by the customer.

- Protection mechanisms the customer can implement to protect him from service provider errors both initially and as the customer network grows due to an increase in the SP's customer base.

- Mechanisms/policies that the customer can implement to protect him from deliberate assaults originating from the service provider network.

Layer 2 and Unmanaged VPN Service Considerations

Clearly, the types of physical network available to interconnect the CE and PE offer varying levels of resilience to intrusion and redirection mechanisms. A serial point-to-point facility is difficult to subvert and intrusions are usually noticeable. When a serial connection of this nature is interrupted, alarms are raised quickly and the two end points are difficult to masquerade.

Private virtual circuit (PVC)-based networks, such as Frame Relay and ATM, are somewhat less resistant in that they are generally controlled by software-based virtual circuit switching and can be readily mis-switched or duplicated. However, even these facilities typically use a serial point-to-point connection between the CE and the telecommunications (telco) central office, making intrusion difficult outside of the telco realm.

Ethernet-based facilities are most readily compromised in that inserting a promiscuous monitoring device within the network is relatively easy. The physical links from the CE to the central office remain directly cabled and consequently intrusion still generally requires telco access.

Of course, you can insert equipment into these physical plants, but the level of expertise required to identify the correct facility, access the physical structures, and unobtrusively insert illicit systems is very high and not readily performed by any but the most determined and well-funded attackers.

The more significant issue with shared physical interface accesses (PVC-based or VLAN-based) is managing the offered traffic loads so that one VPN cannot impact the operational characteristics of other VPNs that are terminated on the same port. To guarantee the performance of the VPNs per SLAs, you must either provision much greater bandwidth on the access port than the expected load or manage the bandwidth available using policing and shaping mechanisms. Typically, this is done through the offering of a limited set of performance options (say, four or five classes) to the customer when he requests the service. Policing controls are then applied to the interfaces based on these predefined classes of service to meet the expectations of the customer. In an unmanaged VPN where different entities control the CE and PE, and consequently neither can be guaranteed to stay within the expected operational characteristics, these controls need to be applied to both routers to ensure that offered loads do not impact the applicable networks.

Design Option Examples

MPLS VPNs offer several network design options to address varying customer deployment needs. These include the following:

- **Central services topology**—In this scenario, either the customer or the SP provides a service at a centralized site that can then be accessed by various VPN entities. For example, the SP might be providing a storage area network (SAN) facility or perhaps an IP telephony call manager service. This necessitates judicious use of MPLS VPN route targets to provide connectivity to these facilities without leaking access between VPNs. The servers providing such support must be carefully managed so that access to these devices does not compromise the various VPNs.

- **Hub-and-spoke topology**—In a hub-and-spoke design, a particular customer site is designated as the focal point for user traffic and also likely provides corporate services to other sites. Examples include server farms and Internet access. These types of implementations have security needs as well.

For example, controlling services that might be specific to particular corporate groups or providing firewall/NAT mechanisms for Internet access. However, MPLS introduces no additional concerns with respect to managing corporate traffic flows in a hub-and-spoke design, and as such, typical network planning approaches can still be applied.

- **Any-to-any topology**—When traffic profiles indicate that sites need to freely communicate with one another, any-to-any connectivity might be appropriate. This is the simplest topology to implement from an MPLS VPN perspective in that the import/export policies of route targets (RT) is the same at all sites within a given VPN.

In the service provider–managed VPN environment, the CE is managed by the service provider. That is, the SP's control extends all the way out to a point-of-presence within the customer's IGP. This section recommends best practice deployment guidelines for the customer edge implementation. When a service provider manages a customer edge, the SP has full control of the CE configuration, including:

- Access to the router itself for configuration and fault diagnostics

- Interaction with the rest of the customer's IGP or routing instance

- Interaction with the SP's PE routing mechanism—that is, the routing instance between the CE and PE

- The gathering customer statistics as required for reporting

This model provides the SP with the greatest degree of control over the potential impact of the customer's operations on the SP's network itself, as well as greater control over issues that might arise and affect other SP customer VPNs. The SP has a single backbone infrastructure for multiple sets of customers.

In addition, this arrangement implies some degree of trust on the part of the customer:

- The customer permits another company (the SP) to have access to its IGP.

- The customer trusts the SP to map its network communications solely to end points approved by the customer.

- The customer assumes that the SP will provide the majority of fault analysis and resolution activity (because its own access is somewhat limited) because the service is managed by the SP.

Additionally, in some environments the customer demands a call for some degree of sharing of responsibility between the SP and the customer. In these situations, the span of control with respect to the previously mentioned parameters can shift from one direction to the other. A customer might have an unmanaged VPN in which an unmanaged VPN is distinguished by the notion that the CE router is owned and controlled by the customer. Although the term *unmanaged VPN* is strictly speaking a misnomer (and perhaps indicative of a more SP-centric perspective), it is widely accepted to mean a network in which the customers manage the CE router themselves rather than the SP. In this scenario, the demarcation point between the SP and the customer is usually the dataset at the customer premises (although the communication facility provider might not be the Layer 3 MPLS VPN provider). The customer has full control of the configuration of the CE router and interacts with the SP's network over some mutually agreed upon arrangement between the SP and the customer.

The SP might have some exposure of the SP network operation to the customer's configurations of the CE router. As such, the SP needs to take additional steps to ensure that its network operations are not disturbed by changes in the customer's network environment or CE router setups.

However, this operative mode might be more palatable to customers who desire to maintain the following:

- Retain complete control of their IGP
- Provide additional fault analysis/troubleshooting information access
- Minimize exposure of the customer network to the SP

From the SP's perspective, the unmanaged VPN environment changes the span of control significantly. This approach impacts the SP in a number of ways, including these:

- The need to protect Layer 3 interconnects between the CE and PE.
- The need to provide the possible requirement to protect the Layer 2 interconnect (if shared).
- There is a requirement for a clear definition of SLA responsibilities between the SP and enterprise customer, due to changes in the span of control. This requirement is a result of the need for the SP to closely interact with the customer in the event of problems that require an additional level of security awareness at the PE router because the CE is no longer under the explicit control of the service provider.

Carrier's Carrier Network and Inter-Autonomous Considerations

Carrier's Carrier (CsC) networks can be viewed as a special case of unmanaged VPNs. In these environments, a hierarchy of service provider operators is used to provision end-to-end connectivity for a customer, where the SP who is directly interfacing with the end customer might not have facilities in place to meet all of the customer's needs completely. As an example, a smaller SP might have been selected to provide MPLS VPN services for a given customer. However, although the particular SP might possess direct facilities to meet the customer's needs at the end points of the network, the SP might not be capable of providing intercontinental or transoceanic facilities. As such, the SP might contract with a carrier who has such networking available through a CsC type of arrangement. Consequently, the top-tier SP views the second-tier SP as an unmanaged VPN client, whereas the second-tier SP might have either an unmanaged or a managed arrangement with the end customer. CsC is usually accomplished by the higher-level SP mapping the secondary SP's traffic through some form of a VPN-LSP path. As such, one essentially has end customer traffic mapped into a VPN by the first SP and then again into another labeled hierarchy by the second SP.

There is also a variation on this approach, usually referred to as an *Inter-AS network*, in which the interconnection between SPs is purely a label-switching mechanism and the end point peering is still accomplished between the CE routers.

CsC network environments present an additional set of interconnection concerns because the following connectivity arrangements are present:

- Connections between customer and provider

- Connections between a provider and its carrier

- Routing and label implementation arrangements between the two SP

In this situation, SLA and security requirements exist amongst three entities, rather than the typical two.

This approach is generally favored by customers who do not want to operate a Layer 3 network or who feel that they can simply use the SP's expertise and support staff to operate the Layer 3 environment. The notion of an SP edge router interconnecting with a customer's network at a Layer 2 level is increasingly popular—in particular, in metro environments. In this design, the customer presents a Layer 2–based interconnect, possibly one or more VLANs, to the PE Layer 3 network. In effect, the SP PE router is the routing kick-off point for Layer 3 service for the customer. The customer has no Layer 3 routing occurring within his own network. Such an implementation allows the customer to focus on the pure switching component of networking his campuses.

To secure this type of connectivity arrangement, several considerations need to be addressed, besides the typical Layer 3 interconnect.

In the case of a LAN-based, Layer 2 interconnect, the PE router must maintain ARP entries for all the end system addresses that are reachable beyond that interface.

The number of entries can be considerable depending on the size of the connected site, and they can considerably impact router CPU and memory. It is generally thought that an excess of 20,000 ARP entries can lead to issues on the connected router; as such you might want to segment a large campus.

In addition, the fact that no Layer 3 CE router exists in this scenario means no reasonable mechanisms are available to ensure that the only accesses into the VPN from this interface are those authorized to access the VPN. That is, given some large number of hosts on this Layer 2 domain, it is difficult, if not impossible, to create access controls that can ensure that only the appropriate traffic sources exist—the Layer 2 domain must be a trusted network space. This must be an operational consideration of the entity controlling the Layer 2 network—be it the customer or the SP. Intrusion into the network at this point gives access to much, if not all, of the entire VPN (depending on the VLAN arrangements).

In addition, because this is a Layer 2 environment, no Layer 3 opportunities are available for controlling DoS issues beyond the PE edge. If an assault or intrusion reaches the Layer 2 space, it must be dealt with at that level. For example, a broadcast-oriented attack would have an immediate impact on all the nodes within the same Layer 2 domain.

The SP must also determine the degree of interaction it wants to have with respect to L2 operations—for example, spanning tree termination and Cisco Discovery Protocol (CDP functions, QoS, trusted ports, and so on).

As MPLS VPNs have become more popular, the need to provide connectivity across different SP or autonomous system boundaries has become apparent. Large enterprise customers are often multinational and, because of their geography, might not always be able to get their full VPN connectivity through a single provider. Even if connectivity can be achieved via a single SP infrastructure, the topology of the network might be split into multiple autonomous systems.

The Inter-AS suite of solutions was introduced to facilitate such connectivity requirements. The three most popular choices are referred to as option A, option B, and option C; they are described in Section 10 of RFC 4364.

Option A is an IP relationship between two AS domains commonly represented by back-to-back VRF constructs.

Option B has become the option of choice for inter-provider connectivity where two SPs under separate authoritative control peer with the intent of directly exchanging VPNv4 routes. Option C, on the other hand, has become the option of choice for Inter-AS connectivity. in which multiple autonomous systems under the same authoritative control peer use route-reflectors and exchange BGP next-hop addresses across the Inter-AS links.

Whichever connectivity model is chosen, the SP must choose how to provision the import/export policies at the PE routers, ASBR routers, and route reflectors (if applicable). The route-target values used to implement these policies might or might not be the same in each autonomous system. Because of this, three different schemes can be adopted for the import/export policies:

Scheme 1—Each SP uses its own route-target value and rewrites the incoming route-target value from an adjacent provider using the RT-rewrite feature at the ASBR router. This enables the SP to configure its PE routers with local route-target values, regardless of whether the VPN is connected to multiple autonomous systems. If an existing VPN requires connectivity via another autonomous system, the SP need only know the route-target value used by the adjacent provider and then rewrite this to the local value at the ASBR boundaries.

Those SPs that prefer a centralized filtering and provisioning methodology generally favor this scheme because they are able to make all the changes at the ASBR routers rather than the PE routers. However, this scheme complicates the filtering configuration and can compromise the security of the local VPNs if the wrong route-target value is configured. This scheme is therefore *not recommended* unless the correct provisioning tools are in place.

Scheme 2—Each SP uses the same route-target values for each VPN that crosses autonomous system boundaries. This scheme requires that the route-target format consist of one or other of their autonomous system numbers. This scheme is *not recommended* for two reasons: (1) Using a route-target value, which belongs to the neighbor provider, might conflict with the filtering scheme used by the neighbor provider; and (2) it is not very practical because the majority of VPNs exist prior to Inter-AS becoming a requirement.

Scheme 3—Each SP configures its PE routers with **route-target import** statements that match the **route-target export** statements for a given VPN within the adjacent autonomous system. This is the recommended scheme because this scheme doesn't require the neighbor provider's route-target value to be associated with the local VPN prefixes. This scheme, however, might require the provisioning tool to update the VRF configurations at all the relevant PE routers whenever the VPN becomes an Inter-AS VPN. Most deployments commence with option A or back-to-back VRFs and move to option B for more scalability. Option C can be deployed in an Inter-AS model in which the provider is under the same trust and administrative domains. In the next section, we identify security attributes to secure the customer edge router connection to the provider edge device.

Customer Edge Router Security Considerations

For the CE router, securing the data plane is pivotal for overall security. The Unicast Reverse Path Forwarding (uRPF) lookup feature should be enabled on each interface of the PE router's CE-facing interfaces and on the CE router's PE-facing interfaces. RPF attempts to verify that the source of an incoming packet is accessible via the interface from which it was received (by checking the CEF tables) prior to switching the packet through.

uRPF is currently available in two operating modes:

- **Loose**—In this mode, if the incoming packet's source address is reachable through any interface in the router, the packet is forwarded.

- **Strict**—In strict mode, the packet must enter via the exact interface through which the source address would be reached prior to forwarding.

The two modes are intended for operation at different points of the network. Loose mode is primarily applicable in network cores, whereas strict mode is intended for use at the edges of a given network.

Because PE and CE routers implement the network edge in an MPLS VPN context, strict mode would be the appropriate choice. However, if the connections are dual-homed, the RPF mechanism must be relaxed somewhat by using loose mode.

Various QoS mechanisms can be used to protect the PE and CE router interfaces from undue traffic volumes. A higher-than-expected traffic flow might be due to a deliberate DoS assault or simply be the result of a misconfigured device somewhere within the network. However, because these mechanisms are inserted directly into the forwarding path, they do have an impact on packet forwarding rates—especially on software-based platforms. As such, these features should be applied with care and due consideration given to the environment in which they are to be applied.

The PE is within the SP domain and could have multiple customer relationships; for example, multiple customer VPNs might be provisioned on a single PE. From a security standpoint, ensuring complete privacy between various customers is of utmost importance for the service provider. Hardening the control and data plane for a PE is required as a security best practice guideline. To manage forwarding information between the PE and CE, some sort of Layer 3 routing must be performed. There are, in essence, two options: static routing and dynamic routing. The pros and cons of each are well understood in Layer 3 routing environments and apply equally to an MPLS VPN network. However, an MPLS VPN PE-CE connection involves a relationship between separate corporate entities, so due consideration must be given to the security and stability implications of such interconnections. For example, the concerns of interconnecting two entities can include the following:

- The PE or CE might be subject to floods of routes from its neighbor.

- Instabilities in the routing protocol processes can adversely affect CPU utilization.

- Invalid routes injected into either network space can cause traffic flows, resulting in suboptimal or insecure pathing.

These issues are no different from those faced by most Internet service providers (ISP) today, although ISPs usually do not use IGPs in their interconnection points. They typically rely solely on BGP for this purpose. MPLS-VPN customers might desire the use of mechanisms other than BGP; as a result, consideration needs to be given to the requirements this might impose. For data plane security, as in the CE, the use of uRFP is recommended for the PE. The uRPF lookup feature should be enabled on each interface of the PE router's CE-facing interfaces and on the CE router's PE-facing interfaces. RPF attempts to verify that the source of an incoming packet is accessible via the interface from which it was received (by checking the CEF tables) prior to switching the packet through.

Implementing security guidelines for both the PE and the core as per *Cisco ISP Essentials* (ISBN 1-58705-041-2, Cisco Press) is highly recommended.

Overall Best Practice Recommendations

The following guidelines summarize best practices for MPLS VPN security:

- For the core (PE+P), secure it with infrastructure access lists (ACLs) on all interfaces.

- Use PE-CE routing where possible to hide topological information or prevent leakage from trusted domains.

- If static routing is not feasible, use BGP or an IGP with an authentication mechanism, such as Message Digest – 5 (MD5).

- Enforce separation of CE-PE links where possible and between the Internet and customer VPN.

- Implement Label Distribution Protocol (LDP) with authentication (MD5).

- For VRF, define the maximum number of routes to proactively monitor traffic patterns within a VPN.

- Use BGP maximum prefix constructs to set limitations on BGP routing traffic to control and monitor where an exceeded limit results in a notification to the NOC.

For Inter-AS implementations, start with a back-to-back VRF implementation (static VPN connections) because this is an easy way to begin. Perhaps at some point (with the deployment of multiple Inter-AS customers), you can migrate to the second option to benefit from the ease of provisioning associated with the second option. For the third option, deploy it only when both ASes are under the same administrative and trust zones.

NOTE	For both CsC and Inter-AS deployments, implement them only on private peerings due to the vulnerabilities under the LAN subsection.
	For Inter-AS and CsC (when labelled packets are exchanged), do NOT use a shared VLAN.
	Best recommendation: Dedicated connection
	Second best recommendation: Dedicated VLAN

Figures 7-6 and 7-7 summarize best practice security recommendations for the deployment of MPLS.

Best Practice Security Overview

- Secure devices (PE, P): They are trusted!
- PEs: Secure with ACLs on all interfaces.
- Static PE-CE routing where possible.
- If routing: Use authentication (MD5).
- Maximum number of routes per peer (only BGP).
- Separation of CE-PE links where possible (Internet/VPN).
- LDP authentication (MD5).
- VRF: Define maximum number of routes.

Note: Overall security depends on the weakest link!

Figure 7-6   *Best Practice Security Overview*

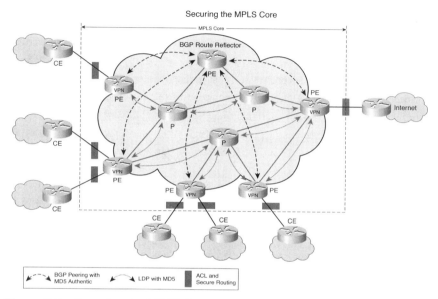

Figure 7-7   Securing the MPLS Core

Summary

This chapter discussed security within an NGN framework and pointed out the Cisco IP NGN vision and architecture overview as an example. Additionally, it identified the three security pillars of architecture, implementation, and operation and the relationship of these three pillars to MPLS security. We explored the security aspects of MPLS and defined common requirements that VPN users have for a VPN service. We have further explored the attack scenarios and recommended best practice guidelines.

The result is that, based on the architecture described in RFC 4364, MPLS VPNs (BGP-VPNs) can be provided securely, meaning that

- VPNs are separated (addressing and traffic).

- The core is protected from miscreant intrusions.

- Protection against VPN spoofing exists.

- The core is invisible to the VPN user.

In general, MPLS VPNs provide equivalent security compared to traditional Layer 2 VPNs, such as ATM and Frame Relay.

We also examined the architectural security of Inter-AS and Carrier's Carrier architectures. Although CsC networks are quite secure, care must be taken with Inter-AS scenarios when connecting different carriers because not all architectures provide the same level of security between providers. Furthermore, a customer can deploy IPSec and MPLS because these are not competing technologies.

A number of issues exist that MPLS VPNs do not address. Amongst those are the internal security of a VPN, attacks from the Internet into a VPN, and VPN data confidentiality. These issues are independent of MPLS and have to be solved separately.

MPLS VPN networks are secure only when the network implementation is correct and when the network is operated correctly.

Standards and References

Behringer, M. and M. Morrow. *MPLS VPN Security.* Indianapolis, IN: Cisco Press.

RFC 4381—Analysis of MPLS VPN Security

RFC 4364—BGP/MPLS IP VPNs, E. Rosen et al.

RFC 2082—RIP-2 MD5 Authentication

RFC 2154—OSPF with Digital Signatures

RFC 2385—Protection of BGP Sessions via the TCP MD5 Signature Option

RFC 3013—Recommended Internet Service Provider Security Services and Procedures

RFC 3031—MPLS Architecture

RFC 2196—Site Security Handbook

RFC 2401—IP Security Architecture

Gartner research note M-17-1953: "MPLS Networks: Drivers Beat Inhibitors in 2003."

Other Cisco Press Security Book References

Cisco Press books and ISBN numbers:

Network Security First-Step (1587200996)

The Business Case for Network Security (1587201216)

Network Security Fundamentals (1587051672)

Designing Network Security, Second Edition (1587051176)

Network Security Architectures (158705115x)

Network Security Principles and Practices (1587050250)

CCSP Self-Study: Cisco Secure PIX Firewalls Advanced, Second Edition (1587051494)

CCSP Self-Study: Cisco Secure VPNs, Second Edition (1587051451)

CCSP Self-Study: Cisco Secure IDS, Second Edition (1587051443)

CCSP Self-Study: Securing Cisco IOS Networks (1587051516)

Cisco Router Firewall Security (1587051753)

Cisco Access Control Security (1587051249)

Cisco Wireless LAN Security (1587051540)

Cisco ISP Essentials (1587050412)

End to End QoS Network Design (1587051761)

IPSec VPN Design (1587051117)

Cisco PIX Firewall Handbook (1587051583)

The Business Case for Network Disaster Recovery (1587201194)

Securing Your Business with ASDM (1587052148)

*Cisco Security Agen*t (1587052059)

CHAPTER 8

TRAFFIC
ENGINEERING

Traffic engineering is a familiar topic in the communications industry. Network operators have used traffic engineering on circuit infrastructure to evenly distribute traffic in the network. In ATM networks, PVCs are placed by operators such that network load is distributed evenly. Even dynamic routing protocols such as Private Network to Network Interface (PNNI) send topology and bandwidth information to the switches, and switches perform admission control when admitting virtual circuits (VC) in the network.

Today most networks are packet-networks, so they also use mesh connections for better redundancy and resilience. If failure occurs, reconvergence causes the IP routing devices to use the new paths in the network. How the new path is calculated is determined by several factors, one of which is link metrics. To perform traffic engineering in an IP network, these link metrics must be manipulated to influence traffic flows. MPLS provides a much needed solution to balance the traffic in the network by building label-switched paths (LSP) and allowing operators to map traffic onto these paths. This chapter describes the IP routing problem and shows how MPLS traffic engineering helps solve that problem. It also investigates the applications of MPLS traffic engineering, where it is used, and how it can help in building a protection solution for better network resiliency. One of the first applications of MPLS was to deliver traffic engineering in an IP network.

This chapter discusses this problem statement: Why is traffic engineering (TE) needed in an IP network? We then provide a technical overview of how MPLS traffic engineering can help address the network congestion by using the nonshortest paths. We examine a main application of MPLS TE for protection and restoration, known as MPLS fast reroute (FRR). You'll also see examples of how MPLS TE is used in networks today to address specific problems, such as IP bandwidth guarantee. The management elements of MPLS and TE are dealt with in the Operation, Administration, and Maintenance (OAM) chapter, Chapter 12, "Network Management and Provisioning."

Problem Statement

To understand why traffic engineering is needed in IP networks, let us first understand what happens in an IP network. As stated earlier, IP routers perform destination-based routing when sending traffic. This implies that the routers use a simple shortest path first algorithm to compute the shortest "distance" between themselves and the destination. This "distance" can be hop count, for protocols such as Routing Information Protocol (RIP), or least total metric (the sum of link metrics added along the path from the network element to the destination). It does not matter whether other alternate paths exist in the network. If there is traffic to send, the traffic always flows through the least cost path or shortest path first. Even if the traffic to be sent is more than the path can accommodate and the path itself is congested, the traffic is always sent on the shortest path. This results in traffic drop, as shown in Figure 8-1.

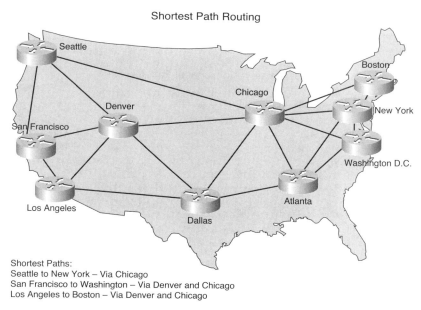

Shortest Paths:
Seattle to New York – Via Chicago
San Francisco to Washington – Via Denver and Chicago
Los Angeles to Boston – Via Denver and Chicago

Figure 8-1   *Shortest Path Routing*

Assuming all links are OC-192 in Figure 8-1, if 8 Gbps of traffic is flowing between Seattle and New York, the network without traffic engineering can accommodate only 2 more Gbps of bandwidth between Seattle and New York on the shortest connection via Chicago. So, if an additional 4 Gbps of traffic now needs to be sent between Seattle and New York, this traffic flows along the Chicago-New York path on directly connected links. This results in a massive 2

Gbps of traffic drop. Even though other links do exist between Seattle and New York, such as via a Denver-Dallas path, these links are not used. In other words, even if other nonshortest paths that might have available link bandwidth exist in the network, because of shortest path first (SPF) computation, the traffic is always routed along the short path (the least distance). The nonshortest paths are not used; therefore, traffic drop occurs along the shortest path.

MPLS TE enables the operator to build a TE tunnel/LSP along the nonshortest path or a path that meets the bandwidth requirements (4 Gbps in the earlier example). In addition, MPLS TE maps traffic to this new path, thereby using links with available bandwidth. For example, in Figure 8-1, traffic going from Seattle to New York can now go through a TE tunnel built via Atlanta, Dallas, and Denver, as shown in Figure 8-2.

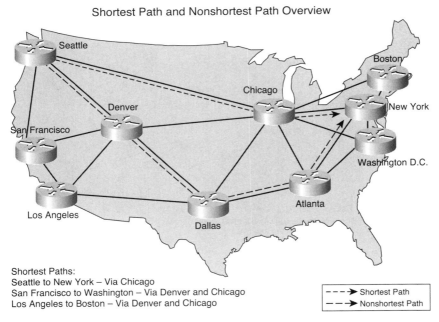

Shortest Path and Nonshortest Path Overview

Shortest Paths:
Seattle to New York – Via Chicago
San Francisco to Washington – Via Denver and Chicago
Los Angeles to Boston – Via Denver and Chicago

Shortest Path
Nonshortest Path

Figure 8-2   *Shortest Path and Nonshortest Path Overview*

Technology Overview

To better understand the process of rerouting traffic on nonshortest paths and setting up of MPLS TE, let us now investigate how the technology works. The previous section described elements of MPLS TE as follows:

1   Network devices must be capable of routing traffic on nonshortest paths.

2   Network devices must be capable of routing traffic based on delay and bandwidth constraints.

3   Network devices must be capable of supporting mechanisms that establish the traffic engineering tunnels. Traffic must now be mapped on these TE tunnels.

Based on these requirements, you can see that routers in a given network must have available link bandwidth information for the entire network. Sufficient bandwidth information can be established by sending available link bandwidth information in the routing protocol updates.

IGP Extensions and Distribution of Constraints

Interior Gateway Protocol (IGP) extensions are needed to flood available link bandwidth information. This flooding ensures that all routers participating in the traffic engineering setup understand which links to use to satisfy the constraint criteria. For example, in our topology all links that do not have 4 Gbps of available bandwidth can be removed from the topology to compute the best available path between Seattle and New York. Because the directly connected links via Chicago have only 2 Gbps of available bandwidth, they are removed from the topology and a new path is computed that satisfies the 4 Gbps bandwidth requirement.

The flooding of available bandwidth information happens via IGP (OSPF or IS-IS) link state advertisements (LSA). This implies that IGPs must be extended to use the new LSA type (Opaque LSA) to flood the information. Other routers in the same IGP learn about the links and available bandwidth on each one of them. The flooding of information can be periodic or it can occur when a significant change occurs in the available bandwidth of a link. The significant change is determined by a defined threshold—for example, when the available bandwidth on a link drops below a threshold value. Thresholds provide a reasonable compromise between information flooded less often versus information flooded every time some bandwidth is taken away from the link.

Signaling of TE Tunnels

After the available bandwidth information is learned by the router, the router computes the set of paths that meet the bandwidth or delay constraint. This computation is often referred to as a constrained-based SPF (CSPF) calculation. After a path is obtained through the constraint-based SPF, a traffic engineering tunnel must be established along that path. To establish the traffic engineering tunnel, a signaling mechanism is required to set up an LSP along the constraint-based path.

During the standardization days of traffic engineering, there was a hot industry debate about which protocol had to be used for traffic engineering. Should LDP be extended to constraint-based routing and admission control or should RSVP—a protocol that has admission control capability—be extended to do label distribution?

After much debate, the industry settled on RSVP as the de-facto standard for the setup of traffic engineering tunnels. RSVP was previously used for per-flow bandwidth reservation in the IntServ QoS model. Because it had the capability to perform admission control and traversed hop by hop for reservation establishment, it could be easily extended to perform label distribution and explicit routing. Other attributes of RSVP, such as shared-explicit (the capability to share the reservation on common links without double counting bandwidth), allow the setup of make-before-break operations without any double counting of bandwidth.

RSVP uses PATH messages to establish state hop-by-hop and reservation messages to perform admission control and reserve bandwidth along the path. In the case of MPLS TE, the same PATH messages traverse hop by hop along the path computed by the CSPF calculation done by the router. For instance, if the CSPF determines that the path going through San Francisco, Denver, and Dallas meets the 4 Gbps bandwidth requirement from Seattle to New York, the RSVP PATH messages from the Seattle routers travel hop by hop to Denver, Dallas, Atlanta, and to New York, as shown in Figure 8-3.

RSVP PATH and MESSAGE Flows

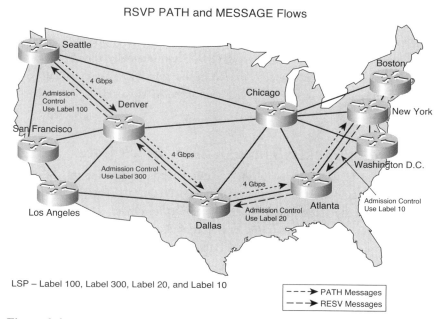

LSP – Label 100, Label 300, Label 20, and Label 10

- - -► PATH Messages
- - -► RESV Messages

Figure 8-3   *RSVP PATH and MESSAGE Flows*

At each hop along the path, a state associated with the TE tunnel is stored. After the PATH messages reach the destination, New York, admission control is performed to see whether the link has the available bandwidth that was requested in the PATH message. If the link has available bandwidth, this bandwidth chunk is removed from the available bandwidth pool, a label is allocated for the TE tunnel, and an RESV message is sent back with the label along the same route on which the PATH message was received. At each hop, the same operation is performed in which the admission control process is performed and a label is allocated for the TE tunnel and chunk of the bandwidth that was removed from the available pool of bandwidth. The RESV message finally reaches the source, or the head end of the TE tunnel. The TE tunnel is not established and labels are programmed into the forwarding hardware that correspond to this tunnel.

If the admission control fails at any hop along the path, an error message is sent back to the head end of the tunnel. The head end router can then pick up a new path and resignal the TE tunnel.

A network operator can decide to bypass the CSPF process, ignore the available bandwidth information on the links, and manually specify an explicit route along which a TE tunnel is placed in the network. This is called *explicit routing* and is analogous to PVC placement of the ATM world.

Forwarding Packets Through the Network Core

After the TE tunnel is established, traffic must be mapped to this TE tunnel. There are multiple ways of mapping traffic onto TE tunnels. The simplest form of mapping is by the static routing of traffic onto a TE tunnel. The TE tunnel is a special interface onto which traffic can be routed. By static mapping the traffic, specific prefixes can be routed onto a TE tunnel.

Another important method of mapping traffic onto a TE tunnel is by using a policy routing mechanism. With policy routing, the operator can specify a criterion that, when matched, results in packets being mapped to a TE tunnel. For example, voice traffic destined to New York can be mapped to a specific TE tunnel using policy routing while data traffic uses the longer route. Policy routing enables the creation of flexible maps for routing traffic in the network.

Another method of mapping traffic is using a feature called AutoRoute. In AutoRoute, the TE tunnel is treated like a link connecting the head end and tail end of the tunnel and is fed into the IGP database with a metric. The IGP then thinks it has direct connectivity to the end node and routes traffic over that link (TE tunnel). However, the IGP does not advertise LSAs over this link (TE tunnel).

The last most important method of mapping traffic onto TE tunnels is using EXP bits in the MPLS label or DSCP bit in the IP header in addition to the destination address. This is also referred to as class-of-service–based tunnel selection. In this procedure, at the head end, the traffic is mapped based on a class-of-service (CoS) value toward a given destination. In Figure 8-2, for instance, there could be two TE tunnels: one for carrying voice traffic and another for carrying data traffic. A packet marked with an EXP value 5 can be mapped to TE tunnel 1, and all other packets can be sent on TE tunnel 2. In this manner, traffic engineering can be used to build low-delay and available bandwidth paths for the efficient routing of traffic in the network core. By placing TE tunnels around network choke points (they can be links or nodes, such as Chicago in our example), more traffic can be routed in the network.

Referring to our example, the only reason an extra 2 Gbps of traffic was accepted into the network is because more traffic could be sent along the nonshortest path. One of the providers terms this capability *additional bandwidth inventory*.

Sequence of Operation

The sequence of steps in establishing a TE tunnel are as follows:

1   IGP reachability is established using a link state routing protocol such as OSPF or IS-IS.

2   The operator enables MPLS traffic engineering on the network elements and configures link bandwidth available for traffic engineering. The operator also configures other attributes, such as SRLG (Shared Risk Link Group is described in more detail later), and link affinity.

3   The MPLS TE configuration triggers the flooding of available link bandwidth information in the IGP. All routers and network elements learn the information and store this in their constraint databases.

4   The operator configures a TE tunnel only at the head end, specifying a destination or tail end of the tunnel, bandwidth, and a path-option (explicit or dynamic).

    – Explicit path-option implies which explicit path a TE tunnel must take from the head end to the tail end. This includes a list of router IDs or hops the tunnel must travel.

    – A dynamic path option implies that the path and the list of hops are computed based on available link bandwidth using CSPF, as discussed earlier.

5   The configuration of the TE tunnel triggers RSVP signaling, and the head end sends a PATH message to the next hop as specified in the path option (it is the explicit node if the path-option is explicit or the computed next hop across the link that had available bandwidth for a dynamic path option).

6   The midpoints store the tunnel ID and bandwidth information and forward the PATH message to the next downstream hop.

7   After the PATH message reaches the destination or tail end, the tail end accepts the TE tunnel if it has the bandwidth capacity. Then it allocates a label and sends a RESV message back toward the head end of the TE tunnel to the previous hop.

8   The RESV message now retraces the same path on which the PATH message was sent. At each hop, admission control is performed to check whether the link has available bandwidth.

   – If the admission control process fails on any of the hops, a reservation error is sent back toward the tail, a path error is sent toward the head end, and the tunnel setup process fails.

   – If the admission control passes, a local label is allocated and RESV is sent upstream toward the head end.

9   After the RESV reaches the head end, the head end programs the labels, and the TE tunnel setup is now complete.

10   The operator must now map different types of traffic onto this TE tunnel via the specified criteria as stated in the previous section.

11   The traffic can now be forwarded onto the TE tunnel. The label is imposed onto the incoming IP traffic, and the packet is forwarded onto the TE tunnel.

12   The traffic is label switched in the network core at the midpoints of the TE tunnel.

13   At the tail end of the TE tunnel, the MPLS label is removed or disposed; the traffic is then natively forwarded to the destination.

TE Tunnel Maintenance

TE tunnels are point-to-point and are analogous to Frame Relay or ATM PVCs. However, they scale far better than PVCs because they carry aggregate traffic from PE to PE rather than individual flows.

Unlike the hard state of ATM PVCs, TE tunnels are soft state and require periodic refresh messages that refresh the state of the tunnel along its path. If the refresh message is not received in a specified time period, the tunnel can be declared inactive and the state cleared and removed. When too many tunnels exist, many refresh messages might need to be processed. A technique called *refresh reduction* is used to reduce the number of refresh messages, thereby increasing scalability to a large number of tunnels.

The soft-state nature of the RSVP protocol is also helpful when resizing TE tunnels to increase or decrease in bandwidth. While the tunnel is operational, a new path message can be sent with the new bandwidth values toward the tail end. The process of signaling and admission control is the same as the establishment of a new tunnel. After the new bandwidth is accepted, the tunnel attributes are updated and the tunnel can now carry more traffic. If the admission control process fails during the resize operation, the resize request is rejected and the TE tunnel continues to operate at the old bandwidth value. This is done in a manner that results in zero traffic loss.

Inefficiencies can occur over a period of time if the tunnels are frequently set up and torn down with various bandwidth values. Each node might look to reoptimize tunnels independently. Periodic reoptimization can be done at a specified interval, or it can also be triggered by the operator or by a significant change in link or bandwidth parameters. Should a provider require global reoptimization of tunnel placement, an offline tool with sufficient intelligence can provide the tunnel placement information to the network elements by specifying the explicit route to which a TE tunnel is placed.

Many more complicated features are available that allow resizing or reoptimization of TE tunnels. For further reference, they are all discussed at length in the book *Traffic Engineering with MPLS*, by Eric Osborne and Ajay Simha (Cisco Press, 2002).

Managing MPLS TE tunnels can be done via the command-line interface (CLI) or via sophisticated network management tools such as Cisco's IP Solution Center—Traffic Management (ISC-TM). ISC-TM enables the configuration and monitoring of TE LSPs via a GUI with sophisticated mechanisms to compute paths under additional constraints and provide the explicit placement of both primary and backup tunnels. Additionally, online diagnostics and troubleshooting capabilities exist that provide the capability to check the liveliness of the TE tunnels. This is discussed at more length in Chapter 12.

TE Applications and Examples

So far you have learned how TE tunnels are signaled and how they can be placed in the network via explicit routing. Although TE tunnels specify tunnel bandwidth, there is no rule that says that each node must police the amount of traffic to ensure compliance to the bandwidth associated with the tunnel. This is done by design; the tunnel bandwidth value used in the control plane is only a means to perform admission control and allow the setup of TE tunnels on the nonshortest paths. In this section, we discuss the requirements for QoS and how TE tunnels help or do not help in QoS in the network.

TE tunnels can be used in full mesh or used sparingly to route traffic around choke points in the network. For example, if only a few links are congested in the network, a TE tunnel can be explicitly placed around the choke points without enabling MPLS TE in the entire network.

Because most networks today are either multiarea or multiarea and multi-autonomous systems, support of TE tunnels across the areas or autonomous systems is beneficial. How TE tunnels are set up across areas and how they work are discussed in the sections that follow.

Intra-Area TE

We stated earlier that MPLS TE requires IGP extensions to flood available bandwidth information, such that network elements can compute available paths for the setup of TE tunnels. Because the IGP information is not flooded across areas or IS-IS levels, the head end node does not have any visibility of the entire path. Hence, the head end node cannot compute the entire path. The TE tunnel information is therefore loosely specified, and the head end node does not have "strict" knowledge of hops beyond its area.

To set up the TE tunnels across the areas, the TE tunnels must be set up from the head end to the area boundary router (ABR) and then from the ABR to the destination or the tail end. A feature called loose explicit provides the ability to set up loose route to the ABR and then let the ABR set up the rest of the tunnel to the tail end. MPLS TE signaling extensions enable the setup of tunnels via the ABR.

More details regarding Inter-Area TE can be found in *Traffic Engineering with MPLS*.

Inter-Autonomous System TE

Inter-autonomous system (Inter-AS) traffic engineering with MPLS can be performed in a manner similar to the inter-area TE. In this case, the TE tunnel is set up from the head end to the autonomous system boundary router (ASBR) and then from the ASBR to the tail end. There are two modes in Inter-AS TE:

- **One flat IGP across the ASes**—Both ASes have the same IGP with no hierarchy areas or levels. All IGP information from one AS is redistributed and flooded into the other AS. Nodes learn the bandwidth and topology information, and TE tunnels can be set up between nodes whether they are in the same or different AS.

- **Different IGP areas in different ASes**—In this case, there might be no IGP connectivity between ASBRs. The ASBRs might connect only via BGP. This is the most common case of ASBR peering, when the ASBRs are directly connected to each other. In such cases, the IGP information must be force-flooded so the head end gets the information about other nodes whether they are in the same or different AS.

The signaling methodology is the same as inter-area, in which a loose route is specified at the head end with ASBRs and the ASBRs in turn expand the route information and signal to the tail of tunnel.

Due to a separation of areas and ASes, the topology change information is sent across areas or ASes. Thus, reoptimization cannot be triggered at the head end when changes occur in the tail end area or AS. To handle this case, a technique called *loose path reoptimization* is used where the ASBR informs the head end of a better available path in the tail end area or AS. The head then decides to reoptimize the tunnel.

Inter-AS TE is useful in building a scenario called Virtual POP. Imagine that a service provider wants to establish a remote POP in a different geographical location to serve its customers. This location might be in a different country or region where this service provider does not have connectivity or facilities access. However, in this geographic location, the service provider has an agreement to transport traffic through the local provider's network. In this case, the SP is AS1 and the local provider's network is AS2. The TE tunnels must be set up through the local provider network to the co-located equipment of the service provider. Hence, the TE tunnels in this case must span AS1 and AS2 from head to tail.

Remember that both inter-area TE and Inter-AS TE signaling extensions of loose hop reoptimization and forced flooding are useful when the dynamic bandwidth control of the TE tunnels is used. An offline tool can also be used to recompute paths and the placement of TE tunnels across the areas. Offline tools provide a global view of the network and can provide better reoptimization. However, offline tools are more static and cannot react to network changes dynamically, though they do provide immense control of the network. As a decision-maker, you must evaluate whether the explicit control and the global network optimization is worth the complexity. In your network and topology, dynamic control might be capable of providing good optimization and reacting to network/topology changes quickly enough that offline tools might not be required.

Quality of Service and TE

So far, we have not specified anything about data plane policing or controlling incoming traffic mapped onto the TE tunnels. This is done by design because the MPLS TE specification does not define any data plane interaction and does not specify any bandwidth reservation. A data plane can be set up for quality of service (QoS) in the same way as DiffServ, whereas a control plane sets up the TE tunnels on links that meet bandwidth constraints. The available bandwidth information is useful in computing available paths to a destination, although that information does not result in queue allocation or scheduler bandwidth change at any given hop.

Traffic Handling of Delay-Sensitive Traffic

By considering link delays as a constraint, TE tunnels for low-delay traffic can be steered onto specific low-delay paths.

The topic of QoS is discussed at length in Chapter 9, "Quality of Service." For the purpose of this chapter, we specify that TE tunnel setup is independent of data plane policing, queuing, and marking. However, packets with specific markings can be mapped to specific tunnels using class-based tunnel selection (CBTS) for routing voice traffic or by delaying sensitive traffic onto specific tunnels bound for a specific destination.

When traffic is mapped to a TE tunnel, based on TE tunnel bandwidth, a policer can be set up to police the incoming traffic and ensure it does not exceed traffic contract (in this case, tunnel bandwidth). Queuing and weighted random early discard (WRED) can be enabled on the head end and mid point nodes so that marked packets get the needed per-hop behavior to ensure the correct delivery of traffic.

Inter-AS TE can also be a means of signaling bandwidth requirements across ASes between providers. By ensuring the appropriate policing of traffic and checking the tunnel counters, providers can determine how much traffic is flowing between autonomous systems and between specific source and destination routers (in this case, the tunnel head and the tail). For example, out-of-contract traffic can be either rejected by the policer or marked as nonconforming to be dropped by WRED thresholds should congestion occur. More details on this and how DiffServ can be used with traffic engineering can be found in Chapter 9.

Protection and Restoration

One of the most popular applications of MPLS TE is fast reroute. FRR is the capability to reroute traffic quickly onto a backup link, path, or tunnel when the primary path fails due to link, node, or primary path failure.

Here is how it works: MPLS allows label stacking where one application label can be stacked onto another label, providing a nested hierarchy of LSPs. This technique is exploited in the fast reroute application to set up a short backup or bypass tunnel around a network element (link, node, or path). When the primary link, node, or path fails, the node detecting the failure quickly reroutes traffic onto the backup tunnel—a tunnel that is set up for this purpose. This reroute can happen very quickly (in 50ms or less), which is comparable to SONET Automatic Protection Switching (APS)—reroute times.

The sections that follow describe the three main types of fast reroute: link protection, node protection, and path protection.

Link Protection

As evident by the name itself, link protection involves protecting against link failures. These days, links have become more reliable, but statistics still show that most unplanned failures in the network occur because of link failures. So, protecting against link failures is necessary in any network. To protect against link failures, you can use multiple circuits or SONET APS–protected circuits. This can result in expensive circuits. Because providing circuits is usually a recurring cost—especially if the fiber circuit is not owned by the carrier—you might want to reduce the operating cost by eliminating the redundant circuits if fast reroute of traffic can be done by using other paths in the network. Link protection enables you to send traffic to the next hop on a backup tunnel should the primary link fail. Off-course link protection does not work if the only means of reaching the next hop is through the primary link (singly connected cases). How does this work?

FRR link protection is an ingenious technique. A node must be configured for link protection, and a backup tunnel is established around the link that needs to be protected to the same next hop. When the link fails, the node detects the link failure and, without changing the labels of the primary tunnels, imposes the backup tunnel label on top of the MPLS packet. When the packet comes out of the backup tunnel, the primary tunnel label is exposed. Because the backup tunnel always terminates onto the next hop, for link protection, the receiving node understands the primary tunnel label and switches the packet onto the destination. This is shown in Figure 8-4.

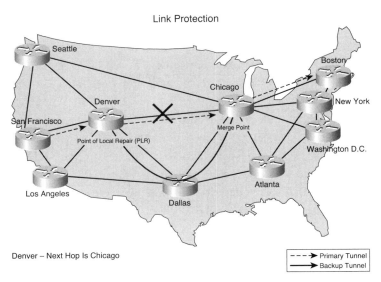

Figure 8-4   Link Protection

For illustration purposes, we have chosen the same topology discussed earlier. In this example, we are trying to protect the link between Denver and Chicago. Primary tunnels flow between other cities via Denver and Chicago over the link to be protected. More than one primary tunnel can be flowing over the link between Denver and Chicago. A backup tunnel is now preestablished between Denver and Chicago via Dallas and is configured to protect the link between Denver and Chicago in Figure 8-4, irrespective of the number of tunnels traversing that link.

When the failure occurs, the following steps follow: The Denver router detects the failure either via loss of carrier or SONET alarm. Then the Denver router takes the MPLS packets destined for Chicago on all the tunnels and imposes a new label on top for the backup tunnel. The Denver router then forwards it toward Dallas. The Dallas router can then swap the backup tunnel label to implicit null due to PHP and forward the MPLS packets to the Chicago router with the primary tunnel label exposed. Finally, the Chicago router looks up the incoming label and switches the packet toward the destination normally.

Node Protection

In link protection, the backup tunnel is always set up to the next hop node and the failure detection is performed based on loss of carrier or SONET alarms. In node protection, the mechanism described is similar to the link protection except that the backup tunnel is always set up to the node beyond the next hop—that is, next-next hop.

Upon detection of failure via a hello timeout, the point of local repair (PLR) node reroutes traffic onto the backup tunnel to the next-next-hop (nnhop). However, when MPLS packets emerge at the tail of the nnhop backup tunnel, they might not have the right labels for the merge point to carry the traffic further. To avoid discarding traffic at the tail of the backup tunnel, the head of the backup tunnel (also known as the point of local repair) swaps the primary tunnel label to the label expected by the merge point and then imposes the backup tunnel label. This ensures that the MPLS packets coming out of the backup tunnel carry the correct labels and hence are switched to the correct destination. This is illustrated by the example shown in Figure 8-5.

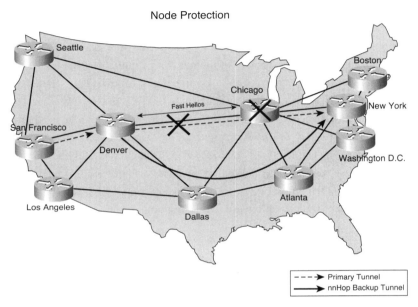

Figure 8-5 *Node Protection*

Again for simplicity, we consider the same topology as before. In this example, we are trying to protect against the failure of the Chicago node. So, from the Denver node, the primary tunnels always flow through the Chicago node. Assume node protection is set up. The Denver node and the Chicago node are configured for hellos and a backup tunnel is placed between the Denver router and New York router via Dallas and Atlanta.

The fast hellos between the Denver node and Chicago node time out when the Chicago node fails. The Denver node had previously recorded the labels used by nodes downstream, such as those used by Chicago, Boston, and New York. Thus, the Denver node now swaps the primary tunnel label to the label expected by the New York node instead of the label for the Chicago node (because it has failed). The Denver node then imposes the label for the backup nnhop tunnel and forwards the packet toward Dallas. When the packets appear at New York from Atlanta, they have the primary tunnel label; therefore, the New York node is now able to switch the traffic to the destination without any problems.

Path Protection

The last type of protection mechanism, called path protection, is the ability to protect one or more end-to-end paths via a preestablished or predetermined backup tunnel. This is always end-to-end protection and is similar to the shadow PVC model often used in the ATM networks of today. The backup tunnel is link and node diverged from the primary tunnel, such that if any element (link or node) along the primary path fails, the head end reroutes the traffic onto the backup path, as shown in Figure 8-6.

Many schemes for backup can be used, such as 1 to N or 1 to 1. In the 1-to-N scheme, there is one backup tunnel for N primary tunnels between the same pair of routers. The 1-to-1 back up implies that for every primary tunnel a backup tunnel exists. The number of backup tunnels needed for path protection is twice the number of primary tunnels.

However, the failure detection time is the longest in the path protection mechanism. This is due to the fact that if any network element fails along the path, the notification for this failure has to reach the head end of the TE tunnel for the traffic to be rerouted.

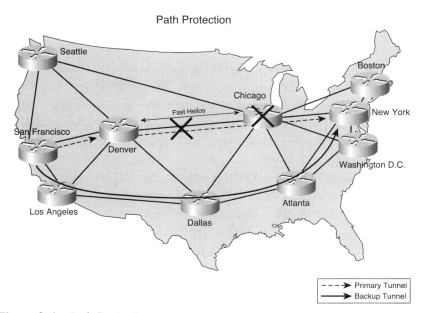

Figure 8-6   *Path Protection*

Usage Scenarios

MPLS FRR can be deployed with or without PE-to-PE or P-to-P traffic engineering. As stated earlier, backup tunnels are set up in the network based on the network element, link, or node to be protected. For traffic to be rerouted onto backup tunnels, it must be associated with a primary tunnel. The primary tunnel can be end to end or be one hop or two hops.

One-hop tunnel implies that the primary tunnel is only to the next hop and no further. Due to PHP, there are no labels for the primary tunnel—a backup tunnel is set up around the link to be protected. When the link fails, the primary tunnel to the next hop fails and the node reroutes traffic onto the backup tunnel. This method of one-hop tunnel can be used to easily deploy link protection. Several details about MPLS FRR deployment are explained in *Traffic Engineering with MPLS*.

Scalability of Protection Mechanisms

In choosing a protection mechanism, you must consider the scalability of each of these mechanisms. Link protection is the simplest approach. It requires only explicitly creating TE tunnels around the failed links and tying them to either one-hop tunnels or PE/P-to-PE/P tunnels. The number of backup tunnels required for link protection is approximately equal to the number of links in the network. More tunnels might be needed should bandwidth protection be required. This is because multiple backups can be required to back up a single link due to the unavailability of a single back tunnel with the same bandwidth as the link being protected. If only connectivity protection is desired, with no bandwidth guarantees during failures, a single backup tunnel backing up all the primary tunnels is sufficient.

In node protection, for each node protected with p degree of connectivity, the number of backup tunnels required is exactly p tunnels assuming no bandwidth protection is needed. So, for a complete network with n nodes, the total number of backup tunnels required is as follows:

$\sum np_i$ for $i=1$ to n, where p_i is the degree of connectivity of the ith node.

In approximation, if the degree of connectivity is a constant p, the number of backup tunnels required is $n*p$. Link protection requires fewer backup tunnels than node protection.

In path protection, the number of backup tunnels corresponds to the number of primary tunnels depending on the protection scheme used. If 1-for-1 protection is deployed, the number of backup tunnels needed is equal to the number of primary tunnels. If an N:1 protection mechanism is required, the number of backup tunnels depends on the number of parallel tunnels between two pairs of nodes. Irrespective of the path protection scheme used, the number of tunnels required is far more than for link and node protection methods. For example, let us consider a network with n nodes.

The number of primary tunnels in the network is $n(n-1)$ n^2 number of tunnels. If a 1-to-1 backup schema is used, the number of backup tunnels required is also equal to n^2. For a small number of n, the number of tunnels for each scheme might be small and manageable; however, for a reasonable number of nodes, the total number of tunnels needed with path protection is $2n^2$.

Path protection, though, is a well-understood model and is analogous to the shadow PVCs model used in ATM/Frame Relay networks of today. Providers have more experience with the shadow PVC model and have developed tools to place PVCs in today's ATM or Frame Relay networks.

Scaling MPLS TE

One of the most common concerns of operators is the scalability of MPLS TE. Some of the common objections used are stated as follows:

Myth: MPLS TE uses RSVP and RSVP does not scale, so how can MPLS TE scale?

Reality: Actually, no per-flow reservation scales well in the network core. However for MPLS, the tunnels are created for all traffic between two nodes of a certain traffic type. For instance, all voice traffic flowing between two nodes flows through one tunnel. Moreover, RSVP used in MPLS TE is different from RSVP signaling used in integrated services (IntServ). In IntServ, RSVP reservations perform per-flow policing and queue reservation; in MPLS TE RSVP signaling is not associated with any queue reservation or policing, by design. Even the admission control is for an aggregate traffic flow between POPs and not per flow. In summary, RSVP for MPLS TE scales well with thousands of tunnels. Cisco has tested up to 2000 head ends and 15,000 midpoints on its core routers.

Myth: RSVP is stateful and is also a soft-state protocol. It requires too much state, and it needs to be refreshed periodically.

Reality: Yes, RSVP is a soft-state protocol. However, after the labels are distributed, the TE tunnel is in place until it is torn down. No per-flow policing is done, and the tunnel state is maintained with periodic refreshes. The protocol has been enhanced to add refresh reduction so that refresh messages can be bundled or aggregated together for efficient processing. This results in far fewer refresh messages. Moreover, with best design practices, this is not an issue and tunnel timers can be tuned to handle the pacing of refreshes and appropriate handling of messages.

Myth: Managing large number of tunnels is too difficult.

Reality: Yes, managing TE is an overhead but not to the degree it is assumed. TE and explicit routing provide some additional gains with respect to additional bandwidth inventory or link, node, and path protection against failures. Tools for management are available. Moreover, configuration is simplified with Autotunnel and Automesh, where the tunnels are set up automatically to the routers in the same domain.

MPLS Traffic Engineering and Multicast

Another emerging application of MPLS traffic engineering is bandwidth-guaranteed multicast for video distribution. Currently, multicast traffic does not use LSPs in the network and traverses natively as IP. Recent developments in MPLS traffic engineering enable the building of point-multipoint TE tunnels using MPLS TE control plane and map multicast traffic to these TE tunnels for efficient packet replication in the core. Here is a simple explanation of how it works.

As you learned earlier, MPLS uses RSVP messages to build traffic engineering tunnels. In the point-to-multipoint case, you have multiple tail ends and a single head end for the traffic-engineered tunnel. To build a point-to-multipoint tunnel, the head end must send PATH messages to all the tail end nodes with the same tunnel ID. The PATH messages are received by the tail ends, and the tail end nodes respond with a RESV message. While the RESV message travels back toward the head end node, along the path, each core node performs admission control and merges the LSP upstream with the matching tunnel indicated by the tunnel ID. The merged reservation continues upstream toward the head end node, thus creating a multipoint tree from the head end to the tail ends. (See Figure 8-7.)

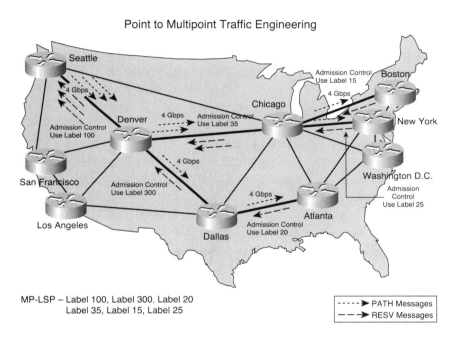

Point to Multipoint Traffic Engineering

Figure 8-7   *Point-to-Multipoint Traffic Engineering*

In this example, we need to send multicast traffic from Seattle to Atlanta, New York, and Boston. Three PATH messages are sent from Seattle to each tail end node in Atlanta, New York, and Boston with the tunnel ID "tunnel1." The tail end nodes reply with a RESV message and label mapping back toward the tunnel head end when the admission control process is complete. The RESV message from Atlanta travels back toward the Denver node and eventually back to the Seattle node. The RESV messages from New York and Boston travel back toward the Denver node via Chicago and then eventually back to Seattle. The Chicago node notices that multiple PATH and RESV messages with the same tunnel ID ("tunnel1") exist. When sending upstream RESV messages toward Denver, the Chicago node merges the two requests coming from New York and Boston with the tunnel ID "tunnel1" when responding with a RESV message to Denver. The Denver node in turn performs a similar merge function for RESV messages coming from Chicago and Dallas, thus creating branching points for traffic at Denver and subsequently at Chicago.

Packets sent from the Seattle node are replicated at each branching point on the tree. The admission control process and the CSPF enable the building of a multipoint tree only on the links that have available bandwidth. Much like the point-to-point TE tunnels for unicast traffic, explicit and dynamic path options can be used for either the explicit placement of P-MP TE tunnels or the dynamic computation using CSPF.

Using point-to-multipoint traffic engineering (P-MP TE), you can efficiently transport multicast traffic across an MPLS network. Video distribution requires the efficient use of network resources—and P-MP TE can certainly help.

Standards and References

The Cisco implementation of MPLS TE supports the IETF standards shown in Table 8-1.

Table 8-1   *TF Standards*

MPLS TE RFCs	RFC Number	
Requirements for Traffic Engineering Over MPLS	2702	Supported
RSVP-TE: Extensions to RSVP for LSP Tunnels	3209	Supported
Applicability Statement for Extensions to RSVP for LSP-Tunnels	3210	Supported
Signaling Unnumbered Links in Resource ReSerVation Protocol – Traffic Engineering (RSVP-TE)	3477	Supported
Framework for MPLS-based Recovery	3469	Supported
Multiprotocol Label Switching (MPLS) Traffic Engineering Management Information Base	3812	Supported
Fast Reroute Extensions to RSVP-TE for LSP Tunnels	4090	Partially supported

Summary

MPLS TE can be useful in networks where links are running close to capacity. Using MPLS TE can help utilize the bandwidth available in nonshortest paths. However, MPLS TE might not be needed if the links have low utilization or if bandwidth can be easily added by lighting up more fiber in the ground (adding more links). Even in networks in which some links are running at capacity, though, MPLS TE can be useful. As illustrated in this chapter's first example, MPLS TE can help redirect traffic in the network, resulting in better utilization and lower traffic loss. It need not always be used in full mesh fashion. For example, MPLS TE can be used just around choke points to redirect traffic in a small portion of the network without adding more bandwidth capacity.

MPLS FRR is the most important application of MPLS TE and is useful in protecting against failures at Layer 3, eliminating the cost of redundant and protected circuits. Many service providers are deploying MPLS FRR, but they are doing so without deploying end-to-end tunnels to exactly achieve a protection solution with one-hop primary tunnels for link protection.

Node and path protection are also useful techniques, depending on the topology of the network. Traffic can also be protected against node failures in distributed platforms using nonstop forwarding of traffic while the control plane is recovering from the failure. Finally, although MPLS TE is not a must-have in the network in which you want to run other MPLS services, it certainly has its benefits. Before deciding on MPLS TE, a cost-benefit analysis must be done to determine whether the benefit it provides is more than the cost it might incur. For smaller networks, metric manipulation can be sufficient for better traffic engineering. However, as the network size grows, metric manipulation can have a number of undesired effects. MPLS TE can be much easier to manage and responds much more dynamically to changing topologies than metric readjustment in large networks.

CHAPTER 9

QUALITY OF SERVICE

Quality of service (QoS) is an important aspect of any IP service offering. QoS helps define an important component of the service level agreement (SLA): packet delivery. The guaranteed and timely delivery of packets is necessary for applications, such as voice and video. The unsatisfactory delivery of packets results in an undesired user experience that might eventually result in a negative perception of the network. The existing user experience of the Internet has defined a grade of service called *best effort*. This Internet grade of service is usually assumed to be best effort packet delivery with no security or bandwidth guarantees but providing ubiquitous presence. Packets are delivered to the destination if they can be with no regard for delay, jitter, or even guarantee of delivery. This might be enough for most applications we commonly use, such as web browsing, e-mail, and Internet chat.

On the other hand, when it comes to the delivery of business-critical traffic, in most cases, best effort delivery of traffic is no longer sufficient. Many applications require bandwidth guarantees, and some also require delay and jitter guarantees. Any service delivered with MPLS must also be capable of delivering QoS to meet the needs of business-critical applications. Applications, such as voice and video, have stringent requirements with respect to jitter and packet loss. These days, highly efficient codecs are used that can mask some delay and jitter with buffering, encoding, and decoding techniques. Nevertheless, despite these efficient codecs, bandwidth, delay, and jitter guarantees from the network are still needed for better quality of experience (QoE).

This chapter discusses the QoS requirements and the available QoS tools and techniques of an IP network. It also explains how the IP QoS can be further enhanced using MPLS components.

Problem Statement

Because a high number of enterprises and service providers (SP) are considering IP/MPLS for their next-generation network (NGN) convergence, the expectation of an IP/MPLS network is high. We have often seen IP/MPLS networks compared to FR/ATM networks and FR/ATM QoS. Enterprises are used with the following bandwidth models:

- Frame Relay committed information rate (CIR).

- ATM constant bit rate (CBR); also referred to as guaranteed bit rate service.

- ATM variable bit rate (VBR) (nonreal-time [NRT] and real-time [RT] for delivery of video services).

- However, no such bandwidth or bounded delay services are possible in a plain IP network. MPLS and QoS can certainly help mimic the FR/ATM QoS behavior, though.

Enterprises commonly use ATM and Frame Relay as access circuits into provider networks, even for IP access. They have an expectation of peak and sustained information rates based on the connection-oriented nature of Frame Relay or the ATM network. MPLS has label-switched paths (LSP), so it is often wrongly assumed that MPLS brings the connection-oriented nature of the circuit-switched world to the IP network. Although this might be true because packets are always sent along a designated LSP, no one-to-one relationship exists between the sender and the receiver for an LSP in packet networks. In fact, at the receiving end, packets can come in from any source along the same LSP. This notion is referred to as the *multipoint-to-point capability* of MPLS. Due to the lack of a one-to-one relationship between the source and destination, not all the connection-oriented QoS models can be applied. However, enough similarities exist between traditional ATM and Frame Relay networks and MPLS networks to pick up a number of components and apply them in the MPLS network. Packet loss is also an important component of service delivery and SLAs. Although packet loss can be tackled on an end-to-end basis using retransmission for TCP, it cannot be handled with the User Datagram Protocol (UDP). Packet loss can occur due to network changes. Although some failures, such as link or node failures, are out of the operator's control, network nodes must not drop packets in the queues unless by design (for instance, dropping low-priority traffic). As an example, hardware must be capable of guaranteeing the delivery of the highest-priority traffic no matter how congested the low-priority queues are. Packet loss within a network node is a function of hardware design and the implementation of queuing, policing, and other QoS functions.

Voice and video traffic needs bandwidth, delay, and jitter guarantees from the network in addition to a low packet loss guarantee. Because of the nondeterministic behavior of packet networks, the QoS guarantees provided are not the same as those provided by circuit-switched networks. IP QoS models, such as DiffServ, provide a method of packet delivery that allows the prioritization of sensitive traffic. This DiffServ QoS model is widely deployed by service providers and enterprises. Given the deployment of DiffServ IP QoS, the constrained based shortest path first (CSPF) capability of MPLS traffic engineering, and the admission control, we must consider whether we can build a model that combines these elements to deliver better QoS than a plain old IP network does and that can mimic as closely as possible the behavior of the circuit-based QoS model?

IP QoS

To address the problem statement, let us first try to understand what IP QoS can and cannot offer and understand some basic building blocks of QoS.

QoS Building Blocks

QoS has a foundation of basic building blocks that allow traffic characterization or classification, policing, queuing and random discard, scheduling, and transmission. Each of these building blocks plays a vital role in implementing QoS in IP networks.

- **Traffic classification and marking**—To provide the right QoS behavior for applications, traffic needs to be classified. Traffic *classification* simply means identifying traffic types for treatment in the network. Traffic can be classified based on any criteria. A simple criterion is by source and destination address; other criteria could be the protocol type or the application type. A third one could be traffic marking, and a fourth one could be by deep packet inspection and the identification of payload types, such as web URLs, transactions, interactive gaming, and so on. After the traffic is classified, it is marked for appropriate treatment in the network. The marking is done by setting the DiffServ field or the IP type of service field in the IP header.

- **Policing**—Traffic policing needs to be done to identify whether the incoming traffic is in contract or out of contract. Traffic is supposed to be in contract if the user is sending traffic at the specified interval and at a specified rate (and not exceeding that rate and frequency). A policer determines whether too much traffic is coming in and sets up traffic for transmission or discard. For example, traffic can be policed and out-of-contract traffic can be re-marked with a different (lower-grade) QoS label for best effort service delivery so that if congestion occurs, the out-of-contract traffic can be dropped. If the operator does not police, it does not know whether the links are oversubscribed. Policing is key to determining the actual over-subscription factor. For better traffic control, policing can be selectively applied to various QoS classes to meet specific QoS delivery targets or traffic contracts.

- **Queuing and random discard**—When the incoming traffic rate is greater than the outgoing traffic rate, the traffic must be queued; otherwise, it is discarded. Traffic can be queued based on individual flows or based on some aggregate QoS groups or classes. For example, 100 voice flows can be queued separately. This results in 100 queues where each queue can be serviced fairly or 100 flows can all be queued into the same class queue, and the class queue can be serviced at an aggregate level with the highest priority. By queuing flows separately, isolation is achieved between flows, so one flow can be prevented from potentially hogging the bandwidth of other flows. Flows cannot hog bandwidth due to standard codecs, but it is indeed true for voice, video, mission-critical data, and best-effort data. A video flow can hog bandwidth and starve the ERP traffic or voice traffic if they are both lined up in the same queue. However, in per-flow queuing, when you have a large number of flows, you need a large number of queues and some weighted fair queuing mechanism—which could be a scale issue. The method most frequently recommended is to queue voice packets in the highest-priority queue and place video and ERP traffic in separate queues to provide isolation and maintain QoS delivery guarantees. Random discard can be applied on a queue when the queue builds up due to a high incoming rate of traffic. Random discard or weighted random early discard (WRED) can be done on a queue to discard lower-priority packets or out-of-contract packets from the queue; with this technique, you can avoid losing the higher-priority packets. Assuming the flows use Transmission Control Protocol (TCP), they can be recovered by retransmitting them even if some packets are lost. For a detailed explanation of random early drop (RED) and the effect it has on the network, see the [RED], RFC 2597 and Figure 9-1.

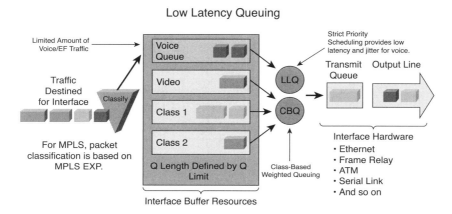

Figure 9-1 *Queuing and RED*

- **Scheduler**—Queues can be serviced at a specified rate. If all queues are serviced fairly, this is called *weighted fair queuing (WFQ)*, meaning queues are serviced in a fair manner such that equal amounts of data are transmitted from each queue in one cycle. The queues can be weighted to provide a bias for the high-priority traffic. If class-based queuing is done, each class can be serviced at a specified rate to provide fairness to all traffic. Alternatively, a *strict priority scheduler* is one in which all traffic in a queue is serviced first until no packets remain in the queue. Only then are other queues served. If the priority queue always has packets to send, other queues could get starved.

- **Transmission**—Packet transmission on the wire is also an important factor. For example, voice packets are small (usually 64 bytes), whereas data packets could be large. Especially on low-speed links, where the serialization delay is large, voice packets becoming stuck behind the large data packets can affect the link delay budgets and ultimately the voice quality. You might want to fragment larger packets into smaller chunks and interleave the voice packets to deal with link delay budgets. These serialization delays don't have any effect on high-speed links. The serialization delay is most pronounced in sub-T1/E1 rates or data rates of 768 Kbps or less.

The building blocks previously described are used in any QoS model, whether it is signaled QoS (specific source signals for QoS) or provisioned QoS (manually preprovisioned by the operator).

By using the previously described building blocks, IP networks can provide a statistical guarantee for the traffic. *Statistical guarantee* refers to a specified delivery of data for a certain percent in time—for instance, a net data rate of X Kbps 98 percent of the time. In contrast, ATM networks can deliver an absolute guarantee by delivering a data rate of X Kbps 100 percent of the time using CBR services.

IETF has developed two main models for delivering QoS. Both use the basic QoS building blocks of queuing, policing, and the discard mechanisms to deliver QoS. The first model developed is a per-flow QoS model known as Integrated Services (IntServ). Because of scalability issues with per-flow models, IETF also developed an aggregate model called DiffServ. Each of these models classifies the incoming traffic, polices it if necessary, queues it and applies WRED, and schedules the traffic on the wire. However, the differences lie in the *granularity*, or the amount of state stored in each of these models. See Figure 9-2 for a quick comparison of IntServ and DiffServ.

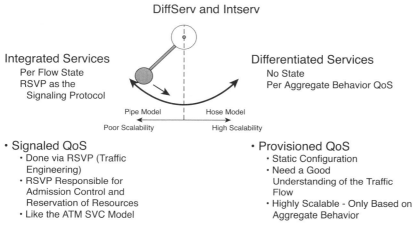

Figure 9-2 *Integrated Services Versus Differentiated Services*

By using these IP QoS models, traffic can be prioritized and delivered to the destination. The next section discusses these QoS models in a bit more detail.

IntServ

As we mentioned earlier, IntServ is a per-flow QoS model. In this model, reservation is made for every flow that is classified by the five tupple (source address, destination address, source port, destination port, and an IP TOS marking, policed for traffic contract, and placed into its own queue. Another important element of IntServ is signaling and admission control.

IntServ uses RSVP signaling for setting up flow information along the path. RSVP path messages are sent from the source to the destination. At each hop along the path, the flow state is initialized. When the PATH message reaches the destination, the destination device can decide to accept the reservation and send a RESV message back to the sender along the same path. Admission control is done at each hop to see whether bandwidth exists on the link and queue space is available on the node. The RESV message travels hop-by-hop back to the source. At each hop, a policer is set up to police the flow for the bandwidth, a queue is allocated, and admission control is performed.

IntServ is a great model for per-flow QoS and is the only model that provides admission control on a per-flow basis. However, at the core of the network are thousands and maybe even hundreds of thousands of flows. Per-flow QoS therefore doesn't scale well at the core of the network due to the amount of state that needs to be maintained for these hundreds of thousands of flows. Aggregation of flows is needed to scale the IntServ model to a large number of flows. This can be achieved by either creating fat reservations that aggregate individual flow reservations or using the traffic engineering tunnels to aggregate the individual RSVP flows. Another form of aggregation could be done by just queuing flows based on classes but still performing admission control on a per-flow basis. We explore this option a bit more in subsequent sections. The admission control capability of RSVP makes this protocol useful in VoIP QoS. It provides a feedback mechanism to voice signaling about availability of QoS from the network when voice calls are set up, rather than transmitting packets only to realize that the network did not have enough capacity. Plus, it breaks down not only the new flow, but also existing flows.

DiffServ

In contrast to IntServ, DiffServ is more coarsely grained and aggregate-based and thus far more scalable. Here traffic is classified into traffic classes, and all traffic grouped into a class requires the same treatment from the network. Each class represents a per-hop behavior (PHB) that can be distinctly identified from other classes. This QoS behavior between classes can vary on any QoS parameter. For example, all voice traffic can be classified into an expedited forwarding (EF) DiffServ class, or all bandwidth-guaranteed data can be classified as an assured forwarding (AF) class. Both EF and AF classes are defined by the IETF DiffServ standard. EF class means data must be forwarded through the node in an "expedited" manner. This class is characterized by low delay and low jitter. Similarly, an AF class is characterized by a bounded delay and is bandwidth guaranteed. For more details on DiffServ, read the IETF RFC 2474, RFC 2475, and RFC 2430.

Packet Handling

As mentioned earlier, a per-hop behavior is characterized by QoS parameters, such as bandwidth, delay, jitter, and packet loss. To achieve these characteristics, the basic QoS building blocks can be arranged in such a way that results in the desired behavior. Traffic must be classified, marked, policed for over-subscription, queued, and scheduled for transmission. By adjusting the service ratios of the queues, a desired bandwidth partition can be achieved for that class of traffic.

The Hybrid Model

DiffServ addresses the problem of scalability over IntServ by aggregating flows. However, DiffServ does not have a key component of IntServ, which is admission control. Admission control is key in controlling the over-subscription. By policing, you can determine only the current state of the network. In a DiffServ model, if the traffic is over-subscribed, it is just dropped when congestion occurs. There is no feedback mechanism to the end user whether the traffic is going through or not. For example, in a voice call model, say the eleventh caller comes in on a link with a capacity of ten calls. Without admission control, the eleventh call might be admitted and could result in degrading the quality of all calls currently in progress.

Using the RSVP signaling of IntServ can provide a means of feedback to the voice gateways and end points that no more capacity exists in the network and that the caller should try the call at a later time.

A hybrid model uses the RSVP signaling for the admission control and the feedback mechanism while maintaining aggregate information in the core of the network. For instance, admission control can be done on the EF class queue with a specified bandwidth for voice calls, and the scheduling can be done based on DiffServ, thereby scaling the QoS model extremely well. MPLS adds some variations to these IP QoS models; they are discussed in the paragraphs that follow.

Other methods of call admission control can be overlaid on the network for voice and video. The most common method is call counting, applied on the voice gateway. It is a simpler method because you preprovision bandwidth and restrict the number of calls on any given link. For simpler topologies, such as hub and spoke networks with predictable traffic patterns, the call counting method works well. However, for large mesh networks, the call counting method does not work at all. The network state, and hence available bandwidth, can change at any given time. The most accurate call admission control is based on network resource status, network-based admission control necessary. Flow-based admission control schemes have appeared recently. However, flow-based admission control schemes do not provide any feedback to the end user/station or call (voice/video) terminal about the acceptance or rejection of the call. A signaling protocol, in contrast, can provide that feedback, distinguishing the line busy condition from the end user busy condition.

MPLS QoS

Because MPLS uses an IP network with IP routing protocols, it also uses the same IP QoS models. MPLS QoS does not change the IP DiffServ model of traffic classification, marking, policing, queuing, scheduling, and transmission. However, the IntServ model of IP QoS is different in MPLS networks.

MPLS DiffServ

MPLS DiffServ is similar to IP DiffServ. In MPLS DiffServ, packets are marked with the EXP field instead of the IP TOS/DSCP byte of the IP header. Packets are queued based on the EXP marking, and WRED is applied on that marking. Other basic building blocks remain the same as in IP DiffServ. The IP header byte contains 6 bits for DSCP marking and MPLS labels have only 3 EXP bits; therefore, the number of classes in IP DiffServ can be $2^6 = 64$. In MPLS based on EXP bits, the number of classes can be only $2^3 = 8$. Mapping IP DiffServ classes to MPLS DiffServ classes can be straightforward. However, the MPLS EXP cannot accommodate more than 8 MPLS DiffServ classes because it does not have enough bits. In this case, the IETF RFC states that label values with the EXP field can be treated together as a class of traffic. For example, 8 LSPs with 8 classes of traffic each can be signaled to provide 64 classes of service. The label inferred class of service allows unique LSPs to be set up that can carry a specified class of traffic. These are commonly referred to as *L-LSPs*. A single LSP that carries multiple EXP markings of traffic is commonly referred to as *E-LSP*. Mapping IP DSCP can be done in many ways, with one-to-one or many-to-one mapping. Table 9-1 shows a simple IP CoS/ToS (class of service/type of service field) mapping.

Table 9-1   *IP Type of Service to MPLS Class of Service Mapping*

IP ToS	MPLS EXP	Comment
7	7	Control and management
6	6	Voice
5	5	Video
4	4	Data—Business-critical
3	3	Data
2	2	Data—E-mail, bulk
1	1	Data—Better than best effort
0	0	Best effort—Web

Another example of label-inferred class of service is shown in Table 9-2.

Table 9-2   *Label-Inferred Class of Service*

IP DSCP	MPLS EXP	MPLS Label	Comment
0–7	0–7	10	Lowest class
8–15	0–7	20	Grade 1
16–23	0–7	30	Grade 2
24–31	0–7	40	Grade 3
32–39	0–7	50	Grade 4
40–47	0–7	60	Grade 5
48–55	0–7	70	Grade 6
56–63	0–7	80	Grade 7—Highest grade

Table 9-2 shows some sample buckets of IP DiffServ classes with MPLS DiffServ. MPLS EXP 5 in Grade 3 is differentiated from MPLS EXP 5 in Grade 4 by looking at the labels of 40 and 50. In this example, the queuing must be done based on label classification. Each LSP is called an L-LSP with label-inferred class of service.

Using MPLS DiffServ has some notable advantages. One is that IP DSCP or ToS information can be copied onto the MPLS label header or the MPLS label header can be independently set irrespective of IP ToS/DSCP value. By default, Cisco's devices copy the information, which is referred to as *uniform mode QoS*.

If the MPLS label header is independently set rather than being copied from the ToS/DSCP byte, then depending on the configuration, the IP header information can be retained as is. In this manner, IP QoS is tunneled through the MPLS network; this is referred to as *tunnel mode QoS*. Tunnel mode QoS is important for the following reasons:

- For an unmanaged service, IP QoS values from the customer might or might not be trusted. The provider has two options: either rewrite the IP header with a new QoS value or tunnel the IP QoS through the MPLS QoS. By using independent classification and marking of MPLS packets, the SP avoids any trust issues and is in control of the network.

- The customer packet marking might or might not coincide with the provider markings. For example, a customer might mark all voice packets with ToS 5, whereas the provider might mark the highest grade of service with a 4 and hold the 5 marking for management traffic. Moreover, the customer might like to maintain the QoS values because their local area network (LAN) infrastructure is configured to accommodate the QoS values. In this case, the customer would look for tunneling of its QoS value through the MPLS network.

Tunnel mode QoS is important for CoS transparency in single or multiple networks. Even if the service spans a single or multiple AS with tunnel mode QoS, the transparency can be maintained. The trick is in not copying the QoS value at the ingress PE and not recopying it back from the MPLS header to the IP packet at the penultimate hop (if PHP is used) or at the egress PE (if the ultimate hop or explicit NULL label is used).

Traffic Engineering and DiffServ

As discussed in detail in Chapter 8, "Traffic Engineering," traffic engineering by design is a control plane function and does bandwidth accounting only in the control plane. Traffic engineering keeps track of where tunnels are placed on different links/paths in the network, and DiffServ ensures that traffic receives priority while traversing each of those paths. In other words, DiffServ can be used for appropriate traffic prioritization, whereas traffic engineering places the traffic on different paths. These two independent functions can be used simultaneously in the same network, and together they can be useful in offering a better SLA. For example, delay-sensitive traffic, such as voice and video, can be routed over traffic engineering tunnels that are set up on low delay paths, with voice and data being prioritized differently.

TE tunnels can be set up with constraints, such as bandwidth, delay, and speed of the links. All links can be configured with DiffServ behavior so that packets are queued and scheduled according to MPLS EXP marking. The queuing and scheduling provides priority to packets with higher markings, whereas traffic-engineered LSP provides a steered path through the network. This combination of DiffServ and MPLS traffic engineering is sufficient for most networks to provide QoS-based services. Because the TE tunnels are set up at an aggregate level and through the network core, the scale issues here are similar to MPLS traffic engineering. This means, for all practical purposes, no scale issues exist.

DiffServ-Aware Traffic Engineering

This is different from TE and DiffServ. In the previous section, you saw that DiffServ and TE can be used independently in the network simultaneously. This application of QoS is the reverse of the previous case. In the previous case, the paths were set up by TE tunnels and traffic flowing through those tunnels was marked with MPLS EXP and queued along the path. In this case, each TE tunnel is set up with a stricter constraint for a class of service with a tightly defined bandwidth pool. Link bandwidth is divided into two or more bandwidth pools. MPLS TE then sets up TE tunnels, taking into account each of those bandwidth pools, and does admission control against multiple pools of bandwidth. For a fuller explanation, let us consider an example in detail.

Assume an operator has voice, video, and data traffic to send. The operator would like to use the lowest delay links for voice and the highest bandwidth links for video. Moreover, to avoid nondeterministic behavior, the operator decides to limit each type of traffic carried over any given link such that over-subscription of voice and video is minimal and over-subscription of data is high. In addition, by limiting the amount of each class of traffic on a link, delay and jitter are kept within design bounds for the desired SLA.

To partition each link, the operator has to configure multiple subpools on the link. Assuming a link of capacity of X Mbps, the subpool can be a fraction of X, such as 25 percent or 33 percent of X Mbps. Now this subpool information is flooded in the IGP in the same way that available bandwidth is flooded in the traffic engineering case.

When a traffic engineering application sets up the TE tunnel, the tunnel is specified to be DiffServ-aware by associating a class/subpool with it. This implies that the admission control and bandwidth accounting are done on the subpool of the links and not on the global pool of bandwidth on the link. By setting up tunnels this way, the maximum number of high-priority tunnels can be capped to the subpool bandwidth on any given link. If no subpool information is specified at tunnel setup, then by default the TE application uses the global bandwidth pool for admission control.

Bandwidth pools can be exclusive of each other, or pools can be stacked on each other. The stacked model is referred to as the *Russian doll model*, and the exclusive model is referred to as the *maximum allocation model (MAM)*. In the MAM, the pools are independent of each other and are static with clearly defined boundaries. For example, in the MAM, a link of 10 Mbps can be partitioned in the following way:

- 3 Mbps for voice traffic
- 2 Mbps for video
- 3 Mbps for business-critical traffic
- 2 Mbps for the rest of the data

When you have no traffic to send in the higher-priority pools—in this case voice—the pool bandwidth cannot be used to set up video or data tunnels for business-critical traffic. In other words, the link bandwidth is "hard" partitioned.

In the Russian doll model of bandwidth allocation, the pools are stacked on each other. Here is the same example with the Russian doll model:

- 3 Mbps for voice traffic
- 2 Mbps for video
- 3 Mbps for business-critical data
- 2 Mbps for the rest of data

Notice that the configuration is exactly the same as in MAM. However, there is a key difference: Assume there is only 1 Mbps of voice traffic and only one voice tunnel is set up on the link with 1 Mbps. Also assume you have more than 2 Mbps of video traffic to send. If there is enough data—both business-critical and regular—to take up the next 5 Mbps of bandwidth, the video tunnels can be set up taking up the bandwidth beyond the 2 Mbps limit and utilize the unused voice bandwidth. This conforms to the following in actual practice:

- 3 Mbps of voice
- Up to 5 Mbps of video traffic (it is only 2 Mbps of video if you have a full 3 Mbps of voice to send)
- Up to 8 Mbps of business-critical data (it is only 3 Mbps if you have a full 3 Mbps of voice and 2 Mbps of video)
- Up to full 10 Mbps of regular data (it is only 2 Mbps if you have voice, video, and business-critical data using its full quota)

Any bandwidth model can be made to work. Operators must choose based on which model best suits their operational needs. Operators can also choose to use preemption to preempt lower-priority tunnels. More details on each of these models and each model's pros and cons and variations can be found in IETF RFC 4128.

DiffServ-aware TE is a powerful technique that can be used when tight SLA guarantees are required from the network. However, DiffServ-aware TE is used at the expense of operation complexity. If such tight guarantees and tighter network control are unnecessary, just DiffServ or DiffServ overlay with TE might be sufficient.

MPLS QoS Service Examples

Among Cisco's customers, a great majority have QoS deployed in their networks. Some of them are fairly simple models, such as access network guarantee only; others are very complicated with SLA measurements on delay jitter and packet loss end-to-end.

Here are some examples of QoS-based services that SPs offer.

Point-to-Cloud Model

In this model, the assumption is that the network core has lots of bandwidth. The only bottleneck in this case is the access link. Usually, Frame Relay or ATM is the access mechanism with CIR or SCR guarantees. The network core is over-provisioned with a lot of bandwidth and has no problem handling 2x or 3x of sum of access bandwidth.

The selling model in this QoS-based service is the same as the Frame Relay model. However, the attraction is this: instead of multiple Frame Relay VCs, only a single VC is needed from the site to the PE device. The same Frame Relay characteristics can be applied to the access circuit. This model is embraced by several carriers today and is called IP-enabled Frame Relay. The end user buys a single VC with a CIR to the provider network. Because the VC is not passing through the provider cloud across to the other site, this is also referred to as the *point-to-cloud QoS model.*

Olympic Service Model

The Olympic service model is a simple model with three classes: gold, silver, and bronze. Gold is of course the highest priority, with silver next and bronze last. Gold service is meant for higher-priority applications such as voice or video. It usually has a distinct bandwidth guarantee and a delay bound. Gold traffic is marked with either a 4 or 5 in the MPLS EXP and IP ToS field and is priority or low latency queued. Similarly, silver is marked with a 3 or 2 in the MPLS EXP and IP ToS field and usually has a bandwidth bound associated with it and no delay or jitter guarantees. Bronze is either best effort or is marked by a loose bandwidth bound if it isn't best effort.

This model is simple to provision and is well understood. The numbers of classes are small, so a distinct demarcation line exists between the various classes. The offered SLA is proven by either packet counters or other probes that deliver bandwidth and delay information.

Traffic-Engineered Voice Model

This QoS model uses both MPLS TE and DiffServ and was described previously in the chapter in the section "Traffic Engineering and DiffServ." The MPLS TE is used only for voice traffic to map it coming from the voice gateways into the TE tunnels. The rest of the traffic is sent using DiffServ mechanisms along the shortest paths.

The voice tunnels are set up with bandwidth guarantees on low delay paths. Traffic is mapped using static routing, policy routing, or CoS values onto the TE tunnel. For example, if all the traffic is marked with QoS 5, all the traffic marked as 5 can be mapped to a tunnel.

This model can be layered with the Olympic QoS model and is usually provided as a value-add for better handling of voice traffic.

Virtual Leased Line

A virtual leased line carries data link frames across packet networks. As described in the Layer 2 VPN section, the most important characteristic of virtual leased line is its bandwidth guarantees. By combining AToM functionality with QoS and the ability to explicitly map an L2 circuit to a specific TE tunnel, a bandwidth guarantee can be obtained.

On-Demand QoS

This is a variation on the previously described models. Usually, one of the basic models described in previous sections is used for the provisioning of QoS. However, in this model the user experience of QoS is on demand. The demand and response times vary with providers. In one model, a service provider uses a web portal to request the bandwidth requirements of users, validates them, and then provisions the back end (routers, queues, threshold values, and bandwidth parameters) automatically by adjusting the QoS parameters on the CE and the PE devices.

Another technique used by providers is to set up TE tunnels for the requested period of time between sites to carry the traffic for which QoS is requested on demand. After the demand subsides, the TE tunnel is cleared. For example, an enterprise needs a lot of bandwidth between its headquarters site and backup site at night for data backup. This enterprise might request bandwidth between these two sites only at backup time. Either through the portal method or by contract, the enterprise customer informs the provider of its needs. Then, at the scheduled time, the TE tunnel can be initiated to carry the backup traffic.

Another variation of this model is combining IntServ for explicit admission control with an MPLS network. This is discussed in the next section.

MPLS and IntServ

If IntServ flows are used for bandwidth reservation, then in the core of the MPLS network, these flows can be mapped to either MPLS DiffServ or MPLS TE tunnels. If no QoS configuration is used, the network core has no knowledge of IntServ packets and these IntServ packets are treated as normal IP packets and are label-switched as any other IP packet.

Traffic Flows to MPLS DiffServ Mapping

IntServ flows can be mapped to MPLS DiffServ at the edge. The core MPLS NGN has the aggregate-based DiffServ configuration with MPLS CoS. At the edge router, admission control of the IntServ flows is done on the available DiffServ class queue bandwidth. For instance, on the edge router, if the designated bandwidth for EF traffic is X Kbps, all flows mapped to EF (voice flows) are checked against the available EF bandwidth (available EF bandwidth = X – total bandwidth of the admitted flows) and queued into the EF queue (low-latency queue). This allows admission control on a per-flow basis with aggregation of flows into fewer DiffServ class queues. This scales well because the core routers no longer maintain any flow information; they maintain only queues based on aggregate MPLS CoS.

Tunnel-Based Admission Control

In this model, MPLS TE with DiffServ or the DiffServ-aware TE model is used in the core of the network. TE tunnels are set up to carry voice traffic only. Voice gateways or end points use classic RSVP or IntServ for bandwidth reservation of individual flows. When an individual RSVP flow is signaled at the PE, the admission control is done on the tunnel bandwidth and the flow is admitted or rejected based on the available bandwidth of the tunnel rather than the interface bandwidth. Using IntServ gives you the ability to provide feedback about the QoS reservation to the voice end point/gateway. This feedback is now more accurate because it is based on the specific tunnel bandwidth.

TE tunnels can be resized or expanded should more voice calls come in. New tunnels can also be spawned to accommodate more traffic. These techniques of call control are out of the scope of this book. Decision makers just need to understand that complicated techniques can be applied for some finetuning of the network to deliver stringent QoS to the users.

Standards and References

This chapter has highlighted several options for network operators and designers. These are all covered in various standards documents. Following is a list of IETF documents that can be reviewed for a detailed understanding of the technology:

- DiffServ in MPLS networks
- MPLS TEg
- DiffServ-aware TE with MPLS
- RSVP aggregation with MPLS

Summary

MPLS QoS is a fundamental component of an MPLS offering. You do not need to have MPLS to provide a QoS in the IP network because of the options through MPLS, such as DiffServ-aware TE and MPLS QoS. However, it is often argued that an MPLS network provides much better QoS than an IP network.

QoS is typically associated with SLAs and performance guarantees. There are two types of guarantees, and in fact the the word *guarantee* as used in an SLA can have two different meanings: an absolute guarantee or a statistical guarantee. In practice, providers of IP services use the term *statistical guarantee* to describe a specified quality level of a certain percent of the time at a given level of demand. This is in fact reasonable because the traffic demand is statistical and in effect unbounded.

An IP/MPLS NGN can provide an SLA that is an almost absolute guarantee for data rates, delay, and packet loss by using a combination of admission control and MPLS DiffServ. The admission control function enables the rejection of calls when the network cannot guarantee QoS. By separating the admission control function from data plane queuing, a compromise is struck between absolute QoS and scalability.

This chapter has covered the basic building blocks of IP QoS and discussed how these building blocks can be used in an MPLS network to deliver QoS to end customers. MPLS QoS provides a means to deliver a stringent QoS model on a packet network. Combined with MPLS TE, MPLS QoS can provide a powerful tool for delivering tight boundary SLAs. For finer control of network QoS, DiffServ-aware TE is a useful tool.

CHAPTER 10

MULTICAST AND NGNs

As networks and services converge toward a next-generation network (NGN) service architecture, you have the opportunity to offer valued-added services to both the business customer and the consumer.

Multicast is increasingly becoming useful for content distribution and video streaming in networks. Further, with the emergence of IPTV, multicast is a key foundation for the development and deployment of IPTV service. From the customer perspective, the network is capable of providing the desired application performance, often referred to as *quality of experience (QoE)* as a metric for "perceived performance value" by a consumer. For the enterprise or service provider (SP) implementing multicast, the expected benefits are bandwidth and server efficiency and network optimization. Gaming and mobile applications also use multicast technology.

Figure 10-1 summarizes the applications that use multicast.

Multicast in NGN Architecture

Three Key Service Trends	Multicast Component
Broadband Consumer Service Enablement	YES
Triple-play, Gaming, Content Delivery	Video component in Triple Play service is 90% Multicast Video
Peer-to-Peer Applications	Multicast Games: Half-Life, Counter-Strike Peer-to-Peer: Multicast Kazaa, Bit-Torrent
Mass Delivery of Customized Services	
Flexible Service bundling	
Evolution of Current SP Offerings to Enterprises	YES
L1 Bandwidth, L2VPN, L3VPN with Value-Added Services	Multicast VPN as a L3VPN Service for IPv4 and IPv6 Multicast over Pseudowire, VPLS
Improving OPEX associated with delivery of ATM, FR	
Customized Service Delivery and Bundling	
Converged Wireless and Wire Line Services	YES
Enhanced Mobility between Fixed and Wireless Services	Multicast and Mobile IP Integration: Department of Defense, Emergency Services, Hospitals Multicast Support for 3G Chipset in CDMA
IMS, 2G Transition to 3G & Integration of Fixed and Mobile	

Figure 10-1 *Multicast in NGN Architecture*

This chapter describes how multicast can integrate into MPLS networks for easy migration from existing environments to MPLS VPN environments. The basic principles of a multicast VPN implementation are discussed. Details of deploying multicast are found in the Cisco Press book *Developing IP Multicast Networks*.

This chapter also provides an overview of multicast and applications that can be deployed with the technology. We explore the security and management issues associated with multicast. The chapter focuses on multicast VPN service constructs as a foundation for Layer 3-based service development.

Problem Statement

The basic service provided by a multicast VPN (MVPN) is permitting an enterprise to transparently interconnect its private network across a service provider's network backbone. The use of an MVPN to interconnect an enterprise network in no way affects how an enterprise network is administered, nor does it change enterprise connectivity with the rest of the world. It is an artifact of MVPN service that the enterprise network is not visible in the backbone.

As a result, private address administration in the enterprise is unaffected, and MVPNs do not alter the existing requirements for communication between private and public addresses. Until recently, only unicast constructs had been supported in MPLS VPN. However, VPN customers now require multicast connectivity because applications such as videostreaming need multicast and service providers do want to offer these value-added services to such customers. Without MVPN, the workaround has been to use point-to-point generic routing encapsulation (GRE) tunnels from CE to CE. Such an implementation, however, ultimately is not scalable due to traffic and administrative overhead. In addition, such an implementation can be linked to similar Layer 2 VPN scalability issues, such as

(N*(N-1))/2), as was discussed earlier in the book. Excessive replication of traffic from a local CE to a remote CE does not provide for efficiency of data flow for the transit of multicast applications across the core, as shown in Figure 10-2.

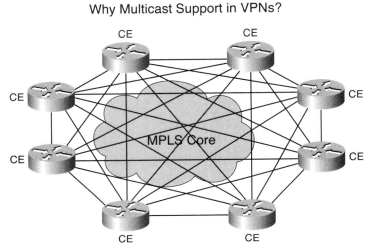

Why Multicast Support in VPNs?

Point-to-point tunneling removes the benefits of multicast.
Traffic has to be replicated by the CE router for each remote CE router.
Traffic in the core will be multiplied by the number of CE routers.

Figure 10-2 *Why Multicast Support in VPNs?*

What are the challenges? Core provider (P) routers should have no knowledge of VPN customer source addresses; this lack of knowledge allows the VPN customer group (and source) address spaces to overlap to provide optimal traffic forwarding in the core. For multicast traffic, this generally implies the use of multicast protocols in the core. Furthermore, core stability must be ensured because multicast applications are sensitive to error conditions—hence, the requirement for MVPN to address these challenges.

MPLS Multicast VPN Overview

MVPN enables a service provider to transport his multicast traffic across MPLS packet-based core networks for IP VPN customers and to implement the "ships in the night" approach with MPLS—that is, the coexistence of separate routing constructs. The SP does not participate in customer multicast routing, and the MVPN configuration is performed only on the PEs, allowing for transparency of the SP network.

Some key components of MVPN include:

- **Multicast domain (MD)**—A domain that consists of a set of VRFs capable of transmitting multicast to each other.

- **Multicast VRF (MVRF)**—A VRF that supports both unicast and multicast forwarding tables.

- **Multicast distribution tunnel (MDT)**—Used to carry multicast C-packets between PEs in a common MVPN. It takes the form of a multicast tree in the core network.

The two additional components used in a Cisco implementation are as follows:

- **Default-MDT**—The Default-Multicast Distribution Tunnel (Default-MDT) group is used for control traffic, and to flood the multicast channel for dense mode and low-bandwidth groups.

- **Data-MDT**—The MDT group is created on demand for MVPN (S,G) pairs, usually high-bandwidth traffic. Every PE router has one or more multicast routing tables and has at least one default table for the provider network. In addition, a multicast routing table exists for each VPN to which the PE is attached.

  A CE router interacts with a PE router in exactly the same way as it does with any other neighboring C routers. A PE router can also have directly connected hosts or Layer 2 switches.

  An interface type called *multicast tunnel* is dynamically created by PIM to build point-to-multipoint tunnels on the backbone network. The delivery (outer) IP header is a multicast group, called the MDT group for the VPN, and is statically configured.

The source address in the delivery header is usually a loopback address on the PE router that is the root of the multicast distribution tree. For every VPN the PE router is connected to, there is one multicast tunnel using the PE router as the root. The PE router also becomes the leaves of multicast tunnels rooted at other PE routers connected to the same VPN. A PE's participation in a VPN is distributed to other PEs by MBGP. PE routers use GRE encapsulation to send packets to other PE routers, and these appear as regular multicast packets to P routers. When a PE router receives these packets, the outer delivery header is stripped and the packet is routed using the MVRF identified by the MDT group in the delivery header.

So, an operation of MVPN can be summarized as follows.

An MVRF is assigned to an MD, and a P-group address is defined for each MD. This P-group address must be unique, and C-packets are encapsulated on the PE routers and sent on to the MDT as P-packets. The encapsulation can be GRE/IPinIP/MPLS. An IP source address is the address of the MBGP update, whereas the group destination address is the P-group address. One state exists in the core for all multicast states within a VPN, therein providing core stability. PIM is a soft-state protocol, so a limited number of states can be supported. However, traffic replication is not optimal because the PE routers without interested receivers still receive all multicast traffic per VPN. This architecture solution does not depend on MPLS as the delivery vehicle, and the current solution permits multicast VPNs within one BGP domain. This architecture also depends on stable multicast routing being enabled in the provider core, which is beyond the scope of this chapter.

Therefore, from a functional standpoint, IP Multicast can be packaged into three solutions. The first of these solutions is Campus multicast or Intradomain Multicast where there is an end station management, or host to router protocols (IGMP), which requests admission to join or leave multicast groups. The second component of this solution is switch membership management via CGMP or IGMP snooping. This ensures that the switch intelligently handles multicast forwarding without flooding the network. The third component is PIM Sparse Mode, which ensures that the network has appropriate information necessary to forward multicast packets down a multicast distribution tree from source to destination. Note also that an Internet Multicast tree includes MBGP for AS to AS multicast routing information and MSDP for third party source discovery across PIM Sparse Mode clouds as shown in Figure 10-3.

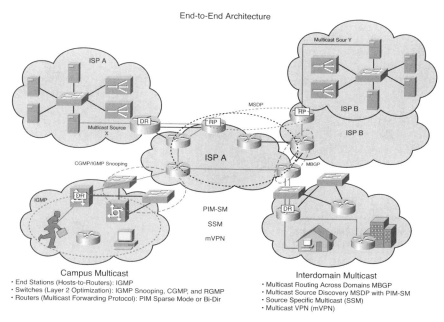

End-to-End Architecture

Campus Multicast
- End Stations (Hosts-to-Routers): IGMP
- Switches (Layer 2 Optimization): IGMP Snooping, CGMP, and RGMP
- Routers (Multicast Forwarding Protocol): PIM Sparse Mode or Bi-Dir

Interdomain Multicast
- Multicast Routing Across Domains MBGP
- Multicast Source Discovery MSDP with PIM-SM
- Source Specific Multicast (SSM)
- Multicast VPN (mVPN)

Figure 10-3   *End-to-End Architecture*

Multicast VPN Operational Details

In MVPN, the P routers form a PIM adjacency with each other; this is a global adjacency. The CE router forms a PIM adjacency with the VRF instance on the PE router. A per-VPN multicast distribution tunnel is established between PE routers in a provider network, and the PE routers form PIM adjacency with other PE routers over a tunnel. This is a VRF-specific adjacency. Multicast packets from CE routers are forwarded over the multicast tunnel, and the PE is always a root (source) of the MDT. The PE is also a leaf (receiver) to the MDT rooted on the remote PEs. The MDT creates an any-to-any distribution tree.

Figure 10-4 summarizes the MVPN concept.

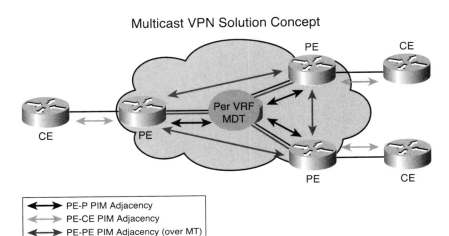

Multicast VPN Solution Concept

Figure 10-4 *Multicast VPN Solution Concept*

For PIM requirements, the service provider might have a preference for a particular PIM mode or already have multicast deployed in the core. Additionally, a VPN customer might have a preference for a PIM mode or already have deployed multicast in its network. Therefore, the customer-facing solution must support all PIM modes.

Available PIM modes are as follows:

- PIM bidirectional (PIM-BIDIR)

- PIM source specific multicast (PIM-SSM)

- PIM sparse-mode (PIM-SM)

- PIM dense-mode (PIM-DM)

PIM-DM is not suitable for service provider core usage because of its scalability limitations and is therefore not supported as a protocol in the core; neither is any other protocol that is not based on PIM (such as dvmrp, mospf, and so on). For a multicast VRF (MVRF) configuration, the MVRF is created when multicast routing is enabled for that VRF. Multicast protocols such as IGMP and

PIM are configured and operate in the context of an MVRF. In fact, PIM-SM is favored by most SPs today for the core.

The MVRF contains the multicast routing information only for the VRFs that comprise a multicast domain. Figure 10-5 depicts the PIM adjacency relationships for the deployment of MVPN.

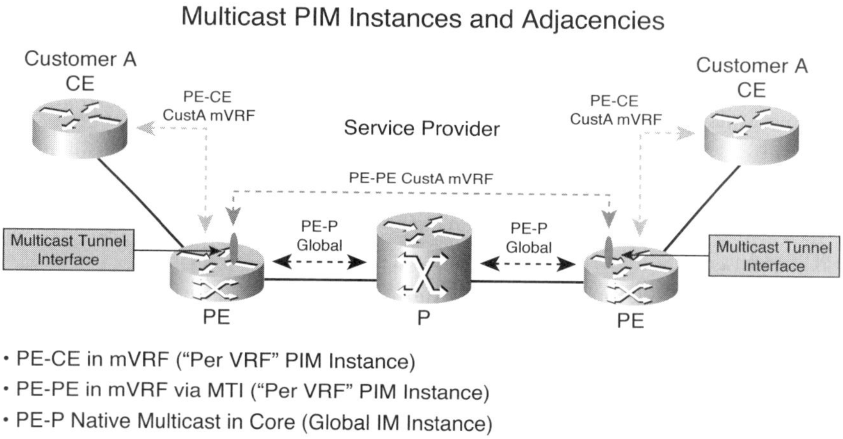

Multicast PIM Instances and Adjacencies

• PE-CE in mVRF ("Per VRF" PIM Instance)
• PE-PE in mVRF via MTI ("Per VRF" PIM Instance)
• PE-P Native Multicast in Core (Global IM Instance)

Figure 10-5 *Multicast: PIM Instances and Adjacencies*

For reverse path forwarding (RPF) considerations, no unicast routing protocol runs over the MDT; therefore, RPF checks need to use other means. For example, the RPF neighbor is determined by checking the BGP next-hop (PE) address to the customer source and the PIM adjacency with the next-hop customer (C) addresses is conveyed by the VPNv4 BGP updates between PEs. For the RPF interface check to succeed, a packet must come in over the RPF interface to the source. One of two scenarios is possible:

• RPF interface is in the VRF and is no different from classical RPF interface behavior.

• The RPF interface is the MD tunnel; that is, the RPF interface check for packets is received over the tunnel interface.

When the PE router receives an MDT packet, it performs an RPF check. During the transmission of the packet through the provider network, the normal RPF rules apply. However, at the remote's PE, the router needs to ensure that the originating PE router was the correct one for that CE. It does this by checking the BGP next-hop address of the customer's packet's source address. This next-hop address should be the source address of the MDT packet. The PE also checks that a PIM neighborship with the remote PE exists. A unique group address is required to be used as the MDT for each customer. A unique source address for the multicast packet in the provider network is also required. This source address is recommended to be the address of the loopback interface, which is used as the source for the IBGP, because this address is used for the RPF check at the remote PE.

If the provider uses MDT-data groups, these also need to be configured. These MDT-data groups must be unique for each customer.

The PE routers must have a PIM adjacency to each other. No other routing protocols can use these MTIs. PE routers are the only routers that need to be MVPN-aware and able to signal information to remote PEs regarding the MVPN. It is therefore fundamental that all PE routers have a BGP relationship with each other or directly or via a route reflector.

The source address of the default-MDT is the same address used to source the IBGP sessions with the remote PE routers that belong to the same VPN and MVRF. When PIM-SSM is used for transport inside the provider core, the PEs indicate that they are MVPN-capable and provide for source discovery via this BGP relationship. This capability is indicated by the updated BGP message.

When a PE receives a BGP update, which includes the RD and group information, it joins the root of that tree, thereby joining the MDT.

The RPF check on the PE is satisfied when the following conditions are met:

- The next hop for the source of the CE data is the BGP neighbor, which is the source of the MDT.

- The source of the MDT is a PIM neighbor.

In summary, while preserving state inside the core network, no upgrade of the core routers is necessary—thus facilitating the deployment of MVPN. However, multicast does need to be deployed in the core. You need to remember that the customer's IP multicast network has no relationship to the provider's multicast network. From the perspective of the provider, the customer's IP multicast packets are merely data to the provider's distinct IP multicast network.

MPLS Multicast VPN Applications and Examples

In the finance sector, an opportunity to reduce the cost of operations exists via the application of hoot 'n' holler onto an existing IP infrastructure. Hoot 'n' holler provides always-on multiuser conferences without requiring users to dial in to a conference bridge. The three major components of a hoot 'n' holler system are transport, bridging, and station apparatus. In most cases, transport is accomplished using dedicated point-to-point circuits provided by a network service provider. Typically, a branch office (financial model) or a station on a hoot 'n' holler network consists of a four-wire, push-to-talk (PTT) handset and a loudspeaker. Standalone speakers are used as well as combination phone/speaker units. When more phones and speakers are required, common equipment (CE) is necessary to distribute the audio and power feeds to the stations. Because the transmit and receive paths are always separate in a four-wire circuit, you must mix the audio (local transmit-out and distant-end receive-in). The CE also provides this functionality.

Currently, most hoot 'n' holler customers pay for separate leased line charges from a common carrier—such as their telephone service provider—to transport their hoot 'n' holler communications to remote branch offices. This recurring monthly charge is usually significant; some larger firms spend more than $2 to $3 million per year just to support hoot 'n' holler feeds.

As these networks have grown from four-wire party lines to global conferencing networks, the sophistication and complexity have increased dramatically. Hoot 'n' holler has proven to be the most cost-effective application for disseminating information across a company in real time. Other applications for MVPN include e-learning via IPTV, videostreaming, and music on hold for IP telephony. Figures 10-6 and 10-7 provide an overview of MVPN-enabled services and the use of multicast for IPTV. In Figure 10-7, we assume 30,000 additional ADSL subscribers per month; this assumption can be used for both retail and wholesale service offerings. Dynamic multicast construct is linked to channel surfing or zap time sequences.

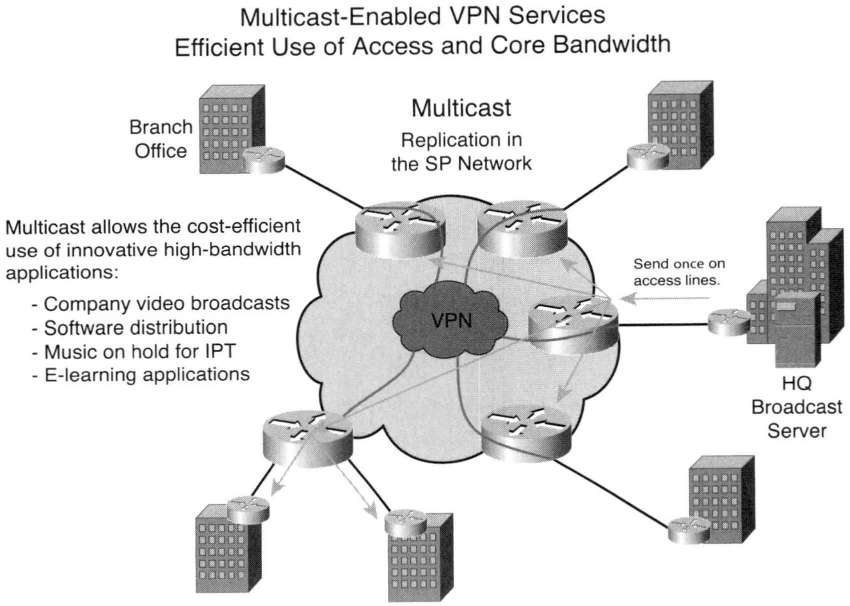

Figure 10-6   *Multicast-Enabled VPN Services: Efficient Use of Access and Core Bandwidth*

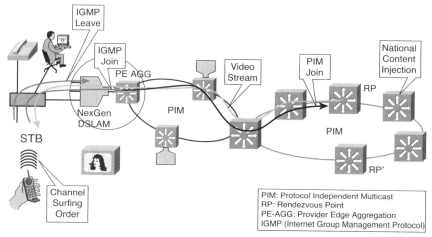

Figure 10-7 *Optimizing Video Distribution Dynamic Multicast*

Multicast Security and Management Considerations

As part of managing services based on technologies such as multicast, it is important to highlight both security and management considerations.

In the context of multicast security, we assume that VPNs remain fully separated; that is, no reachability exists between the VPNS, unicast, or multicast. One cannot spoof the other VPN, unicast, or multicast. Unicast traffic remains separate, as in RFC 4364. This includes unicast PIM packets that are handled per MVRF.

The following list summarizes the multicast security requirements:

- Each VPN can use multicast independently.

- Source and group can overlap with other VPNs.

- Different PIM modes can be in use.

- There is support for the extranet.

- A spoofed PIM remains within VPN; the control plane information is handled in MVPN context only. Each VPN can use the same multicast groups.

- The MPLS core remains secure. It cannot be attacked from VPNs, unicast, or multicast.

In the context of the PE-CE interface the flooding with PIM control messages and multicast traffic (data plane) with possible flooding of data messages are indications of denial-of-service attacks.

In securing the PE-CE interface, you can consider the following best-practice guidelines:

- Limit the access to defined group addresses (access list [ACL]).

- Prevent IP source address spoofing (unidirectional reverse path forwarding [uRPF]).

- Limit sources to known source addresses if possible (ACL function).

Regarding the Rendezvous point function, you should avoid rendezvous point (RP) on PE and avoid a directly connected source/receiver to mitigate against a higher exposure to a denial-of-service attack against the PE.

RP receives join/prune messages, and a corresponding threat exists that an attacker can send a large volume of (*,G) join/prunes with spoofed addresses.

Furthermore, an RP receives register/register-stop messages with a threat that an attacker could fake register messages.

The solution is to filter ip pim accept-register, if designated routers or rendezvous points (DR) are known; in addition, use the command **ip pim register-rate-limit** on DRs (if DRs are trusted).

As for management considerations, current developments within the IETF involve exploring a lightweight connectivity check for point-to-multipoint label-switched paths (these can also be applied to point-to-point LSP) that use multicast technology mechanisms—for example, **draft-swallow-mpls-mcast-cv-xx.txt**.

Standards and References

At the time of writing this book, IETF draft-rosen-vpn-mcast-xx.txt, "Multicast in MPLS/BGP IP VPNs," has been the basis for the development and deployment of MVPNs. The draft describes three approaches to deploying MVPNs:

- **Multicast domains**—Stability of the core is provided by controlling the quantity of PIM states, and native multicast can be used in the core. No upgrade of P routers is necessary.

- **VPN-IP PIM**—Multicast forwarding is deployed in the core.

- **MD using PIM nonbroadcast multiaccess (NBMA) techniques**—No PIM state is created in the core.

Multicast domains comprise the majority of industry deployments because they facilitate the migration of MVPNs to existing infrastructure.

Summary

Multicast integration into MPLS is driven by enterprise applications such as videostreaming, IPTV, and so on and are deployed as VPNs, thus creating MVPNs. We have discussed how an existing MPLS infrastructure can implement MVPNs and have identified the IETF draft (draft-rosen-vpn-mcast), upon which the majority of industry implementations is based. Current IETF-related work involves exploring multicast and traffic engineering constructs to efficiently constrain the multicast flows, in addition to developing a lightweight connectivity check for management purposes. Finally, service providers are using this technology to offer managed services for enterprise multicast applications.

CHAPTER 11

IPv6 AND MPLS

IPv6 is the next version of IP. With a larger address space and more features, IPv6 is the direction in which many service providers are moving—especially in Japan and the Asian Pacific. With the rapid success of the Internet, every device connected to the Internet needs an IP address. Assigning public addresses to all devices is not an option because of the shortage of IPv4 addresses. Hence, the IPv4 addresses must be translated (network address translation [NAT]) using private address space to accommodate all the devices. IETF has standardized a new address family called IPv6 with 16 bytes or 128 bits of address space, a much larger address space than the 4 bytes or 32 bits of IPv4. In addition to addressing, IPv6 also provides improved security and data integrity, auto configuration, multicasting, and anycasting. (Anycasting is the ability of a sender to send traffic to the nearest device within the group. It provides integrated quality of service [QoS] as well efficiency in sending information—for example, to update routing tables.)

The following is an extract of the IPv6 RFC 2460:

1. Introduction

IP version 6 (IPv6) is a new version of the Internet Protocol, designed as the successor to IP version 4 (IPv4) [RFC-791]. The changes from IPv4 to IPv6 fall primarily into the following categories:

- Expanded Addressing Capabilities

  IPv6 increases the IP address size from 32 bits to 128 bits to support more levels of addressing hierarchy, a much greater number of addressable nodes, and simpler auto-configuration of addresses. The scalability of multicast routing is improved by adding a "scope" field to multicast addresses. And a new type of address called an "anycast address" is defined, used to send a packet to any one of a group of nodes.

- Header Format Simplification

  Some IPv4 header fields have been dropped or made optional to reduce the common-case processing cost of packet handling and to limit the bandwidth cost of the IPv6 header.

- Improved Support for Extensions and Options

Changes in the way IP header options are encoded allows for more efficient forwarding, less stringent limits on the length of options, and greater flexibility for introducing new options in the future.

- Flow Labeling Capability

  A new capability is added to enable the labeling of packets belonging to particular traffic "flows" for which the sender requests special handling, such as nondefault quality of service or "real-time" service.

- Authentication and Privacy Capabilities

  Extensions to support authentication, data integrity, and (optional) data confidentiality are specified for IPv6.

As you notice, IPv6 is not just about expanded addressing capability—it is much more. However, the primary driver for IPv6 has been and will be expanded address space. Due to a much larger address space, many carriers are considering allocating IPv6 addresses to mobile devices, such as cell phones. Several providers are actively evaluating IPv6-based services for mobile 3G/4G applications and mobile terminals. In fact, carriers in Japan have already begun this trend and are allocating IPv6 addresses to cell phones for 3G applications.

For carriers who plan to offer mobile services, IPv6 becomes an important protocol for delivering the next generation of services. IPv6 is also popular at universities for the Internet2 (next-generation Internet connecting universities) connections and 6bone (IPv6 backbone).

The options for service providers (SP) are simple—either build an IPv6 backbone or build some translational or tunneling of IPv6 packets through IPv4 networks so that IPv6 edge services are available over an IPv4 network.

Problem Statement

The increasing demand for IPv6 addresses and IPv6-based services is prompting SPs to build an IPv6 network. However, their current network is an IPv4 network with MPLS running on it. The question is, "How best can they continue to offer the existing portfolio of IPv4-based services and layer IPv6 services with it?" Some of the questions providers must ask are:

- Can I build IPv6 edge services without changing the existing IPv4 network core?

- Can I build IPv6 VPNs without changing the IPv4 network core?

- Do I need MPLS? Hence, do I need Label Distribution Protocol (LDP) and Resource Reservation Protocol (RSVP) to be IPv6-capable?

- Can I build an entire network just with IPv6 and layer MPLS on it?

This chapter explores the answers to these questions in some depth. It is not the aim of this chapter to explain exactly why an SP needs to deploy IPv6 or to describe the benefits of IPv6. The Assumption is that SPs need IPv6, and this chapter aims to discuss how an MPLS-based network can carry IPv6 traffic or help provide IPv6 services.

Technology Overview

Let us try to answer some of the questions listed in the previous section. But, before we answer them, let's briefly compare IPv6 header and IPv4 header information, as shown in Figure 11-1, to note the differences.

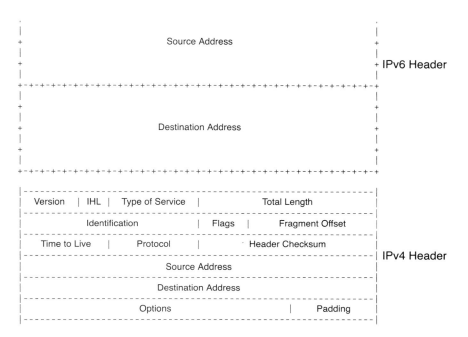

Figure 11-1 *IPv6 and IPv4 Packet Header*

The IPv4 header is 4 bytes or 32 bits. In the world of classless interdomain routing (CIDR), net masks define the network portion of the address rather than the host portion of the address. IPv6 has 16 bytes or 128 bits of address space. The header is slightly different from IPv4 as shown in Figure 11-1.

The flow label is a 24-bit field. It can be used for QoS and is much larger than 6-bit DSCP field in IPv4. The hop limit information is nothing but the TTL field of IPv4. To ease migration and coexist with IPv4, there are capabilities to tunnel or translate IPv6 addresses to IPv4 addresses. Tunneling allows the transporting of IPv6 frames from the ingress of the IPv4 network to the egress without acting on the IPv6 header information.

(291)

IPv6 PE

As mentioned earlier, tunneling of IPv6 packets can be done using IPv4; then the IPv4 frames can be transported across the MPLS network. Another form of tunneling is using the label as an encapsulation instead of another IPv4 header. This method of transporting IPv6 packets across the MPLS network by using the label as a mux/demux field, and the tunneling encapsulation is called IPv6 PE (6PE). Refer to Figure 11-2.

In the 6PE environment, each provider edge router is a dual network stack device with IPv6 and IPv4 stacks. The edge router peers with the customer routers with IPv6 and IPv4 separately. Both IPv4 and IPv6 addresses are exchanged between the edge router and customer routers using a routing protocol. The customer edge devices do regular PE-CE routing via either the dynamic routing protocols or static routing. The PEs peer with each other directly or by using route reflectors for the exchange of IPv6 routes in addition to IPv4 routes. The core routers learn only IPv4 addresses that are advertised in the IGP. The core routers in the network do not have any IPv6 visibility and cannot reach IPv6 addresses. The labeled IPv6 packets are forwarded on the IGP-based, label-switched paths (IGP LSP).

Multiprotocol BGP Extensions

To distribute IPv6 address information between PEs, Border Gateway Protocol (BGP) is extended to carry IPv6 addresses. The address family identifier is used to distribute the IPv6 prefixes within BGP. A label associated with that IPv6 network prefix is also advertised as part of BGP extended communities, similar to the IPv4 VPN extensions. The PEs then exchange this IPv6 prefix and label information via the iBGP session between them, as is done with the L3VPN. Just as the PEs advertise the IPv4 reachability, they also advertise IPv6 reachability with the ability to resolve the IPv6 routes to an IPv4 next hop. (Refer to the Figure 11-2 for details.)

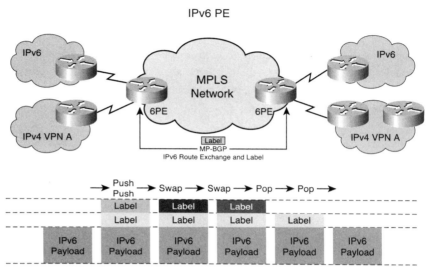

Figure 11-2   *IPv6 Provider Edge (6PE)*

Packet Path

As we stated earlier, the PEs are dual-stack devices that support IPv6 and IPv4 on the same port or on different ports. When IPv6 packets come from the CEs, the PE looks up the v6 forwarding table and finds the IPv4 BGP next hop. It then imposes the IPv6 label assigned to the IPv6 prefix by the egress PE. The PE then imposes the IGP or tunnel label to get to the egress PE (IPv4 BGP next hop) via the PSN tunnel or a label-switched path. The result is the same dual-label stack that we see in VPNv4 (L3VPN) cases. The packet is switched through the network core using the top label, and when the packet arrives at the egress PE, the egress PE looks up the label and forwards the IPv6 packet to the destination interface corresponding to that prefix. This looks exactly like the IPv4 VPN case, but the difference here is that all IPv6 addresses are in one address space.

The packet handling for 6PE is no different from the VPNv4 case, except that all v6 CEs/addresses are in one domain and can be reached via IPv6 unless route filtering is applied. The network core does not understand any IPv6 frames and is running standard IPv4 with IGP routing protocols, such as OSPF and IS-IS. The P routers have no knowledge of the IPv6 label and are only label-switching packets based on the top label or PSN tunnel label. All routing polices that are applicable also apply in this case.

IPv6 VPNs (6VPE)

Much like the IPv4 VPNs, service providers might also want to keep the traffic of one VPN separated from the traffic of another in the IPv6 space. To deliver this traffic separation between IPv6 devices, service providers have two choices. One choice is to perform route tagging of IPv6 routes via the BGP communities and then filter the IPv6 routes based on those tags.

Route Tagging

Route tagging is a technique that allows the PE to assign a tag (community of interest) to any route as part of a BGP attribute. The tag is called a *community.* By assigning route tags, upon import of routes, a PE can then filter the routes to exclude those that do not belong to its community of interest. This prevents routes from being populated in the PEs where these routes are not needed; it also prevents network reachability. This model is simple to understand—all IPv6 traffic belonging to one VPN is tagged with the VPN name. When PEs receive the routes, they filter these routes based on policies. By tagging routes and selectively importing/filtering the routes, extranets can also be built. But as networks get larger and more complicated, efficient filtering techniques are needed to scale this model upwards to address many VPNs and many routes within the VPN.

Virtual Routing and Forwading with IPv6

Another model for IPv6 VPNs is to use the similar virtual routing and forwarding (VRF) structures, as we used in the IPv4 L3VPNs, and separate the IPv6 routes on a per-VRF basis. This separation of routes is similar to that of the

IPv4 model. CEs are connected to the PEs and are placed in a VRF. The PEs have a separate routing and forwarding table per VRF/VPN, and IPv6 routes from the CE are populated in these VRFs. The peering model is similar to VPNv4, in which PEs exchange IPv6 routes in iBGP using the IPv6 address family extension to the MP-BGP. Labels are then distributed in the same way as the IPv4 prefixes are. All the functionality to separate one v6 address from another using route distinguishers and route targets apply here in the same manner. Route targets can be imported or exported in the same manner as IPv4 routes to create intranets and extranets.

Packet Path

When IPv6 packets come in to the PE from the CE of a VPN, the PE looks up the v6 route in the VRF and finds the egress IPv4 BGP next hop and VPN label associated with that IPv6 prefix. It imposes the VPN label and then forwards it onto the PSN tunnel or onto a label-switched path toward the egress PE, as shown in Figure 11-3.

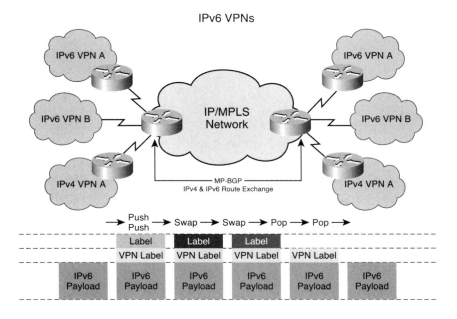

Figure 11-3   *IPv6 VPNs (6VPE)*

The label-switched path between the ingress and the egress PE is set up independently of the VPN route exchange. The network core can be IPv4, and only the PEs are IPv6-capable. This allows layering of IPv6 VPNs services and a rapid start of IPv6 deployments. Alternatively, the network core can also be a complete IPv6 network, in which case the label distribution protocols, such as LDP and RSVP, must be IPv6 capable.

By using 6VPE, the same L3VPN available in IPv4 can also be provided with the same QoS characteristics and flexibility. This means the administration model for IPv6 is no different from the IPv4 model, and the IPv6 model has potentially more flexibility and a much larger address space.

Due to the much larger address space of the IPv6 model, users probably will not use NAT for IPv6 addresses anytime soon. However, tunneling and translation from v4 to v6 and vice versa is certainly necessary. For example, a v6 device, such as a mobile phone, needs access to the v4 Internet for web browsing or other applications. The IPv6 request can go either to a central gateway in the provider network or within the customer network and be translated there into an IPv4 space and sent across the IPv4 network.

The Coexistence of IPv4 L3VPN and IPv6 L3VPN

IPv4 L3VPNs can coexist with IPv6 L3VPNs on the same PE and in the same VRF table. A single VRF table can be used to store IPv6 and IPv4 addresses belonging to the VPN. The CEs advertise IPv4 and IPv6 addresses, while the PE independently advertises IPv4 and IPv6 addresses with route targets.

Allowing the coexistence of IPv4 and IPv6 L3VPNs provides a smooth migration of networks from IPv4 to IPv6. It also enables the seamless coexistence of services regardless of the IP protocol version. Service providers can continue to operate their IPv4 services while introducing new IPv6-based services on their networks. Without MPLS, the network operators have to tunnel IPv6 through the IPv4 network or upgrade the entire IPv4 network to IPv6 or to dual stack. This can be difficult to manage and operate. Using MPLS, IPv6 can be easily layered in the network while keeping the operational paradigm the same as that of IPv4. Mobile wireless integration and residential broadband integration are now possible with a virtually unlimited address space because of IPv6.

IPv6 Network Core

To recap 6PE and 6VPE operations, we know that for 6VPE and 6PE, each IPv6 prefix is resolved to an IPv4 BGP next hop. The setup of LSP to the BGP next hop is done using LDP or RSVP for IPv4 FECs. The traffic mapping to LDP LSPs or TE tunnels is based on IPv4 addresses, and IPv6 is transparent to the TE tunnel setup or forwarding of traffic.

At some point, we hope all networks will become IPv6. To get to that point, all routing protocols and label-distribution protocols need to be IPv6-capable. IGP protocols with IPv6 are already available from Cisco. In the future, LDP and RSVP with native IPv6 support will also be available. Protocol details can be found in RFC3036. With native IPv6 support for LDP or RSVP-TE transport, LSPs will be signaled for IPv6 addresses directly without the layering that is needed for 6PE or 6VPE.

For traffic engineering to be enabled in an IPv6 core, all traffic engineering features (such as autoroute and static route) must work with IPv6 prefix mapping. The forwarding of IPv6 traffic must be done onto TE tunnels, and the tunnels themselves must be signaled using RSVP with IPv6 extensions. The techniques used with fast reroute can also be used to protect IPv6 traffic from link or node failures.

In short, the native IPv6 operation is no different from the IPv4 operation for MPLS because the label space, size, signaling, and forwarding do not change with IP protocol version.

Inter-AS Networks for 6PE and v6VPNs

Inter-AS capability is also important because provider networks are seldom single autonomous system (AS) networks. IPv6 information must be carried across ASes between PEs. The peering model at the Autonomous Systems Boundary Routers (ASBR) is no different from IPv4 peering, but both ASBRs must be configured with IPv4 and IPv6 address families. The three interconnect models discussed in RFC 4364 apply to both IPv4 and IPv6. These interconnect models are briefly described here:

- **Back-to-back peering**—VPNv6 routes can be exchanged within the VRFs or the IPv6 global routing table with logical interfaces between ASBRs. No special arrangement is needed to span the IPv6 services across the ASes.

- **VPNv6 peering**—ASBRs peer with VPNv6 route exchange in addition to IPv4 route exchange. Labels are also exchanged, along with VPNv6 routes, between ASBRs. The packet path in this case is the same as in the case of IPv4, where the ASBR swaps the VPN label to a new label in each AS. Note that both ASBRs must be IPv6-capable.

- **IPv4 peering**—In this model, only IPv4 peering is done between ASBRs. The IPv4 reachability is available between ASes either through leaking PE loopbacks or via redistribution. The IPv6 route exchange happens only between route reflectors (RR) in each AS. In this model, the ASBRs needn't be dual stack. This model is great to start an IPv6 service in an existing IPv4 network irrespective of geography and ASes by simply enabling two PEs with IPv6 address families and configuring the RRs to exchange v6 information only.

IPv6 QoS

QoS is an integral element of the IPv4 service offering; therefore, for any transitional capability to IPv6, all IPv4 services and more must be offered in the IPv6 network. IPv6 has a traffic class field that is 8 bits. This field provides the priority of the IPv6 frame and can easily be mapped from the IPv4 DSCP byte. This traffic class field is designed to use the differentiated services definition; hence, in the MPLS network, it carries the same significance as the IP DSCP field. All the details discussed in Chapter 9, "Quality of Service," regarding marking classification, policing, scheduling, and WRED also apply to the IPv6 frames.

Additionally, a 24-bit field exists in the IPv6 header and is called the flow label. This label is used as a flow designator by the source for special handling of packet sequences, such as nondefault class of service or real-time service. Although this flow designator provides many more options in terms of QoS, it is still under discussion, and the RFC does not clearly define the usage of this flow label. Thus, there is no standard way of dealing with the flow label. Currently, Cisco products do not use the flow label field.

MPLS QoS for IPv6

Because MPLS label information does not fundamentally change for IPv6, the MPLS QoS model for IPv6 does not change from IPv4. The same EXP markings are used to classify traffic from high priority to low priority, and standard QoS techniques are used to deliver MPLS DiffServ for IPv6 packets. In addition, the mapping of the traffic class field is done much in the same way as the mapping of the DSCP field. Refer to Chapter 9 for more details on the DSCP mapping to EXP bits. Should more QoS classes be required, the L-LSP model discussed in Chapter 9 can also be used for IPv6 traffic. Additional mapping of flow labels to MPLS QoS is not defined at this stage.

Management and IPv6

Management and operation, administration, and maintenance (OAM) do not change for IPv6. The same techniques of LSP ping and trace that are applied to IPv4 are also applicable for IPv6. The operation paradigm is similar to the IPv4 case, so the same label stacking, label-based forwarding, and troubleshooting techniques can be applied with no changes to the operational models. The only change is to type or script larger IPv6 addresses.

Service providers currently use large back-end management and operational support systems (OSS) for their operations and management. This management and OSS provide network information, provision the network, perform network inventory, alert you about failure conditions, and provide an interface to billing systems. Adding 6PE or 6VPE to the network requires some changes in the OSS and management systems. The OSS and management systems—in particular, the provisioning systems—need to be updated to reflect the new IPv6 address space. Troubleshooting, fault monitoring, and diagnostic tools must be updated to handle the new IP versions. New MIB objects also must be parsed to understand the network information for billing and management purposes.

The overhead associated with adding IPv6 to the network is similar to the overhead associated with adding a new protocol to it. The assumption is that the benefits of adding IPv6 outweigh the costs in the medium to long term.

Summary

IPv6 can be added to an existing MPLS network with some simple changes without changing the network core or changing the core routing protocols. An IETF draft, "Scenarios and Analysis for Introducing IPv6 into ISP Networks," (draft-ietf-v6ops-isp-scenarios-analysis-03.txt) describes the various migration scenarios in detail and specifies which tunneling and translational techniques are available. IPv6 does not change the fundamental operational model of an MPLS network, and all the currently available techniques can be leveraged in building the IPv6 services to end users. IPv6 VPNs and 6PE are simple extensions to the MPLS VPN model and are designed to accommodate the forwarding of IPv6 frames to IPv4 BGP next hop. In other words, MPLS forms an efficient encapsulation technique to deliver the v6 frames without any 6-to-4 translation or tunneling. IPv6 can also be transparently tunneled across the VPNs or MPLS network as another overlay option with relative ease.

Network operators today have started assigning IPv6 addresses for broadband users or mobile users. Especially in countries such as China and Japan, where the government provides incentives to deploy IPv6, providers are deploying IPv6 services at the edge and using techniques such as 6PE or 6VPE to deliver IPv6 services across an IPv4 core. The U.S. federal government has provided a mandate to its agencies that by June, 2008, all networks must be capable of running IPv6 services. Certainly, IPv4 is here to stay and is unlikely to be phased out in the next decade, but new and upcoming services of the next decade certainly will have a strong IPv6 flavor to them.

PART 4

BRINGING YOUR MPLS PLAN TOGETHER

CHAPTER 12

NETWORK MANAGEMENT AND PROVISIONING

The multiprotocol label switching (MPLS) architecture provides a challenge in troubleshooting and debugging because of the separation of control and data planes. Features, such as MPLS operation, administration, and maintenance (OAM), help in tracing issues and problems that are critical to deploying and managing a service. This chapter describes the management and provisioning aspects for Layer 2 and Layer 3 services. As service providers (SP) evolve their networks and services to IP/MPLS, the requirement for OAM capabilities becomes critical to manage these services.

Problem Statement

We have discussed technology and service overviews in the previous chapters; this chapter focuses on the necessary management aspects when deploying MPLS-based and next-generation network (NGN) services.

As network operators converge multiple services, such as IP VPN, voice, ATM, Frame Relay, and Ethernet over MPLS, the ability for service providers to monitor the LSP integrity, characterize LSP properties, and isolate MPLS forwarding problems becomes critical to their capability to offer services that require service level agreement (SLA) commitments. Traffic engineering, Any Transport over MPLS (AToM), and MPLS IP-VPN are examples of services in which the ability to provide SLA testing and LSP integrity checking might be mandatory (as determined by the network operator managing these services). MPLS OAM plays a crucial role in this picture. Traditionally, SLA testing and LSP integrity checking have been done using Internet Control Message Protocol (ICMP) ping and applications, such as Cisco Service Assurance Agent (SAA), now referred to as Cisco IOS IP Service Level Agreement. MPLS management concerns summarized by customers include the following:

- With all the flow through provisioning, the most complicated part is to ensure that the configuration has worked.

- Solving MPLS virtual private network (VPN) connectivity problems is a complex task for Cisco Certified Internetwork Experts (CCIE).

- You must determine whether quality of service (QoS) configuration is network specific or service specific and whether it is complicated to manage and troubleshoot.

- Troubleshooting performance degradation in MPLS/IP networks is the most labor-intensive NOC activity.

- You must know how to transition PVCs from your ATM core to IP/MPLS infrastructure and how to do so in a multivendor network.

- I need help getting better use of IP/MPLS core—particularly, increased use of existing network bandwidth resource.

Generally speaking, network management and OAM comprise a set of procedures used to diagnose failures; respond to failures; and test, measure, and verify SLAs within a given network. Diagnostics and tests are applicable to both data and control planes, whereas SLA measurement is related more to the data plane—although the combination of the two is often the most comprehensive approach. Having a consistent way of managing and collecting information from the network elements—a way that is access agnostic and possesses a common command line (CLI) interface—becomes critical when managing fault, configuration, accounting, performance, and security aspects.

Cisco MPLS Embedded Management offers a set of tools that work together to provide complete MPLS fault, configuration, accounting, performance, and security capabilities (FCAPS). The MPLS Embedded Management architecture is shown in Figure 12-1; it and its components are the main topics of this chapter.

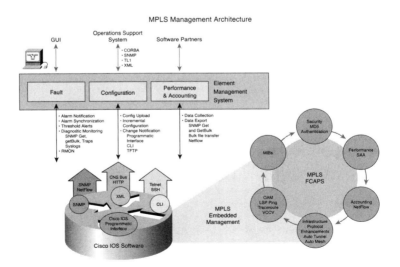

Figure 12-1 *MPLS Management Architecture*

Most MPLS vendor implementations are standards compliant, and, hence, provide incentive for large networks to deploy multiple vendors in the network. Therefore, developing and implementing a common approach to managing and collecting information from the network elements becomes critical to manage FCAPS aspects.

We discuss aspects of the FCAPS model that pertain to MPLS OAM and network management. We commence with fault management mechanisms, such as LSP ping, trace, and virtual circuit connectivity verification (VCCV), for fault diagnosis. We introduce other mechanisms, such as bidirectional forwarding detection (BFD), LSR self-test, and OAM message mapping (for interworking of OAM messages and states) as part of the MPLS OAM toolkit. We also provide an overview of VPN provisioning via the use of The Cisco IP Solution Center (ISC) and examine accounting and performance mechanisms offered by Netflow and Cisco IOS IP Service Level Agreement (Cisco IP SLA).

We conclude the FCAPS section with recommended security mechanisms, such as the use of Message Digest 5 (MD-5) with control plane protocols.

Some organizations are implementing Layer 3 VPNs, namely BGP-VPNs. These require a per-VPN management model for network operations, thus resulting in a more discreet approach to VPN management.

Per-VPN management examples are described in this chapter. We examine SNMP Management Information Base modules (MIB) as applicable to MPLS-based networks for statistics gathering and topology discovery.

Finally, we provide an overview of the relevant drafts and their status as of the writing of this book.

Fault Management, Configuration Management, Accounting Management, Performance Management, and Security Management

This section discusses MPLS fault management requirements that serve as input to developing mechanisms to manage MPLS-based networks. It also covers key attributes required to manage and operate IP/MPLS-based networks within the framework of the FCAPS management model.

Maintaining core integrity is key in identifying requirements for MPLS OAM. The primary objective is to reduce cost by minimizing service interruptions. Minimal requirements include the ability to detect and diagnose a break in the LSP data path and identify the source of the failure.

MPLS OAM

OAM solutions provide the following capabilities:

- **Detection, diagnosis, and localization of broken label-switched path (LSP)**—Any OAM solution should provide the capability to diagnose and detect a broken LSP because diagnosing a broken LSP and isolating the failed resource in the path are required. This is true for misbranching defects, which are particularly difficult to specify recovery. The fundamental requirement, therefore, is to detect and diagnose an MPLS LSP. Additionally, the path trace function *must* have the ability to support equal cost multipath (ECMP) scenarios. ECMP is often used for both load sharing and redundant path capabilities.

- **The OAM mechanism should support equal cost multipath LSPs**— ECMP scenarios appear when several LSPs can be used to carry data from the head end to the tail end. In this particular situation, the OAM mechanism should be able to exercise and verify all those paths that might transport data within a reasonable amount of time. Unfortunately, there is no standard for the load-sharing algorithm, but any function needs to be capable of detecting failures on all operational paths. This is because a failure of any branch can lead to loss of traffic, regardless of the load-sharing algorithm.

- **The ability to raise an alarm when failures are detected**—A defect event in a lower layer should not cause multiple alarms to be raised. This capability is required for alarm suppression and root cause analysis of a fault condition.

  Upon detection of a broken LSP, the correct alarm/notification should be sent to the LSRs or the network management system. For the sake of example, if the LSP is to carry Layer 2 circuits, a defect at the LSP level should not target multiple alarms at the Layer 2 level.

  Those mechanisms are required to measure different aspects of SLAs, such as jitter, latency, and packet loss.

One extra parameter of interest for service providers is the network availability. (The definition of *network availability* likely differs from one provider to the other. At a high-level overview, you can define it as a function of jitter, packet loss, and latency.)

VRF-Aware ICMP Ping and LSP Ping/Trace Mechanisms

VRF-aware ping differs from traditional ping and trace by using the VRF routing table for route lookup, instead of the global routing table, when sending the probe packets. This is mainly used for private addresses. If no source IP address is given, the router uses the first interface that is associated with the VRF.

You can choose a source IP address by using the extended ping command. The specificity of the VRF routing information presents an important consequence: Not all middle routers along the path have such routing information available for the source and destination. Thus, any middle router is unable to respond directly to the VRF interface that sourced the UDP packets. The implementation of VRF-aware ping does not rely on a response from the middle LSRs. In the case of a failure along the path between the PEs, the probe ICMP packet is lost (no response would reach the source) because no ICMP packet can be emitted in response to an error on an ICMP packet.

If a configuration error, such as MPLS not being configured on an outbound interface that results in an improper label pop operation in the middle of the LSP, occurs VRF-aware ping still works because the packet can be delivered and responded to via IP. The operator in this example assumes that the network and corresponding service are still functioning. MPLS LSP ping and trace, discussed in the next section, perform the following tasks: verifying the health of the LSP path, returning detailed information as to the probable defect cause, and further localizing the defect.

MPLS LSP ping/traceroute provides diagnostics and troubleshooting capability for MPLS LSPs. When an LSP fails to deliver traffic, the failure cannot always be detected by the MPLS control plane. For the MPLS data plane verification, as a natural progression, the IP data plane verification tools (that is, ping and traceroute) are extended to work on the MPLS networks. MPLS ping/

traceroute is modeled after the ping/traceroute paradigm. MPLS ping enables the verification of the LSP connectivity and the integrity of the MPLS network.

Ping mode can test the integrity of the connectivity via the verification on the forward equivalence class (FEC) entity between the ping origin and the egress node for this particular FEC. This test is carried out by sending an MPLS echo request along the same data path as other packets belonging to this FEC. When the ping packet reaches the end of the path, it is sent to the control plane of the egress LSR, which then verifies that it is indeed an egress for the FEC. The MPLS echo request contains information about the FEC whose MPLS path is being verified.

MPLS traceroute is used for hop-by-hop fault localization and LSP path tracing. In the trace route LSP verification, the packet is sent to the control plane of each transit LSR, which performs various checks including one that determines whether it is a transit LSR for this path. Furthermore, each transit LSR also returns extra information related to the FEC being tested (such as the label bound to the FEC). This information helps in checking the control plane against the data plane (for example, in checking whether the local forwarding information matches what the routing protocols determined as the path). The traceroute operation is performed via a manipulation on the time to live (TTL) that is decremented to avoid loops.

These tools provide the foundation for the MPLS OAM capabilities and facilitate the operation of the MPLS network.

Dealing with Equal Cost Multipaths

Frequently, LSPs for a given FEC can have multiple "next hops" at transit LSRs. In addition, LSPs can have backup paths, detour paths, and other alternative paths to take should the primary LSP go down. It is useful if MPLS echo requests can exercise all possible paths. Though desirable, this might not be practical because the algorithms that a given LSR uses to load balance packets over alternative paths might be proprietary.

To achieve some degree of coverage of alternate paths, the MPLS ping/trace mechanism can use the 127/8 address as the destination address of the MPLS echo request packet. This address might affect load-balancing in cases where the LSR uses the destination address in the IP header as a decision for load balancing. Further, in the case of traceroute, each transit LSR provides information about how each of its downstream routers can be exercised. The ingress can then send MPLS echo requests that exercise these paths, based on information received from LSP traceroute.

Noncompliant Routers

Because MPLS ping/trace should be compatible with existing infrastructure, if the egress LSR for the FEC stack being pinged does not support MPLS ping, no reply is sent. If in traceroute mode a transit LSR does not support MPLS ping, no reply is forthcoming from that LSR for some TTL—say, n. The LSR originating the echo request should try sending the echo request with TTL = n + 1, n + 2, ... n + k in the hope that some transit LSR further downstream might support MPLS echo requests and reply.

Table 12-1 summarizes LSP ping and trace functions.

Table 12-1 *MPLS LSP Ping/Traceroute*

Requirement	Detect MPLS traffic black holes or misrouting
	Isolate MPLS faults
	Verify the data plane against the control plane
	Detect MTU of MPLS LSP paths
Solution	MPLS LSP ping (ICMP) for connectivity checks
	MPLS LSP traceroute for hop-by-hop fault localization
	MPLS LSP traceroute for path tracing
Applications	IPv4 LDP prefix, VPNv4 prefix
	TE tunnel
	MPLS PE, P connectivity for MPLS transport, MPLS VPN, MPLS TE applications
IETF Standards	RFC 4379

LSR Self-Test

LSR self-test was motivated by a combination of concepts, such as ECMP and liberal label retention. ECMP means that the transfer function of the LSR is MPLS payload dependent. This is unknowable to upstream LSRs, and they must expend a good deal of effort trying to test all the variations of the unknowable. However, the forwarding function is knowable to the self-testing LSR, making it a good option.

In liberal label retention, many labels are offered but few are chosen, and the chosen vary over time. An LSR ensures that the "not yet chosen" actually work when the time comes, which is useful. Instead of dividing the load between the edge LSR, the LSR self-test (see Figure 12-2) divides the load among the LSRs in the path. Another benefit of the LSR self-test is that an operator can validate the condition of unused or dormant paths in the event that the operator would need to use such paths for ECMP.

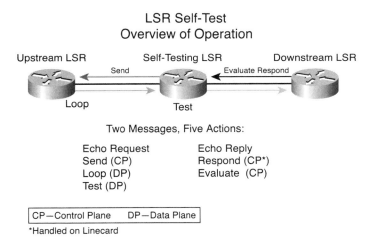

Figure 12-2   *LSR Self-Test: Overview of Operation*

Virtual Circuit Connection Verification and Bidirectional Forwarding Detection

As network operators deploy AToM services, the ability to provide end-to-end fault detection and diagnostics for an emulated pseudowire service is critical for the network operator. Cisco MPLS VCCV enhances the monitoring and troubleshooting of Layer 2 services across an MPLS network. VCCV creates a control channel between the two pseudowire PEs to uniquely identify the connectivity verification packets from the regular Layer 2 payloads. Ideally, such a control channel would be completely in band. When a control word is present on the virtual circuit, you can indicate the control channel by setting a bit in the control header. However, to ensure smooth interoperability between the various devices participating in the pseudowire service, the use of the MPLS router alert label to indicate the control channel is also supported.

In addition, the combination of VCCV and MPLS ping/traceroute allows a simplification of the operation, management, and troubleshooting of the emulated Layer 2 service end-to-end. BFD is a simple hello protocol that offers additional fault detection capability. Within the context of MPLS-based networks, you use the asynchronous mode of BFD. Together with diagnostic mechanisms such as MPLS LSP ping/Trace and VCCV, BFD provides an additional fault-detection benefit. Table 12-2 summarizes VCCV, and BFD is discussed in the next section.

Table 12-2 *Summary of VCCV Applicability*

Requirement	Ability to provide end-to-end fault detection and diagnostics for an emulated pseudowire service One tunnel can serve many pseudowires MPLS LSP ping is sufficient to monitor the PSN tunnel (PE-PE connectivity), but not VCs inside of the tunnel
Solution	VCCV allows sending control packets in band of pseudowires (PW) Two components: Signaled component to communicate VCCV capabilities as part of VC label Switching component to cause the PW payload to be treated as a control packet Type 1: Uses protocol ID of PW control word Type 2: Uses MPLS router alert label Type 3: Manipulates TTL exhaust
Applications	Layer 2 transport over MPLS FRoMPLS, ATMoMPLS, EoMPLS
IETF Standards	Draft-ietf-pwe3-vccv-xx.txt

When offering value-added services, such as MPLS VPN, with regard to OAM, the service provider has at its disposal a set of OAM tools, such as IP ping/traceroute, VRF-aware ping and traceroute, MIBs, and MPLS ping/trace.

Each tool can be used independently for verification and troubleshooting. An example of a troubleshooting sequence when dealing with VPN might be:

1   Use IP ping/trace from the CE to assess connectivity at the VPN level.

2   Use VRF-aware ping/trace to assess connectivity between PEs at the VPN level.

3   Use MPLS ping/trace to assess LSP liveliness between PEs.

4   Simultaneously gather MPLS-related MIBs at the LSR of interest for useful information/parameters. This topic is discussed later in this chapter.

Detection tools tend to be lightweight to minimize the processing load in both inserting and processing the messages and obtaining a useful result. An example of such a detection mechanism is BFD, a fixed hello protocol that is useful for fault detection. Neighbors exchange hello packets at negotiated regular intervals. A neighbor is declared down when expected hello packets do not show up.

BFD control packets are encapsulated in UDP datagram destination port 3784 and source port between 49252 to 65535, where the echo packets use source and destination UDP port 3785. VCCV-BFD can complement VCCV-Ping to detect a data plane failure in the forwarding path of a pseudowire. One point to note when using BFD for VCCV and MPLS LSP is that the mechanism induces a requirement on BFD to scale to a large number of sessions; therefore, distributed BFD implementations enhance scalability. The aggressive detection interval with a large number of BFD sessions increases the chance of false-positives when reporting results. Finally, if MPLS LSPs are fast reroutable, the BFD fault detection interval should be greater than the fast-reroute switchover time. Table 12-3 compares VCCV BFD mode with VCCV. VCCV BFD mode can complement VCCV to detect a data plane failure in the forwarding path of a pseudowire. VCCV BFD mode works over MPLS or IP networks, multiple PSN tunnel-type MPLS, IPSec, L2TP, GRE, and so on.

Table 12-3 *VCCV BFD Mode Versus VCCV*

Method	Data Plane Failure Detection	Control Plane Consistency	Protocol Overhead
VCCV ping	Yes	Yes	Higher than BDF
VCCV BFD	Yes	No	Low

A Word About Interworking OAM

When both attachment circuits (AC) of a pseudowire (PW) belong to the same service type, L2VPN thus formed is referred to as a *like to like*. In this case, because the data plane is still homogeneous (like to like), both end points are of the same L2 encapsulation. Even though there is no data plane interworking, it might involve some kind of network interworking at the control plane during PW setup. Control planes interworking might be required when one attachment circuit is connected to a legacy ATM network (non-IP network) and the other end of the pseudowire (AC) might or might not be connected to the legacy network.

The following are the types of like-to-like L2VPN over MPLS:

- ATMoMPLS
- FRoMPLS
- EoMPLS

Any to Any

Any-to-any L2VPN is formed when both end points of the AC are heterogeneous, meaning they belong to different services. In this case, both end points of an AC belong to different Layer 2 services, such as ATM, FR, Ethernet, and so on. Service interworking (conversion from one type to another) can be performed at either of the end points and can be either signaled or provisioned at the corresponding end points.

Common any-to-any scenarios are as follows:

- ATM to FR
- FR to Ethernet
- ATM to Ethernet

Local Switching

When both ACs of the L2VPN connection are terminated on the same node, this is called *local switching*.

Encapsulation Types and Modes
ATM over MPLS

In this mode, one ATM connection is mapped to a pair of PWs (one for each direction) between the PE nodes. Two types of modes are used for carrying cells over the MPLS/IP network—namely, cell mode and packet mode.

- ATM N:1 Cell mode (VC, VP, port)
- ATM 1:1 Cell mode (VC/VP)

Both of these modes support cell packing for transport efficiency. Similarly, two packet mode encapsulations are defined:

- ATM SDU mode (for AAL5)
- ATM PDU mode (for AAL5)

ATM N:1 Mode

This encapsulation supports the binding of multiple VCCs/VPCs to a single pseudowire. N:1 mode can also be used to carry VCs, VPs, or an entire port. In all these cases, the encapsulation remains the same but the content differs. If used in the context of VC/VP mode, it degenerates into one VC for one PW. To clarify, N:1 here indicates the number of vicks mapped to a single PW and not the number of cells packed in a frame.

ATM 1:1 Mode

In this mode, one VC is mapped to one PW. Because only one ATM VCC or VPC is carried on a PW, the VCI and/or VPI of the ATM VCC or VPC can be derived from the context of the PW using the PW label.

AAL5 SDU Mode

The AAL5 SDU encapsulation is more efficient for small AAL5 SDUs than the VCC cell encapsulations because it does not carry the AAL5 trailer, such as length, CRC, and padding.

AAL5 PDU Mode

The primary application supported by AAL5 PDU frame encapsulation over PSN is the transparent carriage of ATM layer services that use AAL5 to carry higher layer frames. The main advantage of this AAL5 mode is that it is transparent to ATM OAM and ATM security applications.

Frame Relay over MPLS

Currently, two modes of operation are defined for transporting Frame Relay over MPLS:

- **One-to-one mode**—In this mode, one Frame Relay connection is mapped to a pair of PWs (one for each direction) between the PE nodes.

- **Port mode**—FR port mode provides transport between two PE ports, transports of a complete FR frame excluding flags, and frame check. FR VCs are not visible individually to a PE; there is no configuration of individual FR VC in a PE.

A PW can potentially fail for many reasons, and we can't list all the failure scenarios here. However, this section delves into some of the most commonly occurring failures and highlights the various scenarios that can cause these failures to occur. In general, the failures can be broadly classified into line/hardware-related, control plane-related, or OAM- or time-based. Even though, strictly speaking, OAM is not a failure and indicates a failure condition only in the upstream or downstream node, we loosely accept that as one of the failure reasons.

Generic Failure Types

This section discusses generic failure types within the context of MPLS-based networks. These include interface failures, pseudowires, and LSP failure conditions.

Interface Failure

Interface failure events are defined as loss of signal, loss of frame, SONET AIS, and so on. These are also known as *line failures* and usually occur in the CE-PE link. If a line failure occurs on the core side, it usually triggers a change in Internet Gateway Protocol (IGP) adjacency, resulting in LSP tunnel failure.

Pseudowire Failures

PW failures are triggered under the following conditions:

- When the targeted LDP keepalive session between the edge PE fails or times out.

- When a link flap or failure occurs on the core network side resulting in loss of adjacency in IGP. This triggers a tunnel failure cascading into a failure of the individual pseudowires that are carried in the tunnel.

- MPLS OAM-related failures. MPLS OAM techniques, such as VCCV, MPLS, and LSP ping are able to detect the health of the PW.

Tunnel LSP Failures

Any failures on the control plane due to timeouts or link failures in network affect the IGP adjacencies and are reflected as tunnel LSP failures. Depending on whether MPLS fast reroute is configured, the tunnel LSP can be rerouted or an alternate path can be found.

For MPLS to be a viable convergence technology, a number of things need to be achieved when considering replacing it with traditional transport technologies or using it as glue to stitch together different layers and create new services. These are as follows:

- Preservation of necessary operational semantics (for example, consistency at the client layers)

- Common behavior of interworking functions (how it acts does not depend on any peer IWF)

- Minimal messaging to convey all requisite information

- Consistent behavior even under multiple fault scenarios (faults notified promptly and cleared properly)

- No unrecoverable states requiring manual intervention

- Consistent behavior no matter what the chain of interworking is (not limited to attachment circuit <->PW<->attachment circuit)

- Works for all interworking scenarios and mixes of technologies

Therefore, you need to consider these emerging interworking OAM and OAM message mapping mechanisms and applicability when deploying Any Tranport over MPLS-based services.

Configuration Management for MPLS-Based Networks

Deploying and offering MPLS VPN services for enterprise customers requires network resource planning, as well as deployment, maintenance, and configuration of the network elements and services. This manual procedure can be time-consuming and inaccurate. Service providers have expressed the desire to automate these steps to be competitive in this market. For a complete service offering, however, service providers must be able to quickly and effectively plan, provision, operate, and bill for the VPN-based services they offer. Figure 12-3 highlights the challenges in MPLS service provisioning; simply put, manual deployments no longer scale.

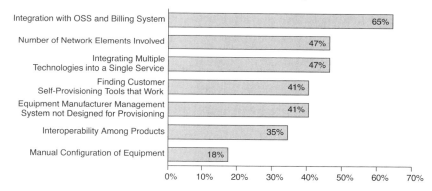

MPLS Service Provisioning Challenge

Challenges in VPN Service Provisioning

Figure 12-3   MPLS Service Provisioning Challenge

Customer priorities for provisioning are as follows:

- Configuration of OAM functions on the network devices depending on the PE, P, and managed CPE roles

- Verification of service after configuration

- Alarm mapping—configuration

- Automation of OAM functionality for proactive monitoring

- Large-scale service provisioning

- Standards-based interfaces to devices—SNMP, programmatic interface

Layer 3 VPNs differ from Layer 1 and Layer 2 VPNs in that the service provider interacts with the customer at Layer 3 and provides routing and forwarding services to the service user, thereby delegating control of the routing architecture of the core transport to the service provider. Layer 3 VPN service providers have multiple Layer 2 access technologies, such as ATM, Frame Relay, serial, Ethernet, and virtual LANs, to provide connectivity to users.

For Layer 3 VPNs, the customer premises equipment (CPE) can be a router or switch because a Layer 3 VPN can consist of an Ethernet segment as a handoff to the customer. In this scenario, the customer might choose to implement an Ethernet switch and use the service provider router as the default gateway between sites. Layer 3 VPNs provide only routed connectivity and do not bridge or forward non-IP protocols.

The routing characteristics of the Layer 3 VPN are strictly defined and enforced within the service provider's network and, more importantly, provide security from other Layer 3 (and Layer 2) VPNs that are defined across the same infrastructure. The degree of scaling achievable within a Layer 3 VPN is provided by the use of extensions to the Border Gateway Protocol (BGP4), a robust, Internet-scale routing protocol that has been extended to support the concept of VPN awareness. We have already discussed these scaling attributes earlier in the book.

Because service providers need to bring services to market quickly, train field operators, and deploy accurate customer services, they are increasingly turning to OSSs or business support systems (BSS) to find solutions. The Cisco IP Solution Center manages a range of Layer 2 and 3 MPLS-related technologies, including these:

- VPNs based on MPLS BGP, IPSec, ATM over MPLS, and Frame Relay over MPLS

- Metro Ethernet services such as Ethernet Virtual Connection Services (EVCS); transparent LAN services (TLS); and Ethernet to the home, building, or campus (ETTx)

Cisco Info Center VPN Policy Manager integrates with Cisco IP Solution Center to enable a deeper understanding of which MPLS VPNs are affected by a network fault, how to prioritize events, and how to effectively and quickly troubleshoot the problem. After the VPN has been analyzed, a report is sent to the Cisco Info Center detailing the affected MPLS VPNs and the customers running across those VPNs. This information is presented to the network operations center (NOC) or VPN user as a specific customer network managed view.

This capability provides clear benefits, including:

- Events (faults) are automatically captured and correlated to clearly identify impacted MPLS VPNs and customers more quickly.

- A set of troubleshooting tools is available to exploit intelligent Cisco IOS MPLS, such as the MPLS Embedded Management toolset mentioned previously for much faster MPLS troubleshooting.

- A system-based combination of event collection, service-level correlation, and sophisticated troubleshooting tools. This gives full life cycle event management and reporting for Cisco-based MPLS networks, focused on the NOC and customer needs from the same data store.

For fault management in particular, Cisco Info Center is integrated with the Cisco ISC Northbound Programmatic Interface (XML over HTTP) to provide fault management functions in a service provider's NOC.

The following fault scenarios are supported:

- Provider edge-customer edge directly connected topology
- In this case, the lists of events that are monitored and correlated include the following:
    - Interface up/down
    - VRF up/down
    - VRF threshold alarms (min., mid., and max.)
    - VRF labels crossing
    - VLAN up/down
    - Syslog messages related to interface, VRF, and VLAN

For all these events (SNMP traps or syslog messages), Cisco Info Center initiates a query via the Cisco ISC Northbound Interface to extract the impacted provider edge, customer edge, site, customer, and VPN information.

In the case of Layer 2 access into MPLS VPN, the added fault conditions are in the Layer 2 Ethernet access domain. VLANs are used to distribute the customer access. Ethernet Relay Service (ERS), Ethernet Wire Service (EWS), and Layer 2 access into MPLS VPN are the services currently supported for the Cisco Metro Ethernet Services. Many customers could be serviced using the same Layer 2 Ethernet infrastructure.

A failure in any given link can potentially impact many customers. In this scenario, Cisco Info Center correlates a single interface failure to many customers and services.

The types of failures include, for example:

- Interface up/down
- VLAN up down
- Device up/down

ISC also has two proactive mechanisms to detect any fault in the network. For all the MPLS VPN and L2 VPN services that ISC deployed, ISC has the corresponding IOS CLI configuration. Network operators can schedule on a periodic basis a configuration audit for the deployed services. A configuration audit connects to all the routers/switches involved in a given service request and verifies the presence of the IOS CLI commands on the network devices.

For MPLS VPN services in particular, ISC can perform a functional audit, which consists of a configuration audit and a routing audit that consists of verifying that the 30 PE-CE IP addresses have propagated to the correct PE. This routing audit is performed in the context of an MPLS VPN hierarchy (full mesh, hub and spoke, or partial mesh). If a problem is detected, ISC marks the service request to the "Broken" state for a routing problem and to "Lost" for a missing configuration. A tool such as ISC can certainly facilitate provisioning for both Layer 2 and Layer 3 VPNs and is a key component for OSS/BSS.

Accounting for MPLS-Based Networks

NetFlow capitalizes on the flow nature of traffic in the network to provide detailed IP accounting information with minimal impact on router/switch performance. NetFlow monitors IP flows in the router/switch and exports the flows in UDP format to a NetFlow collector. The NetFlow collector can correlate, aggregate, and report on the data received from the network. NetFlow data can be used for a variety of purposes, including network management and planning, enterprise accounting, departmental chargeback, usage-based billing, data warehousing/mining for marketing purposes, and so on. The latest version of

NetFlow, version 9, extends it to support MPLS label information, IPv6 details, BGP next-hop data, and multicast information.

MPLS-aware NetFlow can be used to determine and account for traffic to a particular destination in the MPLS cloud. It also supports the complete IP flow information export plus the export of up to three labels and label destination prefix information including the MPLS EXP value. In addition, MPLS-aware NetFlow can also account for MPLS traffic that contains IP or non-IP packets and has the capability to include the MPLS header as part of the accounting information. MPLS-aware NetFlow is an extension of NetFlow accounting that provides highly granular traffic statistics for Cisco routers. It collects statistics on a per-flow basis using the NetFlow Version 9 export format. MPLS-aware NetFlow exports up to three labels of interest from the incoming label stack, the IP address associated with the top label, as well as traditional NetFlow data. A network administrator can turn on MPLS-aware NetFlow inside an MPLS cloud on a subset of provider backbone (P) routers. These routers can export MPLS-aware NetFlow data to an external NetFlow collector device for further processing and analysis or show NetFlow cache data on a router terminal. All statistics can be used for detailed MPLS traffic studies and analysis.

The MPLS egress NetFlow accounting feature captures IP flow information for packets undergoing MPLS label disposition—that is, packets that arrive on a router as MPLS and that are transmitted as IP. One common application of the MPLS egress NetFlow accounting is to capture the MPLS VPN IP flows that are traveling from one site of a VPN to another site of the same VPN through the service provider backbone.

Performance Management for MPLS-Based Networks

Cisco IOS IP Service Level is widely used when network performance measurement and SLA monitoring data such as jitter statistics, packet loss, and RTT are required within an IP-based network. Cisco IOS IP Service Level collects network performance information in real time: response time, one-way latency, one-way jitter, one-way packet loss, voice quality measurement, and other network statistics. It also provides unidirectional and bidirectional measurements and supports measurements per class of service. Also available are proactive notification and threshold violation monitoring for jitter, packet loss, latency, and connectivity. All Cisco IOS Service Level performance statistics are available in the SNMP MIB modules.

In addition, Cisco IOS Service Level provides unique tools that allow monitoring of MPLS Layer 3–based VPNs. Cisco Auto IOS Service Level adds capabilities, such as simplifying the deployment and configuration of the Cisco IOS Service Level probes whenever performance measurement and SLA monitoring for an MPLS Layer 3 VPN infrastructure are required. The extended features include automatic generation of probes to measure performance between MPLS PE routers, proactive monitoring of the MPLS network, and automatic optimization of probe scheduling giving a better scan coverage time. Cisco IOS Service Level uses UDP probes based on LSP ping/trace tools for connectivity and performance measurement (operations that can be configured under Cisco IOS Service Level MPLS LSP monitor are echo, pathEcho, jitter, and pathJitter).

Security Management for MPLS-Based Networks

Security considerations for MPLS-based networks have been described previously in this book. The use of Message Digest-5 (MD-5) for the control plane protocols, such as BGP, LDP, and RSVP message authentication, is advised.

The next section discusses per-VPN management mechanisms as part of the MPLS Management toolbox.

Per-VPN Management

Some of the traditional services supported by enterprise and SP networks include redundancy, security, and IP addressing. These services must be supported in MPLS networks. If an enterprise customer subscribes to services from an MPLS service provider, cohosts services with a service provider, or manages his own MPLS network, the enterprise networks must support the existing IP services seamlessly over the new infrastructure. To facilitate this, some of the services are made MPLS-aware so a single resource can be used to serve multiple VPNs instead of dedicating a resource to a VPN. This reduces equipment investment and operational costs. Several services are made VRF-aware and the portfolio is growing.

The specific types of services that can be VRF-aware are as follows:

- Redundancy: VRF-aware HSRP
- IP addressing:
  - NAT-PE: VRF-aware network address translation (NAT)
  - DHCP/ODAP: VRF-aware DHCP and ODAP for IP address assignment and management
- Security: VRF-aware IPSec

Each of these applications is made VRF-aware by adding an MPLS VPN ID component. Traffic is kept separate using unique VPN IDs, enabling applications to distinguish traffic coming from different VPNs. We discuss VRF-aware DHCP and VRF-aware NAT in this section.

IP Addressing

VRF-aware DHCP IP address assignment and management has been one of the key services required for enterprise networks. Enterprise networks need to support these services in MPLS VPN environments whether MPLS VPNs are deployed locally or the enterprise customer is subscribing to MPLS VPN services from a service provider. The DHCP server needs to be able to distinguish the request coming from hosts located in various VPNs, so that the replies can be sent to the intended host in a VPN. VPN awareness is added to the DHCP applications in the Cisco solution to address the unique needs in an MPLS VPN environment.

Several techniques are available that can be used to assign IP addresses:

- Local pools on Cisco routers
- Dedicated RADIUS server
- Dedicated DHCP server

DHCP can be deployed in various configurations:

- Centralized DHCP server in the enterprise network
- A single DHCP server hosts IP subnets for multiple VPN hosts
- Distributed DHCP servers in the enterprise network
- Having dedicated DHCP servers per remote site
- Co-host DHCP with a service provider
- Outsource DHCP services for all or selected sites

For all three scenarios, a DHCP server can be located in a global table, in a VRF, or in a common VRF. If MPLS VPNs are deployed in an enterprise network and all the services are being managed within this network, having a centralized DHCP server that services hosts within a company's VPNs makes the most sense. This model helps reduce server replications throughout the network, thereby reducing capital and operational expenses; facilitating ease of provisioning, managing, and troubleshooting; and preserving IP address space. The supported VPN topologies are hub and spoke, fully meshed sites, and a hybrid model.

This case does not require VRF-aware DHCP support because DHCP requests and replies do not traverse the MPLS VPN network.

An IP helper address in any case is needed to get the router to forward BOOTP requests. You configure the IP helper address with the VPN option on the PE interface that connects to the clients.

If you have any security concerns—for example, internal or external non-VPN clients reaching the DHCP server—you can put the PE interface that is connected to the servers in a VRF. Additional IPSec techniques to prevent attacks should be used. Notice that the router sends its own interface IP address as a DHCP server address, so the DHCP server address should not be known to the clients.

To summarize, when using a VRF-aware DHCP, it is advisable to:

- Size a DHCP server appropriately based on the number of users the DHCP server will support.

- Make sure overlapping address pools are not used for the hosts in the same VPNs.

- Make sure the DHCP server supports Option 82 SubOption VPN ID if you are using a third-party DHCP server.

- If you're using a firewall or are blocking traffic using access lists in the path, allow UDP port 67 and 69 and allow for BOOTP requests.

VRF-Aware Network Address Translation

For VPNs that use private address space, you need to do address translation for the hosts that need access to public domain or shared services segments. Different VPNs commonly use overlapping private address space. Thus, you must do address translation before the traffic can access public domain or shared services located in a shared data center.

If the enterprise is subscribing to VPN services from a service provider and is using private address space, you must do address translation at the CPE. VRF-aware address translation allows the enterprise customers to offload it to their service provider.

Per-VPN self-management complements VRF-aware central services essential to managing these services discreetly.

Supported MIBs

Standard MPLS MIB modules provide standards-based SNMP interfaces for network operators to rely on vendor element management applications, third-party specialized independent software vendors, or home-grown management applications.

Some key MPLS MIB modules supported in Cisco IOS are MPLS-LSR-STD MIB, MPLS-TE-STD MIB, MPLS-FTN-STD MIB, MPLS-LDP-STD MIB, and MPLS-TC-STD MIB.

Figure 12-4 provides an overview of MPLS network and service MIBs.

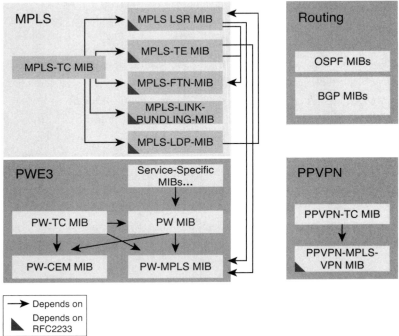

Figure 12-4 *MPLS Network and Services MIB Summary and Concept/ Architecture/Dependencies*

Standards and References

At the time of the book publication, we can enumerate Cisco support for the following drafts and RFCs as these relate to MPLS management:

- RFC 4377, "OAM Requirements for MPLS Networks"
- RFC 4379, "MPLS LSP Ping/Traceroute"

- LSR Self-Test
- Draft-ietf-mpls-lsr-self-test-xx.VCCV, http://www.ietf.org/internet-drafts/pwe3-vccv-xx.txt
- Bidirectional Forwarding Detection for MPLS LSPs, http://www1.ietf.org/internet-drafts/draft-ietf-bfd-mpls-xx.txt
- OAM Message Mapping, draft-ietf-pwe3-oam-msg-map-xx.txt
- Bidirectional Detection MIB, draft-ietf-bfd-mib-xx.txt
- RFC 3812, "MPLS Traffic Engineering MIB"
- RFC 3814, "Forward Equivalence Class Next Hop Label Forwarding Entry MIB"
- RFC 3815, "LDP MIB"
- RFC 3818, "LSR MIB"

Summary

In this chapter we have discussed mechanisms required to manage and monitor MPLS-based networks. These mechanisms correlate to the FCAPS model for network management. We further identified examples of per-VPN management constructs used for VRF-aware central services. Cisco has been driving the development of MPLS management mechanisms in the standards bodies—specifically the IETF—and a list of these IETF drafts and RFCs were provided. Finally, these mechanisms are evolutionary as articulated by customers and will continue to develop to match service management requirements for MPLS-based networks.

CHAPTER 13

DESIGN CONSIDERATIONS: PUTTING IT ALL TOGETHER

In this chapter, we examine overall design considerations when putting together an IP Next Generation Network (NGN) for the service provider (SP) or enterprise. As you learned earlier, L3VPNs require VPN Routing and Forwardings (VRF). This also implies that many other features and protocols used in designing the whole network should be VRF-aware. In this chapter, we consider VRF-aware feature deployments in addition to management and provisioning factors for overall network deployment. We further discuss scalability issues, such as equipment scalability versus network scalability, as factors for designing MPLS-based services. Additionally, we highlight Layer 2 design considerations for planning and implementing an NGN over MPLS-based networks.

VRF-Aware Feature

As identified in Chapter 6, "Remote Access and IPSec/MPLS VPN Integration," the trend is toward discretely defining VRF-aware capabilities as part of a managed central services strategy. Some of the traditional services supported by an enterprise network include redundancy, security, and IP addressing. Simple Network Management Protocol (SNMP) is also VRF-aware to allow "virtual" access to the management and Management Information Base (MIB) information. Currently, Cisco supports VRF-aware SNMP infrastructure with which any MIB can be easily made VRF-aware.

It is critical that these services are supported in the MPLS-based NGN. If an enterprise customer subscribes to services from an MPLS service provider (SP), co-host services with an SP, or manages his own MPLS network, it is imperative for the enterprise networks to support the existing IP services and management capabilities seamlessly over the new infrastructure. To facilitate this, some of the services are made MPLS-aware, so a single resource can be used to serve multiple VPNs instead of dedicating a resource to a VPN. This reduces equipment investment and operational costs. Several services are made VRF-aware and the portfolio is growing.

Each of these applications is made VRF-aware by providing a VRF context for IP lookup within the box. For example, each VRF table is stored separately internal to the box. For any application, the router by default does a lookup in the global table for an IP route, especially if the packets are sourced to and from the router itself. One example is Telnet running on the box and an operator initiates the Telnet session either to the box or from the box to a VPN destination. Then, if Telnet is VRF-aware, the router tries to look up the IP address in the default table (global table). If the application is VRF-aware on the router, then by simply providing the VRF context, the lookup happens in the specific VRF table for packet transmission to the right destination.

Note that services enabled on the PE for shared operation need only to be VRF-aware. All other service within the VPN can operate transparently as long as the PE is not part of those services. In other words, if the Telnet session is between two host nodes inside the VPN and not to or from the PE router itself, there is no need for the PE Telnet service to be VRF-aware. Telnet packets that go from and to destinations inside a VPN pass through transparently via the PE.

VPN-ID as defined in RFC 2685 is used to uniquely identify VPNs across single or multiple ASes. When using shared services across ASes, VPN-ID can be used on the PE to uniquely identify a VPN for appropriate VRF lookup of traffic.

Following is the list of applications and capabilities that are VRF-aware; it is by no means a comprehensive one:

- Ping, traceroute

- Telnet, SNMP

- VRF Static ARP

- Hot Standby Router Protocol (HSRP)

- Dynamic Host Configuration Protocol (DHCP)

- On Demand Address Pools (ODAP)

- Network Address Translation (NAT)

- Service Assurance Agent (SAA)

- Authentication, Authorization, and Accounting (AAA)

- Syslog

- Terminal Access Controller Access Control System+ (TACACS+)

- IP Security (IPSec)

- Public Key Infrastructure (PKI)

- Firewall

- Gateway Load Balancing Protocol (GLBP)

- Virtual Router Redundancy Protocol (VRRP)

- Layer 2 Tunneling Protocol (L2TP)

- Remote Access Software (RAS)

VRF-specific capability helps provide a highly efficient, managed central services capability because, without this, each service needs to be replicated per VPN, as shown in Figure 13-1.

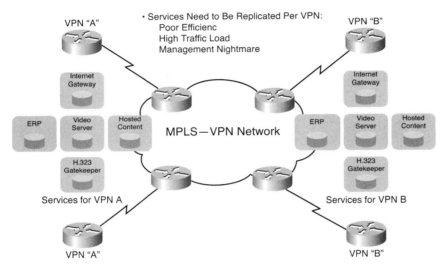

Figure 13-1   *MPLS/VPN: Before Managed Shared Services*

We provide design examples for the following services: DHCP and NAT.

IP Addressing: VRF-Aware DHCP

IP address assignment and management has been one of the key services required for enterprise networks. Enterprise networks need to support these services in an MPLS VPN environment whether MPLS VPNs are deployed locally or the enterprise customer is subscribing to MPLS VPN services from a service provider.

The DHCP server needs to be able to distinguish the requests coming from hosts located in various VPNs so that the replies can be sent to the intended host in a VPN. VPN awareness is added to the DHCP applications in Cisco solutions that address the unique needs in MPLS VPN environments.

Several techniques are available that can be used to assign IP addresses. These are:

- Local pools maintained on routers
- Dedicated Radius Server
- Dedicated DHCP Server

DHCP can be deployed in various configurations, such as the following:

- Centralized DHCP Server in the enterprise network—A single DHCP server hosts IP subnets for multiple VPN hosts.
- Distributed DHCP servers in the enterprise network—A dedicated DHCP server per remote site within a VPN providing DHCP addressing to local sites or a set of sites.
- Co-host DHCP with a service provider—Centralized per VPN. Outsource DHCP services to the SP for all or selected sites.

For all four scenarios, a DHCP server can be located in a global table, in a VRF, or in a common VRF.

If MPLS VPNs are deployed in an enterprise network and all the services are being managed within this network, having a centralized DHCP server that services hosts within a company's VPNs makes the most sense. This model helps reduce server replications throughout the network, reducing capital and operational expenses and facilitating ease of provisioning, management, and troubleshooting, as well as preserving IP address space. The supported VPN topologies are hub and spoke, fully meshed sites, and a hybrid model.

DHCP Deployment Examples

The following examples are DHCP deployment scenarios:

- Dedicated DHCP server per site—This case does not require VRF-aware DHCP support because DHCP requests and replies do not traverse the MPLS VPN network.
- Dedicated DHCP server per VRF in a central location.
- Shared DHCP server for multiple VPNs over MPLS VPN network.

- Cisco IOS as a DHCP server for directly connected clients.

- Cisco IOS as DHCP server on H-CEs or S-CEs.

- Shared or dedicated DHCP server for multiple VPNs over MPLS VPN network.

- Cisco IOS as a DHCP server for nondirectly connected clients.

For cases 2 and 3, Spoke-PE1 is the relay agent. It forwards DHCP requests to the designated DHCP server that is associated with a VRF and replies with an assigned IP address back to the hosts.

This is an example of using the router as a DHCP server in an IPV4 environment. Remember that VPNs originate on PE unless Multi-VRF is enabled on the CE.

Case 6 is an example of supporting sites such as Spoke-Site2 and Hub-Site clients. For this type of connection, use VRF-aware On Demand Address Pool (ODAP) supported with Cisco Network Registrar (CNR5.5 and above). ODAP pool manager downloads pools of IP addresses on appropriate PEs (Hub-PE, Spoke-PE2). The pool can expand or shrink based on address demand. ODAP works with DHCP clients and for devices connected to the PE router using Point-to-Point Protocol (PPP). A PPP session that belongs to a specific VPN is allocated an address only from the ODAP associated with that VPN. These PPP sessions are terminated on a Virtual Home Gateway (VHG)/PE router where the ODAP is configured. The VHG/PE router maps the remote user to the corresponding MPLS VPNs.

Case 7 is an example of having DataCenter-PE act as a DHCP server for any clients. This scenario is not supported yet. Support will be implemented based on demand.

An IP helper address is needed in any case to get the router to forward BOOTP requests. Configure the IP helper address with the VPN option on the PE interface that connects to the clients.

If you have any security concerns—for example, internal or external non-VP clients reaching the DHCP server—you can put the (PE) interface that is connected to the servers in a VRF. You should use additional IP Security (IPSec) techniques to prevent attacks. Notice that the router sends its own interface IP address as a DHCP server address. So, the DHCP server address should not be known to the clients. Figure 13-2 shows a DHCP relay for MPLS-VPNs serving a single VPN, and Figure 13-3 depicts DHCP relays for shared MPLS-VPNs.

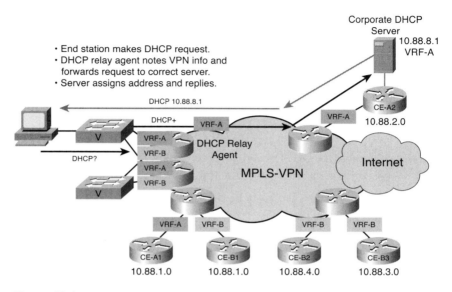

Figure 13-2 *DHCP Relay for MPLS VPNs Serving: Single VPN*

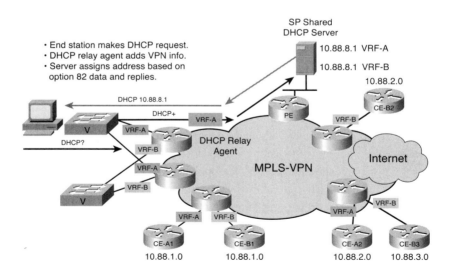

Figure 13-3 *HCP Relay for MPLS VPNs: Shared*

Deployment Guideline Summary

The following list summarizes guidelines for deployment:

- Size a DHCP server appropriately based on the number of users that the DHCP server will support. You must account for all the addresses dynamically assigned by the DHCP server, including any interface addresses, and so on.

- Make sure overlapping address pools are not used for the hosts in the same VPNs.

- Make sure the DHCP server supports Option 82 SubOption VPNID if you are using a third-party DHCP server.

- If you are using a firewall or blocking traffic using access lists in the path, allow for UDP ports 67 and 69 and for BOOTP requests.

- Refer to Cisco Feature Navigator for hardware and software support guidelines.

VRF-Aware Network Address Translation

For VPNs that use private address space, you need to do address translation for the hosts that need access to the public domain or a shared services segment. It is common for different VPNs to use overlapping private address space. Thus, you must do address translation before the traffic can access the public domain or shared services located in a shared datacenter.

If the enterprise subscribes to VPN services from a service provider and uses private address space, you need to do address translation at the CPE. VRF-aware address translation allows the enterprise customers to offload it to their service provider. Enterprise customers who have deployed MPLS VPNs and use private addresses have options to do address translation at various points within the network. This is a generic hub-and-spoke topology. You can dedicate a NAT PE, multiple NAT PEs, or perform address translation in a distributed manner. For example, you can do address translation at

- CE egress interfaces (CE interface connected to PE)

- PE ingress interfaces (on the PE interfaces connected to CEs, labeled with odd numbers)

- On core facing egress interfaces (interfaces labeled with even numbers)

- Dedicated NAT PE with an inside interface, facing the core, and an outside interface, facing (connecting) the Internet gateway and, or a shared data center

- Hybrid model (combination of distributed and central model)

If the address translation is done at the CE1 devices, you do not need VRF-aware NAT. You can do VRF-aware address translation at the points showing odd numbers in this topology. Note, though, that these are ingress interfaces on PE devices for the traffic coming from remote sites. The advantage is that the address translation load is distributed on multiple PEs. In this type of deployment, you need to keep track of the public IP address range used on each PE.

Another approach is to deploy a VRF-aware NAT at interfaces labeled with even numbers in the topology.

Similar principles apply for a fully meshed VPN topology.

A single IP address pool can be used to assign addresses to multiple VPNs. The IP address pool can also be dedicated to a VPN. If you have a large number of VPNs, provisioning could get cumbersome with increased numbers of access lists and pool statements. On the other hand, it is easier to manage and troubleshoot if you use dedicated IP address pools.

Be aware that VRF-aware NAT inherits all the limitations from generic NAT. It supports all the applications supported by generic NAT. In addition, it works the same way as generic NAT. The following section summarizes VRF-aware NAT operation.

NAT-PE System Flow

Now let us take a detailed look at the packet flow for NAT on the PE device. Packets can flow in both directions from hosts in global address space to hosts in private address space. Hosts in global address space are outside hosts, and hosts in private address space are inside hosts.

Inside-to-Outside Packet Flow

In this example, packets from a customer(s) in VPN A and VPN B with overlapping addresses are destined to the data center. After route lookup, NAT performs the translation (static or dynamic) and stores the VRF table ID in the translation entry.

Outside-to-Inside Packet Flow

NAT gets hold of the packet before routing and does a lookup on the translation table. NAT performs the reverse translation and sets the VRF table ID in the packet descriptor header.

This enables the subsequent route lookup to be done on the right forwarding information block.

If the outgoing interface is in a VRF on the same PE, the packet is forwarded an IP packet. If the destination is on a remote PE, the packet is imposed with an MPLS label and forwarded on the core facing interface.

Figure 13-4 depicts NAT and MPLS VPN shared services.

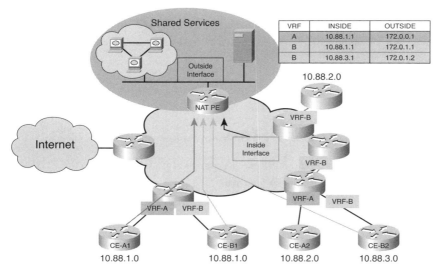

Figure 13-4 *NAT and MPLS VPN for Shared Services*

Deployment Guideline Summary

The following list summarizes deployment guidelines:

- Centralizing address translation makes keeping track of address assignment easier. Multiple NAT PEs might be required for load balancing. If this is the case, make sure public address pools do not overlap. One of the possible disadvantages to centralizing is the amount of redundancy that can be achieved by replication. For example, in a noncentralized environment, one gateway/server failure can result in an outage of only that VPN's service. However, in a centralized environment, a single gateway/shared PE failure can affect multiple VPNs. This drawback can be easily overcome by having multiple PEs that serve as shared gateways, which provide services to the same VPNs. So, you can provide redundancy with shared gateways.

- If VPNs that use overlapping private address space need to access a shared services segment, make sure that private address space is translated somewhere in the path.

- NAT impacts CPU utilization to a degree. Some protocols are more CPU-intensive than others. Therefore, the type of translation being performed could have significant performance impact. The impact is less for newer particle-based routers and more powerful routers.

- As the number of translation entries increases, the throughput in terms of packets per second (PPS) decreases. The effect is negligible for less than 10,000 translation table entries.

- The rate at which a router can add a new translation table entry decreases as the number of entries in the translation table increases.

- As the number of translation entries in the translation table increases, the amount of memory used increases.

Refer to Cisco Feature navigator for hardware and software support guidelines at the following website: http://tools.cisco.com/ITDIT/CFN/jsp/index.jsp.

Management, Provisioning, and Troubleshooting

Scalability affects management, provisioning, and troubleshooting design best practice guidelines such as knowing the minimum, average, and maximum number of equal cost multi-paths (ECMP) in the network and the frequency of Interior Gateway Protocol (IGP) changes within a given topology. Often, customers ask, "How scalable is LSP Ping?" The response depends on a variety of factors, such as the topology characteristics of a network and the device sending the probes with available CPU and memory. We look at a detailed analysis of scale factors a little later.

Management, provisioning, and troubleshooting assume access from the network operations center to the CEs. Although all CEs (customer owned included) should be under the management umbrella, the accessibility of CEs depends on the management model. There are multiple ways of managing CEs. For example, static routes can be configured to reach the CEs in a VRF or all CE and PE loopbacks can be in a network management VRF, called the VPN_Network_Management. Each approach has its advantages and disadvantages, and a detailed network management design is beyond the scope of this book.

The Service Provider Network Management station(s) originates from this VRF. Conversely, each customer VRF should contain the service provider network management station(s) to permit bidirectional communication between the management workstation and the CE router. By creating a management VRF, all CE routers can be managed from a single spot, and by virtue of the transitivity rule (that is, only routes that originate from the VRF are exported and routing separation is guaranteed between CE routers).

In terms of troubleshooting, a distinction exists between detection and diagnostics. *Detection* can involve using a mechanism such as bidirectional forwarding detection (BFD), and *diagnostics* implies the use of tools such as LSP-Ping or virtual circuit connection verification (VCCV) to locate and repair a problem in the MPLS network.

For design considerations, we note the following BFD factors:

- BFD over VCCV—The ability to send BFD packets for VCCV; this induces a requirement on BFD to scale to a large number of sessions.

- Distributed BFD implementations are needed to deal with the scalability requirement.

- An aggressive detection interval with a large number of BFD sessions increases the chance of false positives.

- If MPLS LSPs is fast-reroutable, the BFD fault detection interval should be greater than the fast-reroute switchover time.

Fast detection via BFD for MPLS LSPs and VCCV still requires additional study and operational input to recommend best practice guidelines.

We recommend you use tools such as LSP-Ping or VCCV for diagnostic purposes rather than at high frequency.

These tools are designed for troubleshooting and therefore can impact the performance of the network depending on the platform executing these tools, the number of ECMP paths in the network, and the frequency of IGP changes. The next section focuses more on equipment and network scalability factors that impact network design and the execution of tools and applications.

Equipment Scalability Versus Network Scalability

Scalability is an important factor when considering technology and equipment for deployment. Technology with limited scalability has severely limited applications. Specially, when MPLS is deployed by large service providers, you must understand how well MPLS scales and the role equipment scalability plays in scaling the overall network deployment.

We have stated in earlier chapters that equipment scalability must not hamper network scalability. However, when equipment runs into its bounds, adding more network elements can help scale the network; however, it also means more devices to manage. After a point, even adding more equipment can no longer provide the same linear change that is expected—this is called the *point of inflexion*. The farther the point of inflexion on the scalability chart, the better the overall scale factor. Let us quantitatively define some things.

We have also shown in Chapters 4, "Layer 2 VPNs," and 5, "Layer 3 VPNs," that a network with MPLS network scalability is not an issue because devices can be added, and no single device is a bottleneck in building L3VPNs or L2VPNs.

Assume we are determining the scale factor of an L3 network. To establish the scale factor, we need to understand the network element scalability. The parameters influencing the scale of the network elements are as follows:

- Network element characteristics

- CPU power

- Memory (static and dynamic)

- Buffering capacity

- Number of line cards and interfaces nonblocking (interfaces include Channelized and Clear Channel)

- Network parameters

- Number of L2 VCs

    - FR DLCIs
    - ATM VCs
    - PPP sessions
    - Ethernet VLANs
    - High-Level Data Link Control (HDLC) sessions

- Number of L3 sessions

    - BGP peers (eBGP and iBGP)
    - IGP peers (OSPF, IS-IS, EIGRP, and RIP)
    - LDP peers
    - RSVP TE tunnels (head-end, mid-point, and tails)

- Number of routes

    - IGP prefixes and convergence
    - BGP prefixes and convergence
    - VPN prefixes and convergence

- MPLS scale

    - LDP scale—Number of LDP sessions (neighbor and directed LDP sessions)
    - BGP assigned labels
    - RSVP assigned labels

- • PIM assigned labels
- • GMPLS signaling (RSVP-based)
- • MPLS forwarding
- • SNMP Gets/Sets (simultaneous)

Network element characteristics determine the maximum number of network parameters possible on a device in isolation. However, even if a device is capable of supporting large numbers of each of these parameters in isolation, the device will not necessarily scale well in a real network. This is simply because none of these network parameters will be deployed/configured in isolation within the network. In a real network, the combination of these parameters matters. Hence, as an example, a device must not just be able to support a million prefixes, but must also support a large IGP table; label allocation for all those routes using LDP, BGP, or RSVP; thousands of L2 VCs; and hundreds or even thousands of IP interfaces all at the same time while passing traffic on each of the data paths.

You might think such a network device is nonexistent. In an ideal world, a network element can be configured with all the previously mentioned parameters with huge scale numbers for each and be able to pass traffic at line rate on all ports. However, practically speaking, irrespective of the vendor, it is rarely the case. Hence, the operational paradigm is important to determine what the reasonable scale numbers for a network element are. Decision-makers evaluating equipment for NGN must find their operational sweet spot. Having a highly scalable network element can drive the CAPEX up by running up the cost per unit, and whether it really drives the OPEX down is unclear because fewer devices are required in the network for the same customer base. This is because the OPEX is mainly associated with customer end-point management rather than network core or network edge (PE) management.

Moreover, configuring all services with large numbers of VPNs and L2 circuits equates to placing all your eggs in a single basket. The decision-makers must also determine whether the risk of placing all the services on a single node warrants the benefit gained by the cost reduction that can be attributed to using fewer devices for the same subscriber base. Should the highly scalable device fail or need to be taken out of service for any reason, the failure can affect many users.

Figure 13-5 shows the plot of network elements versus management cost. The fewer the network elements, the lower the management cost.

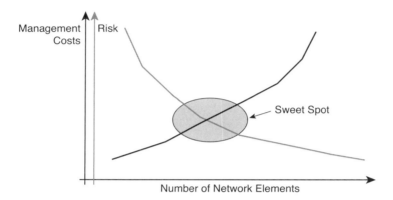

Figure 13-5 *Management Costs and Risks*

However, the fewer the network elements, the higher the risk of outage for subscribers.

Network Element Characteristics

Additionally, IP NGN managers and decision-makers must also determine how these network elements interact in the network. What happens when the IGP is too large or when a VPN is too large? They must design routing such that the network is appropriately segmented in areas or ASes such that any change in network does not impact the entire network but only that portion of the network where the change has occurred.

Let us now briefly discuss each of those parameters that determine network element scalability:

- CPU power—With the hardware-based forwarding common in network elements today, CPU power is mainly used in handling control plane activity. Hence, the higher the CPU power, in terms of processing, the faster the network element can process routing updates, calculate paths, perform SPF, handle management, and converge. However, after custom

ASICs and fabric, CPU is the single most expensive component in the network element. This implies that the higher the CPU power, the more expensive the route processor on the network element.

- Memory, static and dynamic—Memory is required on network elements to store routes and MAC tables in addition to operating system parameters. Assuming the implementation is good, the larger the available memory on the box, the higher the number of routes that can be stored in the network element. The transient memory usage is also important to determine network element load conditions. Better transient usage enables the device to handle a larger churn in the network.

- L3 interfaces—The number of Layer 3 interfaces supported on the network element determines the number of ports and customers that can be connected to this network element for an L3 service. (The total number of L3 customers that can be connected to the network element equals the total number of L3 interfaces—the number of L3 interfaces used to handle core/edge adjacencies and VRFs.) It is common these days to find devices with 3000 to 5000 IP interfaces. In broadband aggregation devices, this number can grow to more than 10,000 interfaces.

Network Parameters

This section discusses network parameters and their scale requirements that must be met by network elements in designing a robust IP NGN.

- L2 VCs—In providing L2 services, L2 VCs provide a measure of the number of L2 circuits that can be transmitted across this device. For a multi-service edge device, this number can be reasonably large with as many as 10,000 VCs supported on a single network element. These L2 VCs can be Frame Relay DLCIs, ATM VCs, Ethernet VLANs, or PPP or HDLC connections.

- L3 sessions—A high number of L3 sessions must be supported to build large networks. For example, a network element can support up to hundreds of IGP adjacencies, thousands of BGP sessions, and thousands of TE tunnels and directed LDP sessions. Today, typical large-scale deployments have seen up to 1000 BGP sessions (eBGP for customer connections), tens of IBGP sessions if full mesh for L3VPNs. The largest IGP seen is 32,000, and the maximum number of IGP neighbors for any given node is 32. These are real provider numbers. For most networks today, the actual numbers might be less. However, for a decision-maker, setting a realistic expectation is important. For example, when evaluating equipment, it is important to buy equipment that provides room for growth, based on expected service demand and current network factors.

For example, increasing the degree of connectivity for IGP to be greater than 2x is unrealistic. Having IGP prefixes increase by 2x in the network, however, is realistic. Decision-makers must consider all these factors carefully and weigh how much the factors strengthen manageability against equipment scale.

TE tunnels also need to scale well. For example, with a network of 1000 PEs and a full mesh of TE tunnels, you need 999 TE tunnels from each device to connect to all the other devices. However, you must analyze how realistic this scenario is. Again, the largest deployed number today is 130 tunnel heads and about 3000 mid-points on any given network element. In network design you must consider how long a network element with a capability to signal 1500 to 2000 tunnels will last if the tunnel growth is 2x, or even 3x. Remember, these tunnels are not per subscriber or per user, but per PE-PE or P-P pair for a class of service as a worst-case scenario.

- Number of routes—The number of routes/prefixes supported by a network element is extremely important for deploying a scalable service. Despite the fact that with L3VPNs, equipment scale does not impact the network scale in a negative manner, having too many devices in the network can cause other issues, such as lower convergence and more control plane activity. For example, a network element can support one million VPN prefixes, the Internet table, and a 35,000 to 40,000 IGP table all at the same time.

- MPLS scale—This is a generic category for MPLS control plane scale and MPLS forwarding scalability. Network elements must be capable of supporting a large number of LDP sessions for L2 scalability. When offering an L2VPN service using AToM (Any Transport over MPLS), LDP signaling must take place between PEs. If the number of PEs is large, say n, then the maximum number of directed LDP sessions required on any given PE is n-1. So, for a 1000 PE network, you need a network element to support 1000 directed LDP sessions. Similarly, based on the degree of connectivity, the number of neighbor sessions required for LDP is in the order of 100. Moreover, the network elements should be able to allocate the full label space for each application. With 20 bits of label space, the maximum number of local labels that can be allocated is one million.

In reality, no application to date requires the full label space. Remember that the labels are local to the box and are allocated by the box. So in reality, the number of labels needed is equal to the number of connected prefixes, attachment circuits, or TE tunnels. This number is far lower than one million, even for the most densely packed interfaces in a network element. Another element of MPLS scale is the ability to store a large number of labels and process packets for those LSPs. The requirement here, however, is to support a large number of labels. So, if a network element supports one million prefixes, the same network element must also be able to store labels for these one million prefixes and forward packets to them on the label-switched paths. Anything short of that could result in supporting fewer than one million VPN routes in actuality.

Combinations of one or more factors can compound the effect on the router, and scale is affected. For example, in isolation a router might be able to handle 5000 QoS policies. However, when combined with BGP sessions, traffic engineering tunnels the number of QoS policies supported might be lower than in an isolated case. When sizing equipment, you must take these things into consideration. Perhaps the best and surest method for SPs, especially when scale is an issue, is to create a lab environment and test it with the configuration with which the router is going to be deployed.

Network-Wide Scale

Having discussed the various parameters required for the scale of network elements, let us also briefly discuss the network-wide scale issues:

- Similar versus dissimilar network elements (multi-vendor network)—Having multi-vendor networks is common these days. However, with multi-vendor networks come interoperability issues. In particular, interoperability issues associated with implementation differences can cause scalability problems at a network-wide level and limit the usage of a device in a certain location or a certain role. For example a device that cannot process many routes and labels for all those routes might have difficulty speaking to another device that can do it. If a network element allocates one label per prefix and another allocates only one label per VRF due to other constraints, some scale issues might exist when these two devices talk to each other. The device that supports per-prefix label allocates many labels, and the device that supports per-VRF labels allocates only far fewer labels. If this device also cannot process many labels, it might not be able to accept all the route advertisements and labels from its peer that is allocating per-prefix labels.

- Full mesh of BGP sessions versus route reflectors—Although the detailed technical discussion of this topic is beyond the scope of this book, a brief description is warranted here. Full mesh of BGP sessions allows a faster update of the information between peers. However, the number of peers that can be supported per device limits the total number of routers that are in a BGP mesh. If the networks scale to a large number of PEs, having full mesh of BGP sessions might not be an option. Route reflectors allow reflection of VPN routes and labels to PEs. Because router reflectors exchange control plane function only with PEs, they can potentially peer with a large number of PEs. On the PE side, they need to peer only with a few route reflectors to obtain information about routes and other PEs. This reduces the number of BGP sessions required on the PEs but introduces a BGP hop in the control plane. This means network convergence is slower when compared to the full mesh of BGP sessions, so you are trading convergence for scalability.

- Hub and spoke design versus full mesh—Most Frame Relay and ATM VPNs are hub and spoke, and with MPLS L3 VPNs, building full mesh connectivity is much easier. However, with large VPNs, some aggregation might be required, hence, a hierarchical design might be needed—for example, a combination of hub and spoke and full mesh design in which remote sites are hubbed to a regional site and regional sites are meshed together.

Management and Scalability

Network elements must support, at a minimum, manageability with MIBs and applications. The degree of support acceptable is dependent on the provider. ILECs and PTTs require full SNMP support and full MIB support with counter information on packets, bytes, and LSPs including per VPN and per class of service. However, network elements must scale well when the network management (NM) stations poll these devices for statistics. The ability to process NM requests accurately and the ability to inform NM stations during failure conditions via SNMP notifications are critical to the operation of the network element.

Other scale issues in managing large networks exist when thousands of sites and thousands of VPNs are deployed. These factors are network and operation dependent. Having a provisioning system that can provision thousands of CEs and PEs to connect the VPN sites together is important. Operators cannot rely on the CLI and **show** commands anymore. Automated management and monitoring tools become necessary—not just necessary, but mandatory—as networks grow larger.

"I think that this (management systems) is actually the biggest issue in provider scalability. Once the hardware architecture is in place, if the network is designed well, network scalability can be achieved by adding more and/or bigger network routers and ancillary devices. However, if the management systems do not scale, the attempt is usually to try and use manpower to overcome the system's limitations. This usually results in high install failure rates. Managing over 10,000 ports with install rates of 500 to 1000 a month means that, without the proper provisioning and management system, installations are slow and problematic. A solid provisioning and automated service activation system is mandatory. The greater the manual intervention at high install rates, the greater the chance of misconstructed VPNs and dissatisfied customers. A look at recent Telemark studies will show that most providers don't fare well in this area as evaluated by customers." —Joe Fusco, BT Infonet

When building IP NGN, decision-makers must evaluate which factors are most important to their operational environment and which factors provide the margin to grow their network up to the next upgrade period. As we all know, in reality no network elements can last through network growth forever, and therefore, a determination must be made on how to strike the right balance. A simple rule is to pick the sweet spot based on operational experience and to maximize the return on investment based on that sweet spot. For example, if 10,000 VCs are provisioned in the current Frame Relay edge switch for subscribers, the multi-service device may also support a similar number of VCs (maybe not the same because the multi-service edge [MSE] network element might also support Layer 3 services at the same time).

Layer 2 VPNs—What to Expect

Often service providers worry whether they will be able to offer the same grade of service on a packet network with multi-service devices using MPLS that they offer today in the traditional Layer 2 switched networks. This is a valid concern. In addition, enterprise customers also would like to know how their service is being delivered and what to expect from the provider. In this section, we deal briefly with this topic and outline some points that decision-makers must consider to set the right expectations.

Same Grade of Service

Today SPs offer multiple grades of services on the Layer 2 network. These range from zero CIR for FR and unspecified bit rate (UBR) ATM service to well-defined bandwidth bounds using variable bit rate (VBR) or CBR services. The SPs also offer a leased connection with PPP or HDLC framing with a clocking/bandwidth rate on a Layer 1 network. Therefore, the question is whether this all can be emulated easily across a packet network. The answer, however, is not a simple one. Although some services such as UBR service or zero CIR service can easily be emulated, perfectly emulating a CBR service on a packet network is difficult, especially the cell delay variation tolerance (CDVT). However, providing a bandwidth bound equivalent to a VBR service is certainly possible. In small quantities, a CBR service is also possible, depending on the available bandwidth on the links in the network core during transient periods. For example, a provider might be able to get away with offering an ATM CBR service on an MPLS packet network by reserving a good deal of bandwidth to account for transient spikes in the network load or if the core links in the network are lightly loaded even during peak-hour traffic bursts.

Offering bandwidth guarantees on a packet network requires QoS capabilities on the network elements. The ability to police traffic per VC and rate shape traffic becomes important to keep the bandwidth bounds of the service. QoS techniques combined with MPLS TE and maybe even DiffServ TE becomes necessary to build a Layer 2 service with similar QoS guarantees as a traditional Layer 2 network. More details on this can be found in Chapter 4, "Layer 2 VPNs" and Chapter 9, "Quality of Service."

Enterprise customers expect to be able to do the same things as they do on a traditional Layer 2 network. As long as their traffic contracts are met, they do not care how the service is delivered across the network.

Planning and Sizing

With spatial and temporal gambling (also called *statistical multiplexing*), service providers overbook their capacity or use. With spatial gambling, service providers overbook and assume that not everyone uses the same space. Temporal gambling allows them to overbook the same space in different time slots, assuming not every one uses the network at the same time. This overbooking concept is well understood and is used in sizing the trunk capacity of the Layer 2 network.

The same calculation might not apply to MPLS networks. MPLS networks use load balancing techniques, and they transport Layer 3 traffic. These planning and sizing tools need to be modified to account for the nature of packet networks. We do not mean to scare you by presenting all the issues up front, but our aim is to ensure that you understand the issues involved and find your way around them.

Density

Current Layer 2 switches have a very high density of aggregation of Layer 2 VCs, be they Ethernet VLANs or ATM VCs. Current-generation hardware in the multi-service switches cannot match the same densities of traditional Layer 2 switches for Layer 2 services. The Layer 2 density is built to accommodate Layer 3 services. So, an MSE is not a direct replacement for a traditional switch; hence, the operation model must adjust to the new device densities. However, we have stated earlier that as providers are converging network architectures using MPLS, they are primarily using the cap and grow model, whereby they cap investment on the traditional Layer 2 networks and grow the multi-service network for all services.

Management

Current Layer 2 networks have evolved over a decade. The problems are well understood and there is considerable operational experience today with the current Layer 2 model. The management tools have also evolved to provide robust provisioning, configuration, and fault and diagnostics management. Many providers use these tools to provide fault monitoring and isolation as well as for billing, including usage-based billing. For IP networks, ubiquitous connectivity is more critical than usage-based connectivity. The two models are rather different when it comes to management, and the models have not come together. Network management vendors are making a concerted effort to allow provisioning of L2 and L3 VPNs and to provide a consistent feature set. It is only a matter of time before tools evolve to support both services in a consistent manner. Decision-makers must evaluate what is mandatory and what is highly desired when it comes to Layer 2 services.

Summary

In this chapter we have tried to tie the technology subjects listed earlier together. This chapter also provided some insight into the challenges facing decision-makers in designing and building an MPLS network to offer Layer 2 and Layer 3 services. We have seen the VRF-aware services model and discussed in detail the impact of equipment scalability on network scalability. Within bounds, we certainly think an MPLS network can replace the traditional Layer 2 services and, as newer-generation hardware arrives, more of the traditional services can migrate to the converged MPLS network. For example, today circuit emulation services are rarely being carried across an MPLS network. As hardware becomes more robust in retrieving and synchronizing clocks from external, line, or GPS sources, and circuit emulation over IP is standardized, more implementations will be available to carry even the traditional T1 circuits across the packet network, making Layer 1/Layer 2 service more closely resemble traditional networks.

Management tools and techniques have also been evolving rapidly to accommodate the needs of service providers and enterprises. Further evolution of management tools will only make the two approaches of L3 provisioning and L2 provisioning and diagnostics more consistent. All these can be deployed today with considerable ease because products are available from Cisco Systems, Inc., and its partners.

CHAPTER 14

MPLS CASE STUDIES

We have discussed multiprotocol label switching (MPLS) technology and its service attributes throughout this book in the context of its use as a base technology for next-generation networks (NGN). This chapter focuses on proof points of the business impact for organizations that deploy MPLS or subscribe to services based on MPLS technology. We first explore Equant, a large and well-established global service provider (SP) with international points of presence. This chapter provides information on its background, business drivers, services, a return on investment (ROI) model, and lessons learned to help you understand the process of deploying MPLS. The purpose of this chapter is to provide a real case study that captures the essential building blocks highlighted throughout this book regarding NGNs and MPLS technology. Further, the chapter acts as a bridge to the last chapter, which focuses on the future of MPLS as we move forward in the twenty-first century.

The Background on Equant

Equant is a service provider, part of the France Telecom Group, with a network reaching into 220 countries and territories. Equant has the local support of its 9500 employees in approximately 165 countries and manages more than 152,000 user connections across the world. In using Equant as a case study example, we are not trying to promote a specific company or product, but rather to use the SP case study as a model that can represent other SPs.

Building on extensive experience in data communications, Equant serves more than 3700 large businesses. At the 2003 World Communication Awards, it was named Best Global Carrier and its IP VPN was named Best Managed Service.

Equant has the industry's most extensive portfolio of communications services and network solutions, including the market-leading IP VPN used by more than 1300 multinationals today. Equant was one of the early adopters of MPLS technology, with its deployment commencing in 1999. It has been a leader in developing and deploying new services based on MPLS.

Equant Business Drivers

Economies of scale have been a key driver for Equant to deploy an MPLS-based network—that is, the capability to offer multiple services over a converged IP/MPLS backbone.

Equant Services

Equant's portfolio includes VPN services, voice and video services, mobility services, managed services (including security and IT services such as server management and messages), integration services, and professional services. Equant has more than 1300 companies across the globe that subscribe to its managed IP VPN service. Convergence is clearly one of the main reasons MPLS IP VPNs are revolutionizing the telecommunications landscape. During 2003, Equant witnessed a shift from an "early adopter" to a "mainstream" attitude by major multinational corporations (MNC). No longer are Fortune 2000 global firms opting for converged voice and data networks simply to future-proof themselves for the technologies and applications on the horizon. Rather, they are seeing the move as crucial to their ability to compete and meet their bottom line numbers.

The economic case for converged voice and data has become so strong that most big companies cannot afford the luxury of waiting. When more than a few international sites are involved, convergence can dramatically lower their total cost of ownership (TCO)—that is, their overall costs factoring in investment. An Equant customer based in Georgia, for instance, recently replaced its separate voice and data networks with a single converged MPLS-based IP VPN network and is now saving $29,000 per month just on voice calls between its Brazilian sites and its U.S. headquarters.

Just as important is the fact that the quality of VoIP calls on an MPLS-based IP VPN network is now as good as the quality of those on the public switched telecommunications networks (PSTN) in developed countries—and it is actually better than PSTN calls in many developing countries. In addition, the any-to-any capabilities of MPLS IP VPNs allow companies to easily add or remove sites from their networks without dealing with the cost and complexity of reconfiguring routing tables. Because of these compelling factors, most multinational corporations are not debating whether to migrate to a converged MPLS-based IP VPN, but rather, when to migrate.

Here is a case study of Equant and one of its customer.

VPN Bridge Case Study

A European consumer goods company plans to integrate while also preparing to spin off.

- Customer name: Nondisclosable
- Business: Consumer products, foods, and tobacco
- Number of sites: More than 350

Background

The customer is a very large corporation with more than 350 offices in all parts of the world. Its network is divided into three major regions, each with a major data center. Within the regions, the different companies share the network back to the data centers but generally have different office locations within the region. The customer has a long history with Equant, which provides FR to the customer within Europe. Within the other regions, other competitors are the main providers.

About one and one-half years ago, the customer issued an RFP to build a network to connect its three regions and data centers. It wanted any-to-any connectivity and a single provider because it felt it would be easier to support major application initiatives with such an architecture. An ERP application, SAP, was the leading application that drove the need for better cross-region connectivity. Equant won the RFP with IP VPN (MPLS).

Customer Issues/Objectives

More recently, a major issue for the customer has been preparation for a possible divestiture of subsidiary companies. The divestiture of companies and the resulting separation of the networks were the compelling events that required the customer to take action.

The account team had a good relationship with the customer. Therefore, as they became aware of the looming divestiture issue, they decided to take the initiative to develop a solution for their customer. As the incumbent provider of service within Europe, Equant had everything to lose. If the customer went out to bid, the risk of loss was significant.

Any major migration to separate the existing networks would likely require significant investment in terms of dual infrastructures for a period of time and in terms of nonrecurring charges. The account team developed a plan that would greatly reduce these charges through the creative use of Equant's new feature: the VPN bridge.

The VPN bridge is designed to act as a bridge or link between an FR network and an IP VPN. Using the VPN bridge for the customer's FR network within Europe, the account team was able to develop a plan to separate the customer's individual networks without the need for duplicate local access circuits, new access routers, or most of the one-time charges the customer would have incurred if it had tried to replace the existing Equant network with another provider's network service. Avoiding these expenses proved to be a strong motivator and was ultimately instrumental in keeping the customer's business.

The Account Team's Keys to Success

The account team credits their success in retaining the customer to several items.

The following success factors are examples:

- **Account management**—It should be no surprise that good account relationships depend on good account management. This account is no different. Successful mapping of the key decision-makers was important. The account team spent significant time and effort to understand the key decision-makers and influencers within the customer organization. One of the competitors did a poor job of account management, and this contributed to their loss; they spent time speaking with the wrong people, even to the extent that their interactions with the wrong people hurt their relationships with the right people.

- **Building trust**—The account team built trust with the customer in several ways. One was simply doing what they said they would do. Another was being honest with the customer by telling them things that the account team felt Equant could *not* do well and identifying areas that included some risk. Finally, the account team stated that they cut through marketing hyperbole to tell the customer what they needed to hear. Primarily, this meant providing customer case studies showing how Equant had helped other customers.

VPN bridge—As mentioned earlier, the VPN bridge was an important part of building a creative and technical solution that, in the end, allowed the customer to deal with its compelling event in such a way that the cost and risk were minimized compared with the alternatives that other providers offered.

- **Price**—Equant offered a competitive price, particularly with regards to the nonrecurring charges. Again, this was thanks in part to the capabilities of the VPN bridge.

- **End results**—The account is worth more than $19 million in revenue per year. Equant provides the following services to the customer:
  - FR/IP VPN
  - Consultancy
  - IPSec
  - Private DSL
  - Project management
  - Dial service
  - Planned: IP telephony or IPT and application-aware VPNs

Case Study Conclusion

To summarize, from an SP account and opportunity relationship perspective you should always:

- Look for the compelling event and then address it better than anyone else.

- Build the strongest possible relationship with your customer/prospect.

- If at all possible, avoid the RFP because it is too difficult to win.

- Note that divestiture is as much a driver as mergers are and that hub site reconfigurations are difficult!

Summary

This chapter has shown one important case study that demonstrates how a service provider can help a customer with the connectivity and migration from an existing Layer 2 network to IP-based VPNs. Further, the case study is an example of MPLS deployment for SPs as they migrate IP/MPLS-based networks as part of an overall NGN strategy. As the next generation, therefore, we can ask the question as to the future of MPLS technology and whether a new packet-based bearer technology exists that will replace MPLS. The last chapter explores this very question—the future of MPLS.

CHAPTER 15

THE FUTURE OF MPLS

As service providers proceed along the path to deploying their Next Generation Network (NGN) networks and services, IP/MPLS is and will be a key architectural component of voice, video, and mobile data services for these NGN networks. This chapter discusses the future of MPLS and the role of IP NGN and MPLS. Finally, two experts from the industry who have been active with MPLS technology from the beginning offer a view on the future of MPLS. First is George Swallow, distinguished engineer at Cisco Systems and Internet Engineering Task Force (IETF) MPLS Working Group co-chair. Second is Adrian Farrell, who has been active at the IETF, particularly in Common Control and Measurement Plane (CCAMP) where Generalized MPLS (GMPLS) is discussed. Is there life after MPLS? The conclusion is left to you.

You have seen that MPLS packets can run over a link layer and a link layer packet (Ethernet, ATM, Frame Relay (FR), Point-to-Point Protocol (PPP), and so on) can also be run over MPLS. You have also seen that Layer 3 (L3) packets run on MPLS and MPLS frames can be run over IP packets. This implies that MPLS is neither a Layer 2 protocol nor a Layer 3 protocol. In fact, Yakov Rekhter, one of the inventors of MPLS has said, "MPLS doesn't fit in the OSI layer at all." So the question must be asked, "Where does MPLS fit, and what is its future?"

MPLS is emerging as a widely acceptable technology for network convergence. Evolving from Cisco tag switching, MPLS has become the defacto standard for delivering services on IP networks. More than 250 Cisco customers, service providers, and large enterprise customers have deployed MPLS for Layer 3 VPNs, traffic engineering, or Layer 2 VPNs.

As noted, MPLS follows a simple paradigm of control and forwarding plane separation. We have also seen that the forwarding plane uses simple shim headers as labels. The complexity is entirely in the control plane w.r.t label distribution and management.

This simple paradigm of control and forwarding planes can easily be extended to other transport networks, such as ATM, Frame Relay, and optical networks. In fact, the ATM MPLS networks has not been discussed in this book due to the fact that fewer and fewer deployments exist, but ATM MPLS networks have been around for more than five years. As shown previously in Chapter 3, "Technology Overview," the label is carried in the Virtual Path Identifier/Virtual Channel Identifier (VPI/VCI) field of the ATM cell in the case of ATM MPLS networks. Similarly, the label can be carried in the Frame Relay data-line connection identifier (DLCI) field for a Frame MPLS network. Remember that with ATM MPLS and Frame MPLS, references are not to networks running either MPLS over ATM or MPLS over Frame Relay, but rather to the setup of virtual connections (LSP) using MPLS as a control plane with each Frame Relay switch and ATM switch behaving as a Frame Relay Label Switch Router (LSR) and ATM LSR.

One other important area to which this concept can easily be extended is the time-division multiplexing (TDM) and optical space. For example, by designating channel numbers or optical tributaries as labels and using a GMPLS control plane to set up the cross connects of channels, you can set up a label-switched path (LSP) in a TDM or an optical network. This cross connection of TDM channels or setup of optical paths across the network is analogous to a packet LSP that is set up across the LSR. In this chapter, we explore in detail this generalization of MPLS, known as GMPLS and find out how this can help integrate IP and optical networks and bring efficiency in provisioning Layer 1 circuits.

Also discussed in this chapter are other applications and enhancements to MPLS that help build other services in the future such as guaranteed bandwidth multicast for video distribution, ubiquitous transport of MPLS VPNs across IP networks, and dynamic setup of security adjacency for better encryption in the MPLS VPNs environment.

Integrating IP and Optical Networks (Transport Area)

In building networks today, a circuit or path setup requires touching multiple transport networks and technologies. For example, in creating an IP connection of OC-12 bandwidth from New York to San Francisco, a Layer 2 circuit must be available, in addition to the IP equipment and connectivity. To provision that Layer 2 circuit, you might have to provision optical connections on the Synchronous Optical Network/Synchronous Digital Hierarchy (SONET/SDH) network and provision Dense Wavelength Division Multiplexing (DWDM) long-haul for this OC-12 connection.

Each specific technology has its own control protocol and, as a result, each set of control protocols does not communicate directly with the others at a peer level. Instead, as we see in our example, networks are layered one on top of the other creating overlays at each layer to collectively provide end-user services—DWDM long-haul that connects multiple OC-192s via wavelengths, a SONET/SDH Optical Add and Drop Multiplexer (OADM) that multiplexes OC-12s to OC-192s, and an MPLS LSP that provides IP layer connectivity. Obviously, this process requires knowledge of each technology domain, provisioning of each layer, and separate management of per-domain operation functions.

A unified control plane with a common set of control functions that can tie in all transport types and provision across all technologies can make the provisioning process simple and efficient. The use of such a control plane enables quick deployment of IP services and applications, and providers no longer need to separately provision connectivity across technologies. The common control plane signals appropriate parameters across different types of transport networks. The common control plane uses IP-like routing and signaling and allows topology discovery and connection setup, as well as a sharing of resource and state information across different technology domains.

How Does it Work?

Although all the details of GMPLS and Unified Control Plane (UCP) are beyond the scope of this book, we briefly describe how this works to understand how the future deployment of MPLS and GMPLS is shaping up.

To understand the basic concepts of GMPLS, let us first understand the layering model. What is commonly represented in the network diagrams of connectivity between two routers via an OC-12 or OC-192 link is much more than that. The OC-192 from the router usually terminates onto an optical add-drop MUX. Multiple add-drop MUXes aggregate to DWDM equipment that are connected by long-haul fiber. In other words, in the layering concept, at the lowest layer are the devices that connect long-haul fiber—a DWDM network. Layered on top of this are the OADM devices that provide the SONET framing optical grooming and Optical Carrier Level n (OCn) connectivity to the routers. (See Figure 15-1.)

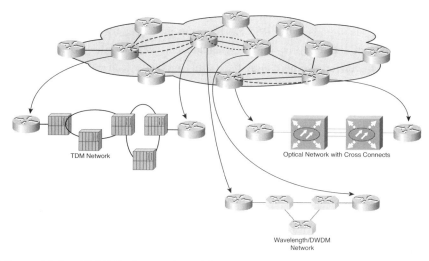

Figure 15-1   *GMPLS—Layered Model*

A common control plane network that connects the IP routers, SONET/SDH MUXes, optical cross connects, and DWDM gear provides the signaling of parameters such as wavelengths, TDM channel numbers, and fiber ports in the GMPLS signaling. Here the TDM channel number or the wavelength lambda is the label. The signaling is done by extending RSVP-TE to carry optical network parameters, and admission control is performed based on available bandwidth (optical channel, fiber port, or light wavelength), as shown in Figure 15-2.

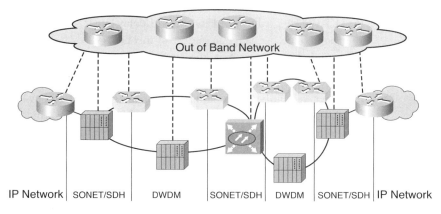

Figure 15-2   *GMPLS—Out of Band Control Plane*

The optical light path setup is similar to an RSVP-TE tunnel setup where the head-end node signals using RSVP. The setup messages travel the network and initialize bandwidth (ports, optical channels, or wavelengths) to the tail end. However, the difference here is that signaling messages can either travel in band or out of band through a control network or control channel. In optical networks an out-of-band network commonly carries the provisioning and management information; sometimes a dedicated control channel provides this information in band. By using a common signaling protocol with appropriate technology, specific extensions, light paths, or TDM connections can be dynamically triggered when a demand exists for bandwidth at the IP layer.

NOTE   While writing this book, we recalled a conversation that happened with a service provider. We paraphrase this conversation to demonstrate the difficulty providers face in provisioning circuits between two cities or points and the management challenges they face.

In discussing the provisioning times of circuits in general, we were surprised to hear that it takes the provider between three weeks and three months to light up an OC-192. They create a service request and toss it over to the transport group. Depending on the geography, available capacity of fiber, free channels, cross-connect capacity, and so on, the transport group provisions this request and tosses the connections back to the IP group. Because these networks, transport networks, and IP networks are managed and supported by different groups within this provider, the IP group has no control over where the OC-192 gets provisioned and what its delay budget is. In fact, the IP group notices a change in reroute of this OC-192 by monitoring the variation in ping times of this link.

This shows the challenges faced by the provider and the difficulty they have in rapidly provisioning and managing circuits. If they had the ability to control the placement of this OC-192 (along which optical path) and the ability to provision it rapidly (inline with the demand of the IP capacity), their bottom line would be much better. Delays in availability of network capacity mean higher operations costs, which affect the bottom line.

Bandwidth On-Demand Service

In addition to providing a rapid provisioning of circuits, GMPLS can be used as a standard interface like a network-to-network interface (NNI) to provide a service-like bandwidth on demand to other regional or national providers or large enterprises.

Let us consider a facilities-based provider that has a transport network. This provider wants to offer bandwidth on-demand services to regional ISPs or large enterprise customers that need loads of bandwidth for bulk data transfers for relatively short periods of time. The transport provider needs the ability to rapidly or instantly provision circuits, depending on the demand. The transport provider has two choices.

First, if the optical and TDM equipment is capable of GMPLS control plane, then you enable the control plane, create an NNI with the regional providers, and react to signaling requests from the regional providers using the GMPLS network. The dynamically signaled requests from the customers are authenticated and honored by setting up the cross connections and allocating OCn channels from the ingress to the egress of the network.

The second choice is this: If the existing optical and TDM equipment is not capable of being upgraded with the unified control plane and GMPLS signaling, you might be able to create a proxy function that can translate the GMPLS requests coming from the regional ISPs or customers and translate this to the provisioning mechanisms of the equipment. A proxy function behaves similarly to the GMPLS peer and responds to signals in the same manner as a real GMPLS network. The proxy function translates the request to the existing provisioning systems to set up the OCn channel or light path hop by hop.

Due to the dynamic nature of this signaling, circuits can be signaled and torn down on demand based on customers's needs. Such a service can be attractive to service providers.

Challenges Faced with GMPLS and UCP

Any new protocol has its set of challenges with respect to operations and management. Moreover, GMPLS challenges the fundamental assumptions of network operations. Service providers have separate groups managing different network components—one that manages the transport network and another that manages the IP network. Almost all ILECs, IXCs, and PTTs operate this way. Integrating the transport network with the IP network is a massive challenge for these providers for political and operational reasons. After the providers overcome their political and operational problems, GMPLS can help build an efficient network.

Future Layer 3 Services

The idea of a single forwarding plane and different control planes is powerful. Exploiting this idea, newer control planes can be invented to provide newer services. Following are a few ideas on where we see MPLS technology adopted to build new services.

Label-Switched Multicast

One such idea being discussed in the IETF at press time is the ability to set up point-to-multipoint label-switched paths to carry multicast traffic. By providing bandwidth guarantees to label-switched multicast traffic using appropriate signaling extensions, multicast services for video, TV, and other applications can be easily built. Current IP multicast and multicast VPN do not use MPLS LSPs. Hence, for multicast you cannot use the excellent capabilities of MPLS, such as fast reroute for link protection, node protection, and bandwidth protection. However, if multicast traffic is also carried across MPLS LSPs, MPLS traffic engineering and fast reroute can also be used to protect unicast and multicast traffic simultaneously.

An increasing number of providers are standardizing on MPLS and GMPLS for their next-generation networks. They have a requirement to carry all traffic—unicast and multicast—across label-switched paths. By having a common data plane, you get an operational savings and increase in network efficiency in terms of bandwidth and resource utilization. Extending either the multicast routing protocol or the MPLS TE signaling to perform label distribution, to build point-to-multipoint trees for efficient multicast transmission across the network, can lead to several new services for customers.

Dynamic Encrypted VPNs

As seen in previous chapters MPLS VPNs provide excellent full-mesh connectivity to build IP VPNs. We have also seen that MPLS VPNs provide a separation of traffic from customer A to customer B. However, we have also seen that MPLS VPNs do not encrypt traffic. For some banking applications or when traffic is transited over a public network, encryption is desired for VPN traffic. One way to add encryption to MPLS networks is to overlay a mesh of IPSec tunnels between CEs. This overlay, however, is not efficient and defeats the purpose of MPLS VPNs: Single-peer connectivity from the CE to PE.

Dynamic encrypted VPNs provide the ability to encrypt any traffic between CEs without running a tunnel overlay. The security information is either statically provisioned or exchanged within BGP via some new extensions to BGP. After the security adjacency is learned, the encryption is set up for traffic flowing only to that prefix. This creates a flexible method of dealing with encryption requirements in an MPLS VPN network.

Content-Based Services

Other types of VPN services include content-based services and broadband services integrated with the MPLS-based VPNs. In a content-based case, each VPN can represent a content service and subscribers subscribe to this service or VPN. The subscriber traffic is intelligently mapped to a content VPN without compromising the connectivity between the content VPNs themselves. The key here is the ability to map customers to VPNs. Appropriate policy routing with label distribution can help accomplish this capability.

Adaptive Networks for Integration of Voice and Video

MPLS TE allows the creation of TE tunnels with bandwidth. RSVP is also an excellent protocol for admission control and per-flow QoS. For VoIP and video, RSVP can be used to provide per-flow admission control for each voice call or video session. When these RSVP reservations arrive at the MPLS network, the admission control is performed on a bandwidth pool that is manually adjusted by the operator. One future enhancement is to perform admission control on the TE tunnel interface so that the correct number of calls is admitted on the TE tunnel.

In addition, the TE tunnels themselves could be resized when the VoIP calls or video sessions increase either automatically (with some intelligence in the PEs) or manually at the instructions of the operator. This form of aggregation of RSVP reservations onto a TE tunnel is referred to as tunnel-based admission control (TBAC). Adding a call control function to TBAC to allow the automation of tunnel setup and resizing and reoptimization of tunnels can help build a network that dynamically "tunes" itself to incoming voice or video calls.

Security Enhancements

With Layer 3 services, in the future you can expect to see the following examples of security enhancements: more robust handling of labels; the detection of, response to, and prevention of denial-of-service attacks; the authentication of sessions and peers; and the prevention of misforwarding that is caused by state changes. Security is the single most important aspect of building a reliable VPN service. Handling all possible security situations, such as denial-of-service attacks, is a must when it comes to operating an IP-based service.

Another form of Layer 3 service that is catching attention these days is using IP NGN for video distribution. Using efficient multicast techniques and marrying IP multicast with label switching allows the building of efficient Point to Multi-Point (P-MP) LSPs that use newly developed techniques, such as Multicast Label Distribution Protocol (MLDP) or RSVP-TE.

Future Layer 2 Services

Several enhancements to the current Layer 2 VPNs are being discussed for MPLS networks. The following sections discuss some examples that can shape the future of Layer 2 VPN deployments.

ATM-MPLS Interworking

The migration of Layer 2 VPNs from current ATM networks to new MPLS-based Layer 2 VPNs has its own set of challenges in terms of provisioning, management, and cutover. Flash cutovers from an old network to a new network are not an option. This means that during the migration phase, some nodes must be on the old network and others on the new network. The migration process might be much simpler if the two networks spoke to the same control plane. Given the fact that an ATM network uses ATM UNI/PNNI signaling to set up SVCs and SPVCs and an MPLS control plane uses LDP to set up pseudowires, you need to interwork the two control planes to be able to set up Layer 2 connections and VCs across the ATM and MPLS networks. This requires a control plane interworking function at the edge; the interworking function translates the ATM UNI/PNNI signaling to the MPLS LDP pseudowire that is set up dynamically. More intelligence can be added to the interworking point to set up TE tunnels or to perform admission control for VCs to provide the correct QoS behavior. For more details, please refer to the ATM Forum Specifications.

Layer 2 VPNs Across Multiple Provider Networks

The setup of Layer 2 VPNs across multiple ASes and providers is not obvious when it comes to building pseudowires. Some proposals include building two segment provisioning systems, where each provider builds its own pseudowire segment for the Layer 2 connection and there is either a native handoff of Layer 2 frames or these pseudowires are stitched together at the boundary. Having a stitching model helps each provider maintain control of its network without disclosing the network loopback addresses. More redundancy options can be added by allowing setup of backup pseudowires where traffic is mapped when primary pseudowires fail due to either a path or PE failure.

VPLS Service Across a NonEthernet Last Mile

VPLS requires an Ethernet end point as it bridges LANs together. However, remote sites might need to be connected to this VPLS network. These remote sites might have only FR or ATM connectivity. Having the ability to do VPLS forwarding at this remote node over a Frame Relay circuit allows a flexible connectivity option that easily extends the Ethernet service to any attached end point. Therefore, you do not need to have an Ethernet connection between PE and CE to offer a VPLS service to CEs.

Future Enhancements in Provisioning and Management

Several enhancements are possible to the configuration, provisioning, and management of MPLS networks. You can create cookie-cutter templates for some standard configurations for some simple deployments. For example, VPN configurations can be simplified if the requirement is always full-mesh connectivity between sites. Many vendors, including Cisco, also offer several management applications that can help manage MPLS services, including some complex computations that can help place TE LSPs explicitly and provide bandwidth guarantees in failure conditions.

Adaptive Self-Healing Networks

Failure detection is extremely important to make re-routing decisions and reconverge on a topology. With MPLS embedded management capabilities, both control and data plane liveliness can be monitored. The liveliness data can be combined with some intelligence in software to make the following:

- Fast reroute decisions

- Automatic invocation of a trace to find the location of fault

- Isolation of that fault by re-routing around that failure, using FRR or other mechanisms

This creates a powerful network paradigm that heals itself when it detects failures. A liveliness check of the LSPs and TE tunnels helps distinguish control plane from data plane failures. An automatic invocation of traces helps find the fault location in the network and, by changing routing metrics and re-routing of traffic, this can be achieved around the failure within a short time—thereby creating the powerful notion of a self-healing network.

Increasing Enterprise Deployment of MPLS

As we have seen in Chapter 5, "Layer 3 VPNs," MPLS VPNs can also be deployed by enterprises for network segmentation or VLAN/VPN requirements. 802.1X authentication, which is widely used in the enterprise, can be mapped to trusted VLANs, and these VLANs in turn can be mapped to VRFs and VPNs for campus-wide and network-wide segmentation of users within the enterprise. Many financial houses and airport authorities are deploying MPLS VPNs in their networks to provide VPN services to their respective departments. In the future such deployments will increase the need to more ubiquitously connect MPLS networks together with provider networks or connect MPLS privately using the Inter-AS connectivity model. Such demands might lead to MPLS interconnect or exchange, or even clearing houses whose business model will be to seamlessly connect MPLS networks together.

Summary

We have described both the MPLS technology components and the related business applications for organizations that deploy and use MPLS. The increasing number of MPLS adopters only confirms the success of the technology in the industry as a service driver. Further, more than 100 IETF drafts and RFCs on MPLS and related technologies have been written. In addition, a dedicated ITU study group on NGN architectures exists, and one of the prime discussion items is MPLS for next-generation networks. Several providers building next-generation architectures have standardized on MPLS and GMPLS for their networks to converge Layer 2 and Layer 3 services, including broadband aggregation, multicast, IPv6, and VPLS.

So, What Is the Future of MPLS?

As we have described in this chapter, several enhancements are expected in the future with MPLS implementations and services. Some of them might be fundamental changes, such as the addition of new control planes, with multicast routing protocol PIM, and others might be enhancements to either the configuration or operation of existing MPLS features. MPLS is the de-facto protocol for network convergence, and MPLS and GMPLS have become the key to next-generation network architectures. MPLS has proven itself such a flexible technology for service deployment that opportunities for MPLS to adapt and evolve in the future are extensive. One thing is certain, though: MPLS is here to stay.

A View from George Swallow

In 1999, Dr. Tony Li wrote, "The long-term impact of MPLS is difficult to anticipate because of the innovations that it enables." Although many innovations have now been revealed, the statement remains essentially true. MPLS is not just a new data-communications technology; it is a new kind of technology. Spawned out of the otherwise ill-fated marriage of IP and ATM, MPLS offers the tight control of ATM while not losing the flexibility found in IP routers. In fact, MPLS adds flexibility to routers. Although a number of important architectural elements contribute to MPLS's success, two aspects have a direct bearing on its future.

The most salient MPLS innovation is its intentionally loose coupling of the control and data planes. In fact, one can barely speak of the MPLS control plane because the intersection of control elements between L3-VPNs, traffic engineering, and pseudowires is minimal. This loose coupling has allowed the independent creation and evolution of multiple MPLS applications. Yet, not only can these applications run in the same network, but they can also be used in conjunction with one another. VPN data flows can be traffic-engineered completely independently of the VPN control plane. On the other hand, QoS preferences can be applied to any particular VPN.

This loose coupling offers service providers the flexibility to create a wide range of service offerings and enables the rapid evolution of service capabilities.

It also offers equipment vendors architectural freedom in creating new applications.

The second architectural element is that MPLS—unlike ATM—was not created as a standalone self-contained system. Instead, MPLS is closely bound to IP. Not only does MPLS coexist in the same network as IP, but MPLS also depends directly on IP protocols for its control plane(s). IP has come to dominate the world's data communications and, as the trend progresses, it appears destined to dominate communications of all forms. With such ubiquitous acceptance, any technology that pretends to compete head-to-head with IP will be a nonstarter for the foreseeable future.

MPLS, however, does not attempt such competition. Instead, it coexists with and complements IP. It enables value-added services above and beyond what can be offered with IP alone. Further, it adds value to basic IP services. Traffic engineering and particularly the fast reroute capabilities of MPLS TE are being deployed in IP networks. As the volume of voice and video traffic grows on IP networks, users will begin to demand higher levels of service. These demands can be met only by the capability to reroute around failures quickly enough to not noticeably degrade service. In fact, the performance of MPLS TE is so good that some providers are eliminating their Sonet/SDH multiplexers and running IP+MPLS directly over DWDM.

Service providers have long sought to have a single, converged network upon which they can offer all services. ISDN and B-ISDN gave us Frame Relay and ATM but failed in their quest for an integrated services digital network (ISDN). Frame Relay and ATM have been, and remain, important technologies, but their primary mission has been to carry IP traffic. IP is the world's only ubiquitous data communications technology; supplanting that infrastructure would be a monumental task. Inserting MPLS into that infrastructure is simply a natural evolution and an evolution that is well underway.

MPLS is enabling IP networks to efficiently and effectively provide IP VPNs, carry Frame Relay and ATM traffic, emulate Sonet and other circuits, and of course provide Internet connectivity all on a single infrastructure. Through MPLS TE, this infrastructure can be made sufficiently robust to meet the requirements of voice and video traffic. Truly we are entering the day of converged networking. The future belongs to IP+MPLS.

For more information, read Tony Li's "MPLS and the Evolving Internet Architecture," *IEEE Communications Magazine*, Volume 37, No. 12, December 1999.

A View from Adrian Farrell

The MPLS data plane would appear to have earned its place as a useful part of the IP network, but it continues to come under attack from the IP forwarding community. It is certainly true that many of the reasons initially cited in support of MPLS (for example, forwarding lookup performance) ceased to be valid almost as soon as MPLS was invented, but the current crop of advanced IP forwarding techniques (such as IP fast reroute and Layer 3 switching) do not look as though they will make any impact on the validity of MPLS as a data plane technology.

Recent industry reports suggest that the revenue generated by providers from MPLS services will "almost double" between 2004 and 2007, representing a predicted growth of 20% per annum. However, such a rate of increase probably simply reflects a continued rollout of existing MPLS technologies and the steady migration of current services to MPLS, rather than the deployment of new MPLS features. Thus, as MPLS is increasingly used to provide connectivity for VPNs, we might expect to see a corresponding dip in the revenues for IP services.

Without a doubt, MPLS is gaining momentum in the core of providers' networks. The ease with which it can offer virtual connectivity services in a wide array of configurations means that it is attractive to providers who want to offer virtual private wire, pseudowire, virtual private LANs, and VPNs across the same network. We can certainly expect to see an increase in these services as the standards settle down, and pseudowire, with its ability to establish end-to-end connectivity through LDP while encapsulating any data technology, is letting providers offer new services over their MPLS packet networks.

As MPLS VPNs bed in with many successful deployments, questions are being asked about how to support multicast VPNs in an MPLS environment. Initial deployments function adequately but are known not to be scalable. More work is required to develop techniques and standards to provide multicast support without placing an undue burden on any of the provider's routers, and without overloading the network with either control or data traffic. This is a rich seam to be tapped because the use of multicast IP within enterprise networks is on the increase.

In fact, the whole area of multicast support in MPLS is currently under investigation by the IETF and seems like an urgent area for research to catch up with the increased demand for the transport of IP multicast. Currently, no support exists for the distribution of MPLS labels for routing-based multicast, and work will likely be developed to bring the multicast and MPLS technologies together— perhaps by extending the PIM routing protocol to support label distribution. Work has already begun to extend MPLS traffic engineering to support point-to-multipoint flows, and this will be a useful tool in the support of MPLS multicast VPNs.

Traffic-engineered MPLS (MPLS-TE), it must be said, has seen a relatively slow start, certainly compared to the routing-based MPLS achieved by LDP. However, as MPLS networks begin to carry increasing traffic loads, traffic engineering will gain in popularity to build virtual links within the network so that traffic can more easily be balanced. At the same time, MPLS-TE will be seen as providing a useful toolset for aggregating traffic flows and graded services. The fact that MPLS-TE can be used to set up DiffServ-enabled LSPs and to make better guarantees of QoS surely confirms the importance of this technology.

As market pressure forces service providers into more cooperative arrangements, we will see an increase in deployment of traffic-engineered LSPs across autonomous systems. VPNs will need to span multiple networks while guaranteeing QoS, and providers will place "virtual PoPs" within their neighbor's network to offer local connectivity outside their sphere of influence. In both cases, the establishment of TE LSPs through untrusted domains will call for new technologies and rationalized peering agreements.

However, MPLS-TE must improve implementation before it is thoroughly useful. In particular, the current resource reservation techniques that are based on simple statistical models need to be replaced by real admission control functions that genuinely reserve and dedicate resources to a traffic flow and that thereby can make absolute QoS guarantees. When this technology is made available, MPLS-TE will take off as a technique for high-grade delivery across core networks.

One of the biggest challenges facing MPLS deployments over the next five years is the migration of MPLS-TE control planes to GMPLS. GMPLS is a protocol family that extends the MPLS-TE protocols to support multiple nonpacket technologies such as TDM and WDM, but GMPLS also continues to support packets. Moving to a GMPLS control plane will bring a large number of benefits to the packet switching network, each of which represents an opportunity to provide new services that can open revenue streams.

- Support for nonstop forwarding so that the data path can be maintained even after a failure of the control channels or of the control plane software, so that the control plane can recover from such failures and continue to manage the data plane

- Bidirectional LSPs

- Link bundling and hierarchical LSPs providing scalability efficiencies in the configuration of devices with many parallel links and in the management of core links with large amounts of bandwidth

- An assortment of protection schemes to allow data services to be rapidly recovered in the event of network failures

- Integration of packet networks with nonpacket transport technologies for the automatic provisioning of end-to-end bandwidth

As can be seen from this list, many of the features that GMPLS offers enable MPLS-TE to be considered more as a transport technology. Services provided over a GMPLS packet network will be more capable of being robust and reliable. This will mean that service level agreements can offer better guarantees not just of throughput and traffic quality, but also of availability and recovery.

To successfully enable reliability, protection, and recovery service within MPLS networks, we need to see increased deployments of MPLS OAM technologies. Not only will operators need to quickly diagnose faults with an array of MPLS tools, but (more importantly) the network itself needs to be capable to detect, isolate, and report problems so that it can automatically recover in the rapid times required by high-function service level agreements.

Index

A

AAA (authentication, authorization, and accounting), 166
account management, VPN bridge case study, 361
accounting, MPLS-based networks, 306–308, 322–323
ACs (attachment circuits), 40
additional bandwidth inventories, 231
address management, dial access, 166
address translation, VRF-aware feature, 338–339
addresses
    IPv6, 288–289
        basics, 290–299
        management, 299
        problem providing IPv4 services, 290
    network assignment, 334–335
Any Transport over MPLS. *See* AToM
anycasting, 288
APS (automatic protection switching), 34
ATM (asynchronous transfer mode), 27–28
    like-to-like transport, 117–118
    MPLS interworking, 375
ATM MPLS networks, 366
ATM over MPLS (ATMoMPLS), 41
ATMoMPLS (ATM over MPLS), 41
AToM (Any Transport over MPLS), 111
    Layer 2 VPNs, 111–112
        packet forwarding, 114
        pseudowires, 112–113
attachment circuit values, LDP signaling, 128
attachment circuits (ACs), 40
attacks, security scenarios, 189–201
authentication, authorization, and accounting (AAA), 166

automatic protection switching (APS), 34
availability, security considerations, 183

B

bandwidths, on-demand service, 371
best effort grade of services, 250
best practices, security, 217–218
BFD factors, network design considerations, 342
BGP (Border Gateway Protocol), 65, 292
    IPv6 PE, 292
    Layer 2 VPN provisioning, 128–131
Border Gateway Protocol (BGP), 65, 292
    IPv6 PE, 292
    Layer 2 VPN provisioning, 128–131
bridged encapsulation, DSL remote access, 171–172
British Telecom, 7
business drivers, service convergence, 9–10
    enterprise customers, 10–11
    Layer 3 services, 11–14

C

cable, remote access, 172
campus multicast, 276
Carrier's Carrier (CsC) networks, Layer 2 VPN security, 212–215
cases studies, Equant
    company background, 358–360
    customer VPN bridge, 360–362
CBQ (class-based queuing), 67

W-Z